A **FALCON** GUIDE®

Road Biking™ Series

ROAD BIKING™

Western Pennsylvania

Jim Homerosky

FALCON®

GUILFORD, CONNECTICUT

HELENA, MONTANA

AN IMPRINT OF THE GLOBE PEQUOT PRESS

A FALCON GUIDE ®

Photos by the author unless noted otherwise

Maps by Trailhead Graphics © The Globe Pequot Press

Library of Congress Cataloging-in-Publication Data
Homerosky, Jim.
  Road biking Western Pennsylvania / Jim Homerosky. — 1st ed.
    p. cm. — (Road biking series)
  ISBN 0-7627-2659-8
    1. Bicycle touring—Pennsylvania—Guidebooks. 2. Pennsylvania—Guidebooks. I. Title. II. Series.

GV1045.5.P4H66 2004
796.6'4'0974—dc22
                                                            2003056970

Manufactured in the United States of America
First Edition/First Printing

ROAD BIKING ™

Western Pennsylvania

Help Us Keep This Guide Up to Date

Every effort has been made by the author and editors to make this guide as accurate and useful as possible. However, many things can change after a guide is published—roads are closed, regulations change, techniques evolve, facilities come under new management, etc.

We would love to hear from you concerning your experiences with this guide and how you think it could be improved and kept up to date. While we may not be able to respond to all comments and suggestions, we'll take them to heart and we'll also make certain to share them with the author. Please send your comments and suggestions to the following address:

The Globe Pequot Press
Reader Response/Editorial Department
P.O. Box 480
Guilford, CT 06437

Or you may e-mail us at:

editorial@GlobePequot.com

Thanks for your input, and happy travels!

For Wendy,
My wife. My friend. My stoker.

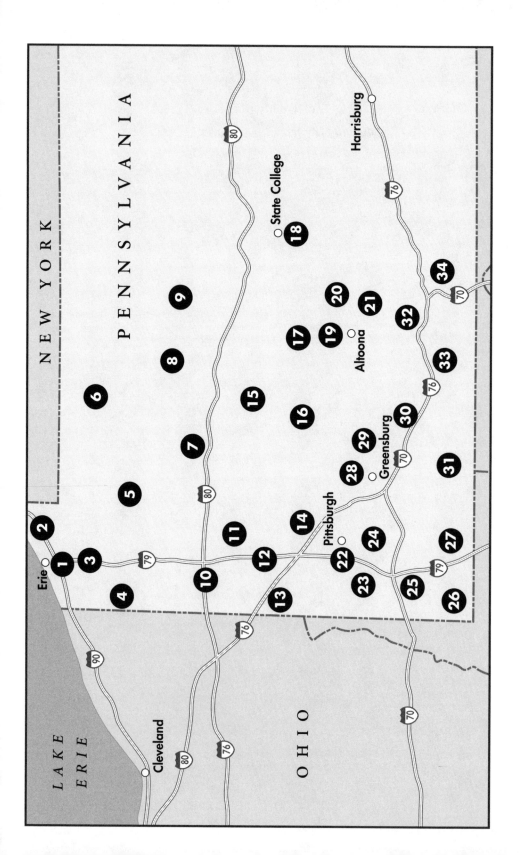

Contents

Preface

It wasn't easy choosing the rides that best represent Western Pennsylvania. The challenge was selecting the rides that best present the variety of scenery, history, and biking conditions that Western Pennsylvania has to offer.

Starting locations for all rides were chosen for the presence of free and adequate parking, proximity to provisions and visitor centers, and, most of all, safety. Routes were designed that struck a fine balance of secondary road riding with scenic and historic highlights along or near the route. Of course, terrain, traffic volume, and road conditions played a significant role. You will find that most rides in the book are extremely rural. For variety I added city rides in Pittsburgh and Erie. I intentionally avoided other major population areas or found suitable routes through the few cities that the rides do pass. As you move farther south and east, the mountainous terrain and rural nature of the region result in fewer options for route development; occasional compromises had to be made.

My research was made easier by utilizing Pennsylvania Department of Transportation county maps, *DeLorme Pennsylvania Atlas & Gazetteer*, and commercial mapping software, particularly Microsoft Streets and Trips and DeLorme Topo. But even the latest technology would not have enabled successful completion of this book without the help of many wonderful people and organizations.

My deep gratitude goes out to Tom Mantle of TRM Cycles, Bill Metzger, Tom Maggio of the Erie–Western Pennsylvania Port Authority, Emily Beck of the Erie Area Convention and Visitors Bureau, Dave and Ruth at Lake Country Bike, and Bob Cramer of Country Side Cycles. Much thanks also to Linda Devlin of the Allegheny National Forest Vacation Bureau, Carla Wehler of the Northwest Pennsylvania Great Outdoors Visitors Bureau, Harry Parker of the Pennsylvania State Archives, Dave Love of Love's Canoes, the Western Pennsylvania Wheelmen; and Ken Mason, current Road Captain of the WPW. The Allegheny Mountains Convention and Visitors Bureau, Bedford County Visitors Bureau, Centre County Convention and Visitors Bureau, Greene County Tourist Promotion Agency, Cycle the Southern Alleghenies, Altoona Bicycle Club, Snitger's Bicycle Store, Laurel Highlands Visitors Bureau, and the Centre Region Bike Coalition, provided invaluable assistance, as did Bill

Minsinger, Mark Vicker, Tim Langston, Steve Turets, Tom King, Ron Hafer, and Mike Williamson. Also thanks to the many other fine ladies and gentlemen of visitor centers, local museums, and attractions throughout the state and the many stores, restaurants, hotels, and bed-and-breakfasts that supplied information—and to any others I may have left out.

But most of all, thanks to my dear wife, Wendy, who helped in every phase of this project. I could not and would not have done it without her.

Introduction

From the Lake Erie shore to the ridges of the Laurel Highlands, Western Pennsylvania has much to offer the cyclist—varied terrain and historic cities, countless lakes and mountain streams, state parks and national forests, quaint villages and quiet country roads. Western Pennsylvania is a region that is blessed with scenic beauty, interesting in its history, proud in its heritage, and superior in its road cycling opportunities.

If you're looking for flat cycling, head to Erie and Crawford Counties. Though not pancake flat, this northwest region offers the mildest terrain in Pennsylvania. As a rule, the farther east and south you go in Western Pennsylvania, the hillier the terrain becomes. Lots of effort went into designing road routes that would be suitable for beginners and recreational cyclists—not an easy task in Western Pennsylvania. Though some rides utilize out-and-back routes or rail trails, others are confined to valleys and never venture very far up the ridges bordering them.

Crossing one of Western Pennsylvania's many wooden bridges. Photo courtesy of Bill Metzger

Pennsylvania can boast numerous recreational areas and tourist attractions. Note that several rides are offered in such areas as Ohiopyle, Ligonier, Pymatuning, and the Allegheny National Forest. Road routes in these popular areas were designed to accommodate cyclists of varying ability levels. In addition, those spending more than one day at these popular areas will enjoy additional cycling options during their stay.

Though Pennsylvania enjoys four distinct seasons, you'll most likely be cycling only three of them. Winter conditions in Western Pennsylvania are extreme, and though it is possible to squeeze in an occasional ride, snow and poor road conditions make winter riding here unpleasant. Summer, though hot and humid, remains a popular time to cycle in Pennsylvania. Morning and late-day rides that avoid the afternoon heat are best. Be sure to carry lots of water during the warmer months. Expect larger crowds throughout Pennsylvania's state parks and recreational areas during the summer.

Spring is a wonderful time to cycle Pennsylvania. Crowds are down, and so are prices. With pleasant spring temperatures, Pennsylvania's natural beauty is augmented by its full bloom of azaleas, rhododendron, laurel, and wildflowers. After a winter slowdown there is no better renewal than a bike ride in the Pennsylvania springtime.

Autumn may be the perfect time to bicycle Pennsylvania. Temperatures are moderate, humidity and rainfall are low, and the fall colors are extraordinary. However, for many of the rides in the northern forests and the Laurel Highlands, you can expect many more tourists flocking to festivals and chasing the turning leaves.

The fifty-four rides presented here offer a varied cross section of Western Pennsylvania routes. You can challenge some of Pennsylvania's toughest mountains or leisurely cruise along the Lake Erie shoreline. Cycle through fields full of tomatoes, corn, or sunflowers and past tranquil farms of horses, cows—even llamas. Keep a lookout for white-tailed deer, and hope to spot the elusive black bear or one of Pennsylvania's free-roaming elk. Plan on attending one of the state's prized festivals or tour a restored village depicting early American life. You will have an opportunity to cycle among Amish farms and through regions where the pace of life isn't much faster than the speed of your own bicycle.

Water will be your companion on many Western Pennsylvania bike rides—from small farm ponds and mountain streams to recreational lakes and expansive rivers. And let's not forget Lake Erie and the countless acres of vineyards blanketing its shores. You will cycle through sleepy mountain villages that time seemed to have forgotten; through proud cities with deep roots in the oil, steel, and railroad industries; and through some of America's best university towns and cities.

Make your bike ride a two-day outing, and spend the night in a cozy country inn or at a state park campground. Enjoy conversation with your inn's gracious hosts, or fall asleep under the stars and the flickering of fireflies. Cycle through the spectacular Allegheny National Forest as well as numerous state, county, and municipal parks. Bike through a covered bridge or along one of Pennsylvania's prized rail-trails. Stop and sample the wares of North East's wineries, or learn about the inner workings of a gristmill. Challenge yourself to a century ride—English or metric. Take a break from cycling to acquaint yourself with the local people and history; stop at the town's coffee shop or visit its local museum. Pennsylvania has a lot to offer—Pennsylvanians, even more so.

ROAD AND TRAFFIC CONDITIONS

Pennsylvania is an exceptional state in which to cycle. Unfortunately, the state's bicycling facilities still lag behind some other regions of the country. Several communities, such as Erie, Altoona, and State College, constantly strive to improve conditions for cyclists. However, don't expect much in terms of bike lanes and wide shoulders once you leave the city limits.

The lack of bike lanes and shoulders is offset by an extraordinary network of secondary roads. These roads are mostly indicated with a four-digit state route identifying number (SR) and make up most of the routes in this book. Though also lacking shoulders, these secondary roads are generally very rural, making them suitable, safe, and very pleasant to cycle. Occasionally a ride will use a primary road when no suitable alternative route is available. These state and U.S. highways usually are indicated with a one-, two- or three-digit number. Use caution on these roads, and remember to follow safe cycling practices.

The Pennsylvania Department of Transportation has developed a network of biking routes that connect all corners of the state. The routes are well mapped on the PennDOT Web site and are well signed on the road. It definitely is a big step in the right direction for Pennsylvania. The drawback to these routes, however, is that they are all linear. They're perfect for a long-distance ride across the state or a several-day jaunt from Erie to Pittsburgh. But most bike outings are made by those out for a day ride, and for those rides loops work best. Those seeking long-distance, linear Pennsylvania trips can find their routes on PennDOT's Web site.

Rides located in tourist areas will naturally have heavier summer traffic. Also take into consideration the fall foliage season when planning rides in the Allegheny National Forest region and the Laurel Highlands. Motorists are twisting their necks to look for that perfect photo, not looking out for cyclists.

Many of the rides in Western Pennsylvania involve considerable climbs. Remember that what goes up, must come down. Many routes will involve negotiating switchbacks or tight turns on the descent. Keep your speed under control, and make sure your brakes are working properly *before* your ride. Pay particular attention to the Terrain and Traffic and hazards sections of each chapter's ride specs for more detailed safety instruction.

SAFETY AND COMFORT ON THE ROAD

Pennsylvania laws governing bicycling are similar to those of most other states. Bicyclists must ride with the traffic on the right side of the road, as close as practical to the right edge of the roadway. Bicyclists may ride on road shoulders but are not permitted to ride on Interstate highways and other controlled-access highways in Pennsylvania.

Every bicycle ridden between sunset and sunrise must have proper lighting. Bicycles ridden on roadways must have brakes that will skid the wheels on dry, level, clean pavement (consider this before attempting some of the mountain rides in the book). Pennsylvania law also requires cyclists to properly signal intentions to stop or turn.

Most of all, ride defensively. Stop at all stop signs and red lights, and keep an eye out for motorists turning into your path. Listen for vehicles approaching you from behind. Anticipate that cars will continue their progress as though no cyclist was present. Even though motorists may be in the wrong, you'll never win in a collision with one.

Pennsylvania law requires all youths less than twelve years of age to wear a helmet. Though no laws require helmets for adults, play it safe—*always* wear a helmet. Remember that it is not a matter of *if* you will fall but *when*. Today's helmets are lightweight and come in bright, visible colors. Hey, they even look cool. Your local bike shop can make sure that your helmet is properly fitted.

Consider wearing padded cycling gloves. They help buffer road shock that can lead to hand numbness. Long-term riding this way can increase the risk of nerve damage. Gloves will also help minimize abrasions should you fall.

Use a rearview mirror to monitor traffic behind you. Various styles are available that will mount to handlebars, eyeglasses, or helmet. Experiment with the different styles until you find one that you can use safely and comfortably.

Note that you will not find a bike shop in some rural areas of Pennsylvania, so at least pack the tools necessary to repair a flat tire. This would include a patch kit (or spare tube), tire levers, and a pump. I recommend that every cyclist also carry a multitool, which usually includes Allen wrenches, a spoke wrench, tire levers, and screwdrivers—enough to solve most roadside problems. Of course, the tool is worthless if you don't know how to use it.

Cycle clothing can also help increase comfort while you're in the saddle. Bike jerseys not only provide increased visibility but their fabric helps wick perspiration and keep you dry. They usually are equipped with convenient rear pockets to carry supplies, and a longer cut in back provides adequate cover in

Cyclists enjoying one of Pennsylvania's forests.

the stretched-out position. Padded shorts may look funny and invite stares, but they definitely reduce saddle soreness and protect your inner thighs from chafing. Biking shorts are one item you never want to compromise. Nothing can ruin a ride faster than saddle sores and blisters. Invest in the best you can afford.

All the routes in this book are suitable for cyclists with road, hybrid, or mountain bikes, with the exception of the unpaved rail-trails. Here, 28mm-width tires or greater are recommended. Cycling unpaved trails for 10 or more miles with skinny road tires would be uncomfortable and unsafe. All other routes in this book utilize paved roads. Though the condition of Pennsylvania's roads can be suspect, they can be ridden safely with any width tire.

Finally, always carry at least one water bottle with you. A good rule is to drink one bottle of water for every hour of cycling. Most bikes are equipped to carry two bottles; and hydration systems that cyclists can strap to their back are widely available and becoming extremely popular. It's a good idea to carry a few Fig Newtons or energy bars with you on any ride. Review the Miles and Directions section of a ride before you head out, and know beforehand whether stores are available and where they are located. Bonking is no fun. Be prepared and bike smart.

A lone cyclist pedals up one of Western Pennsylvania's notorious hills.

HOW TO USE THIS BOOK

The fifty-four routes in *Road Biking Western Pennsylvania* are divided into four categories according to degree of difficulty. These classifications are subjective, taking into account the combination of distance, road grade, and bike-handling skills necessary to negotiate the full tour. Each route's name indicates its relative degree of difficulty.

Rambles are the easiest and shortest rides in the book, accessible to almost all riders, and should be easily completed in one day. They are usually less than 35 miles long and are generally on flat to slightly rolling terrain.

Cruises are intermediate in difficulty and distance. They are generally 20 to 50 miles long and may include some moderate climbs. An experienced rider will generally complete a cruise easily in one day. Inexperienced or out-of-shape riders may want to take two days, with an overnight stop.

Challenges are difficult, designed especially for experienced riders in good condition. They are usually 40 to 60 miles long and may include some steep climbs. They should be a challenge for even fairly fit riders to complete in one day. Less experienced or fit riders should expect to take two days.

Classics are long and hard. They are typically 60 miles or more, with some exceeding 100 miles. They can include steep climbs and high-speed descents. Even fit and experienced riders will want to take two days. Unless done in shorter stages, these rides are not recommended for less fit and experienced riders.

Remember that terrain is as much a factor as distance in determining a ride's category. The 41-mile Pymatuning Cruise is actually a lot easier than the shorter 31-mile Oil Creek Challenge. Examining the elevation profile of a ride together with the distance will enable you to select rides most appropriate for your ability level.

Don't let the distance of a longer tour dissuade you from trying a ride in an attractive area. Out-and-back rides along portions of a route provide options that may be well suited to your schedule and other commitments. Likewise, don't automatically dismiss a shorter ride in an interesting area.

Directions in the route narrative for each ride include the cumulative mileage to each turn and to significant landmarks along the way. It's possible that your mileage may differ slightly. Over enough miles, differences in odometer calibration, tire pressure, and the line you follow can have a significant effect on the measurement of distance. Use the cumulative mileage in connection with your route descriptions and maps.

The selection of these routes is the result of extensive reading and research; suggestions from bike shops, cycling clubs, friends, and local experts; and a lot of bicycling. Some of the routes are well-known cycling venues; others are less frequently ridden. Taken as a whole, the routes in this book offer a cross section of the best riding locations in the state, indicative of the wide variety of roads and terrain Western Pennsylvania has to offer.

To the greatest extent possible, each route has been designed with specific criteria in mind, although not all criteria could be addressed in every instance. Starting points are normally easy to find, with convenient parking and reasonable access to provisions. Roads should be moderately traveled, be in good repair, and have adequate shoulders where traffic volume requires. I've also made an effort to guide the reader to interesting places along the route.

Construction, development, improvements, and other changes are commonplace on Western Pennsylvania roadways. The route descriptions and maps in this book, therefore, can only be records of conditions as they once were; they may not always describe conditions as you find them. Comments, updates, and corrections from interested and critical readers are always appreciated and can be sent to the author in care of the publisher.

ELEVATION PROFILES

An elevation profile accompanies each ride description where there is an elevation differential of 250 feet or more. The ups and downs of the route are graphed on an elevation grid, with FEET ABOVE SEA LEVEL on the sides, and MILES PEDALED across the top. Note that these graphs are compressed (squeezed) to fit on the page. The actual slopes you will ride will not be as steep as the lines drawn on the graphs (it just feels that way). Also, some extremely short dips and climbs are too small to show on the graphs. All abrupt changes in gradient are, however, mentioned in the mile-by-mile ride description.

HOW TO READ THE MAPS

The individual route map is your primary guide to each ride. It shows all the accessible roads, points of interest, towns, landmarks, and geographical features. The selected route is highlighted, and directional arrows point the way.

The rides in *Road Biking Western Pennsylvania* lay an excellent foundation for a bike route. Using a little creativity and additional maps, any cyclist can change the ride direction or add turnarounds or shortcuts. In addition, rides can begin at any point along the course described in the route directions. You can always leave the route to explore interesting side roads and create routes more suited to your individual taste.

Map Legend

	Featured Route
70	Interstate Highway
40	US Highway
999	State Highway
	County or Local Road
	Trail
	Water Route
○ Punxsutawney	City Center
■	Point of Interest/ Structure
3.5 •	Mileage Point
	Reservoir or Lake
	River or Creek
	State Line
State Park	Park

Presque Isle and Erie Ramble

The Presque Isle and Erie Ramble is a delightful and easy spin around one of Pennsylvania's most popular state parks. Stop for a picnic, and go for a swim at one the park's many guarded sandy beaches. Enjoy miles of shady cycling as you encircle the entire peninsula on bike lanes and multiuse paths. Continue on bike lanes through the easily negotiated and bike-friendly city of Erie. Stop and tour the U.S. Brig Niagara and learn its history at the Erie Maritime Museum. Get a bird's-eye view of the region by climbing the Bicentennial Tower at Erie's Dobbins Landing. End your ramble with a relaxing water taxi ride across Presque Isle Bay.

Presque Isle State Park is a 3,200-acre sandy peninsula that arches outward into Lake Erie. Meaning "almost an island" in French, the peninsula is a National Natural Landmark because of its six distinct ecological zones, each with different plant and animal communities. Each year more than four million visitors experience Presque Isle's beaches, recreational opportunities, and natural beauty.

The Presque Isle and Erie Ramble can be done several ways. You can simply ride around the entire peninsula for an easy 13-mile spin, as most visitors to Presque Isle do. You will be rewarded, however, by following the directions here for a slightly longer ramble through the city of Erie. Riding in Erie is a breeze—flat and entirely on bike lanes or multiuse paths. When your ride ends at Dobbins Landing, hop on the water taxi that will transport you and your bike across beautiful Presque Isle Bay and right back to the starting point at Cookhouse Pavilion. Thanks to Tom Maggio of the Erie–Western Pennsylvania

Start: From the Cookhouse Pavilion parking lot, Presque Isle State Park.

Length: 16 miles.

Terrain: Mostly flat; suitable for all ability levels.

Traffic and hazards: All cycling is on paved bike lanes or multiuse paths. Use caution when cycling the shoulder bike lanes once you leave the state park, as there is more traffic through the city segment of the ride. Walk your bike across the Bayfront Parkway at Mile 13.8 to access the multiuse path.

Getting there: From points south follow Interstate 79 north until it ends in Erie. Pick up Pennsylvania Highway 5 and follow it west 1.5 miles to Peninsula Drive. Turn right and travel approximately 1 mile to the Presque Isle State Park entrance. Go another 2.8 miles to the Cookhouse Pavilion lot on the right. Also located here is the Waterworks boat launch and water taxi station. There is no entrance fee to the park, and parking is free and plentiful. (About 0.5 mile before the cookhouse, there is a park office on the right. Stop here for a park map and other information on the area. The staff is very helpful.)

Port Authority for submitting this ride. So many bicyclists come to the region and never leave the state park; Tom has mapped out a remarkable ride along some of Erie's fine bike lanes that showcase the city's many attractions.

Plan lots of time to complete your tour of Presque Isle and the city of Erie. There are many picnic areas scattered throughout the park, as well as 7 miles of guarded, sandy beaches. Presque Isle's lakeside beaches have been named among the "Top 100 Swimming Holes" by *Condé Nast Traveler* magazine. The Perry Monument makes a nice rest stop and photo op. Lighthouse lovers will delight in both the North Pier and Presque Isle Lighthouses, as well as exhibits. Several scenic boat tours leave from the peninsula. Numerous hiking trails traverse the ecological reservation, and fishing hot spots are both numerous and popular.

As you leave Presque Isle State Park, Sarah's and Joe Roots Grill are both located on the left and will fuel you for more riding. After several miles on a well-marked bike lane along West Sixth Street, you'll turn left at Mile 13.7 on Cranberry Street. When you reach Bayfront Parkway, please walk your bike across this busy freeway. Hop on the multiuse path and notice how Erie is sprucing up its waterfront. Additional developments and bikeways are planned, and in time longer rides with even more attractions will be possible utilizing a well-designed bike path network.

When you reach State Street at Mile 15.4, consider a detour straight for 1 block to the Erie Maritime Museum, home to the reconstructed U.S. Brig *Niagara*. It was aboard the *Niagara* that Commodore Oliver Hazard Perry defeated the British squadron in the 1813 Battle of Lake Erie. This pivotal battle in the War or 1812 led Perry to report, "We have met the enemy and they are

The wonderful bike facilities of Erie and Presque Isle.

ours." The Erie Maritime Museum not only illustrates *Niagara*'s history but also the region's rich maritime heritage.

Back at Dobbins Landing, consider one of several fine restaurants located at the waterfront. For great views of the city, Presque Isle, and Lake Erie, climb the 187-foot Bicentennial Observation Tower. Then hop on the Port of Erie water taxi, pay the $3.00 one-way fee, and enjoy a relaxing twenty-minute boat ride across the bay to Presque Isle. And don't forget about the stunning sunsets from the western beaches of this peninsula. Whether you come to Presque Isle/Erie for a history lesson or to enjoy nature, swim, picnic, or bike, you're sure to find this region simply Eriesistible.

LOCAL INFORMATION

♦ Erie Area Convention and Visitors Bureau, 109 Boston Store Place, Erie, PA 16501; (800) 524–3743 or (814) 454–7191.
♦ For Water Taxi information call (814) 881–2502 or (814) 899–9059. Boats normally leave Dobbins Landing on the hour, with a 6:00 P.M. final departure. Call ahead to be sure.

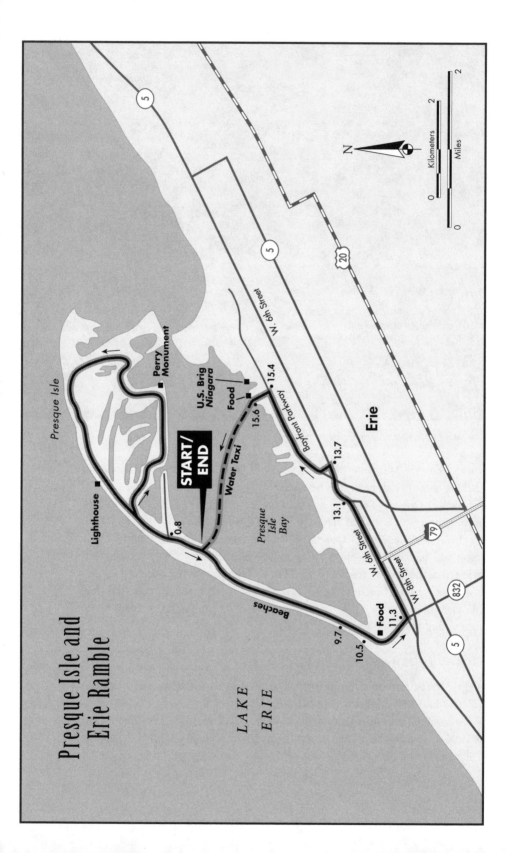

0.0 From the Cookhouse Pavilion parking lot, head toward the water to pick up the bike path. Turn left.

0.8 Stay straight toward the Perry Monument.

1.8 On the right is the East Pier, with fishing, picnic areas, and restrooms. Note that the bike path frequently crosses the park road. Though traffic speeds are very low, use caution.

2.7 The Perry Monument is on the right. Located here are more picnicking areas, restrooms, and a concession area.

4.6 Beach areas begin on the right; numerous access points for the next 6 miles.

6.0 There is an attractive circa 1872 lighthouse to the right.

9.7 Visitor and nature center here.

10.5 The bike path rejoins the main park road. If you are just cycling the state park, go straight another 50 yards. Cross the park road at the painted crosswalk and turn left. The path will take you back to the Cookhouse Pavilion parking lot in 2.8 miles.

10.7 Just outside the state park on the left are two restaurants, Sarah's and Joe Roots Grill.

11.0 Waldameer Park (amusement) and Water World are on the right.

11.3 Turn left at the stoplight onto West Sixth Street. Exercise a little more caution cycling through the city. Nice bike lane the entire length.

13.1 Bear slightly left to continue on West Sixth Street. Keep the playground and tennis courts to your right.

13.7 Turn left onto Cranberry Street. Follow for 0.1 mile until you reach the Bayfront Parkway. Walk your bike across this busy highway and turn right on the multiuse path on the opposite side. Follow the trail along the Bayfront Parkway. In about 0.5 mile, Liberty Park will be on the left, as well as Shakespiers Restaurant.

15.3 After you pass the Presque Isle Yacht Club, the bike path merges with a driveway/access road. Follow it, keeping the railroad tunnel just to your right. Enter a parking lot; cycle through the lot and out through the exit to the stop sign.

15.4 Turn left onto State Street if you want to head directly to the dock. Consider a detour here by going straight on East Front Street. In 1 block, you can visit the Erie Maritime Museum and the U.S. Brig *Niagara*.

15.6 Arrive at Dobbins Landing. Several restaurants and the Bicentennial Observation Tower are located here. Just beneath the tower is where you will find the Port of Erie water taxi. Pay the fee and enjoy the boat ride back to Cookhouse Pavilion on Presque Isle.

LOCAL EVENTS/ATTRACTIONS

♦ Discover Presque Isle. Held the last full weekend in July at Presque Isle State Park. A celebration of the beauty and recreational opportunities of the park. Nature programs, craft displays, competitions, live music, bonfires, and more; (814) 833–7424.

♦ Erie Days Festival. Mid-August. Erie's largest downtown festival with lots of food, art exhibits, games, performances, and fireworks. Call the visitor center for information; (800) 524–3743.

♦ U.S. Brig *Niagara* and the Erie Maritime Museum, 150 East Front Street, Erie, PA 16507; (814) 452–2744. Museum depicting the history of the *Niagara* as well as the region's maritime heritage.

RESTAURANTS

♦ Sara's, 25 Peninsula Drive, Erie, PA 16505; (814) 833–1957. Popular eatery on the route just outside the state park.

♦ Waterfront Seafood and Steak House, 4 State Street, Erie, PA 16507; (814) 459–0606. Convenient location at the end of your city riding at Dobbins Landing.

ACCOMMODATIONS

♦ Sara Coyne Campgrounds, 50 Peninsula Drive, Erie, PA 16505; (814) 833–4560. Located on the route just outside Presque Isle State Park.

♦ The Boothby Inn B&B, 311 West Sixth Street, Erie, PA 16507; (814) 456–1888 or toll-free (866) 266–8429. This upscale inn was voted one of the Top 30 Great U.S. Inns by *Travel & Leisure* magazine.

BIKE SHOP

♦ Frontier Bike Shop, 1712 West Eighth Street, Erie, PA 16505; (814) 456–9803.

RESTROOMS

♦ Mile 0.0: Cookhouse Pavilion
♦ Mile 0.0 to 9.7: numerous locations throughout Presque Isle State Park
♦ Mile 10.7: Sara's restaurant
♦ Mile 15.6: various locations at Dobbins Landing

MAP

♦ *DeLorme Pennsylvania Atlas & Gazetteer,* map 27

North East Wine Country Rides

The North East Wine Country offers two delightful rides—a ramble and a cruise—through the vast grape-growing fields of this Lake Erie shoreline region. Stop at one of several wineries to experience the winemaking process and, of course, to taste. Detour to Halli Reid Park and take a refreshing dip in Lake Erie at Freeport Beach. Meander along the rural country roads through one of the highest concentrations of wineries in the country. Time your visit with the renowned Wine Country Harvest Festival for a celebration of the wine industry and lots of grape-stomping fun.

Thanks to the good folks at Lake Country Bike, located right in North East, for submitting these fabulous rides. In addition to your biking supply needs, Lake Country will provide maps and cue sheets for additional rides in the area. Stop in and say hello.

A hundred and fifty years ago, two men suspected that the climate and growing conditions of this Lake Erie shoreline region would be well suited to growing grapes. There were correct. Today there are thousands of acres of vineyards with five thriving wineries. It is not only a major industry for the region but also a source of identity for its residents. Even the sports teams honor their proud heritage—they are called the "Grapepickers."

Two rides are detailed here for the North East wine country; a 22-mile ramble and a 34-mile cruise. The longer cruise encompasses the entire ramble route and adds an additional 12-mile loop. Though the additional loop is not difficult, the additional miles place the ride in the more difficult cruise category. Some rolling hills will get the blood pumping, but overall the rides are not too difficult; even a beginner should finish without much difficulty. Your deci-

Start: From the parking lot located at the junction of North Lake Street/Pennsylvania Highway 89 and Gibson Street in downtown North East.

Length: 22 miles for the ramble; 34 miles for the cruise.

Terrain: Flat to gently rolling. Some gradual climbing on the front end of the ride. Beginners will receive a workout but should have no problems completing either ride.

Traffic and hazards: Use caution while on the short segments of U.S. Highway 20. All roads are paved and are either rural or have an adequate shoulder. Use caution on the several rough railroad crossings.

Getting there: From Interstate 90, take the exit for PA 89 North and go 2.1 miles to the intersection with Main Street in downtown North East. Go 1 block to the parking lot on the right, directly across from Gibson Street.

sion to do the extra 12 miles doesn't come until very late in the ride, so you can see how you're feeling and then decide.

Of the 34 miles in the cruise, about 30 are within sight of a vineyard, and cycling through them is absolutely enchanting. Just 3 to 4 miles into the ride will put you on a high bluff. Views looking down over the colorful vineyards with stark-blue Lake Erie on the horizon are extraordinary. Take the camera with you—you'll be using it. A gradual descent brings you into New York State and the village of Ripley. Here is an opportunity for a rest stop; a restaurant and convenience store are located here.

At Mile 17.6 plan a visit to Mazza Vineyards. A tour will take you through all steps of the wine-making process. Easy on the tasting, however; there's more cycling to do. At Mile 19.7 Freeport Restaurant will be on the right. This popular eatery is the northernmost restaurant in Pennsylvania and is worth a stop just to pick up its historic menu. By detouring to the right on Freeport Road at this intersection, you can enjoy a pleasant rest stop at Freeport Beach and Halli Reid Park (named for the first woman to swim across Lake Erie). Besides the beach, there are picnic areas, a volleyball court, restrooms, and shady spots that allow you to cool off and unwind.

Mile 20.0 is decision time. Turning left on North Mill Street will take you back to town in 2 miles. Continuing straight on Pennsylvania Highway 5 West will add an extra 12 miles to the ride. The scenery for the additional loop is the same—vineyards. You'll have the opportunity to stop at Penn Shore Winery, one of the largest and longest established wineries in the state.

Back in North East, take the opportunity to stroll this fine town listed on the National Register of Historic Districts. Stop at the excellent Lake Shore Railway Museum located in an 1889 passenger train station. Plan to spend the night in one of many B&Bs during the town's autumn salute to wine, the Wine Country Harvest Festival.

LOCAL INFORMATION

♦ North East Area Chamber of Commerce, 21 South Lake Street, North East, PA 16428; (814) 725–4262.

LOCAL EVENTS/ATTRACTIONS

♦ Wine Country Harvest Festival. Hosted by the chamber of commerce, the festival is a celebration of the region's grape industry. Usually held the last weekend in September; expect music, food, artisans, wine tours, tastings, seminars, and grape stomping. Call the chamber for information at (814) 725–4262.
♦ Welch's Harvest Classic. A United States Cycling Federation Bike Race held in mid-August. Call Lake Country Bike for more information; (814) 725–1338.

RESTAURANTS

♦ Freeport Restaurant, 11104 East Lake Road, North East, PA 16428; (814) 725–4607. Family-style restaurant located on the route; breakfast, lunch, and dinner.
♦ Johnny B's Restaurant, 37 Vine Street, North East, PA 16428; (814) 725–1762. Casual Italian-American cuisine in the heart of town.

One of several wineries in the North East region of Erie County.

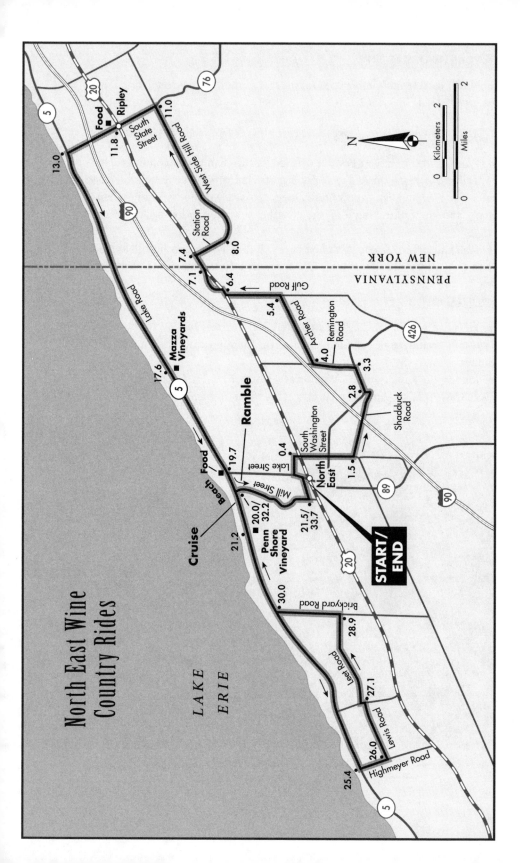

North East Wine Country Rides

N

Kilometers 2

Miles

NEW YORK

PENNSYLVANIA

Ripley

Food

20

76

5

South State Street

11.8

11.0

West Side Hill Road

13.0

90

Station Road

7.4

8.0

7.1

6.4

Gulf Road

5.4

Archer Road

Remington Road

426

4.0

3.3

2.8

Shadduck Road

Lake Road

Mazza Vineyards

17.6

5

Ramble

19.7

Lake Street

0.4

South Washington Street

North East

1.5

89

Food

Mill Street

Beach

20.0/ 32.2

21.5/ 33.7

90

Penn Shore Vineyard

START/ END

20

Cruise

21.2

30.0

Brickyard Road

28.9

LAKE ERIE

Leet Road

27.1

Lewis Road

26.0

Lewis Road

25.4

Highmeyer Road

5

0.0 Turn right out of the parking lot onto PA 89/North Lake Street. Go 0.1 mile and turn right on East Division Street.

0.4 Turn right onto South Washington Street. After crossing Main Street, use caution when encountering your first set of rough railroad crossings.

1.5 Turn left onto Shadduck Road.

2.8 Turn right at stop sign on Pennsylvania Highway 426.

3.3 Turn left onto Remington; nice photo op here.

4.0 Turn right onto Archer Road.

5.4 Turn left at stop sign onto Gulf Road. Use caution on upcoming railroad crossing.

6.4 Turn right at stop sign onto US 20, then take an immediate left onto Gay Street, just across from the House of Potter.

6.7 Turn right at stop sign onto Stinson Road.

7.1 Turn left at the stop sign onto US 20. Use caution on busy US 20 for the next 0.25 mile. Enter New York State and pass Kelly Hotel and Restaurant on the right.

7.4 Turn right onto Station Road. Use caution in the next mile; there are several sets of rough railroad tracks.

8.0 Bear left onto West Side Hill Road.

11.0 Turn left onto Highway 76 North/South State Street. In 0.75 mile there's another rough railroad crossing.

11.8 Go straight at the stoplight in Ripley. A Citgo convenience store is to the left and the Corner Restaurant and Bar is on the right.

13.0 Turn left at stop sign onto New York Highway 5 West. Enjoy a nice shoulder and great Lake Erie views.

15.3 Lakeside Campground is on the right. Just past the campground reenter Pennsylvania.

17.6 Mazza Vineyards is on the left.

(continued)

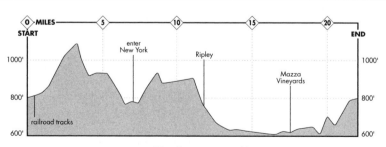

Ramble elevation profile

19.7 Continue straight on PA 5. The Freeport Restaurant is on the right. For a detour to the beach, turn right here and go 0.3 mile. Halli Reid Park has restrooms and picnic areas as well as a nice Lake Erie beach.

20.0 Turn left onto North Mill Street. (*Note:* The cruise route continues straight here.)

21.5 Turn left onto Gibson Street.

22.0 Go straight at stop sign to cross North Lake Street and enter parking lot.

CRUISE MILES AND DIRECTIONS

0.0 Turn right out of the parking lot onto PA 89/North Lake Street. Go 0.1 mile and turn right onto East Division Street.

0.4 Turn right onto South Washington Street. After crossing Main Street, use caution when encountering your first set of rough railroad crossings.

1.5 Turn left onto Shadduck Road.

2.8 Turn right at stop sign onto Pennsylvania Highway 426.

3.3 Turn left onto Remington; nice photo op here.

4.0 Turn right onto Archer Road.

5.4 Turn left at stop sign onto Gulf Road. Use caution on upcoming railroad crossing.

6.4 Turn right at stop sign on US 20, then take an immediate left onto Gay Street, just across from the House of Potter.

6.7 Turn right at stop sign onto Stinson Road.

7.1 Turn left at the stop sign onto PA 20. Use caution on busy PA 20 for the next 0.25 mile. Enter New York State and pass Kelly Hotel and Restaurant on the right.

7.4 Turn right onto Station Road. Use caution in the next mile; there are several sets of rough railroad tracks.

8.0 Bear left onto West Side Hill Road.

11.0 Turn left on to New York Highway 76 North/South State Street. In 0.75 mile there's another rough railroad crossing.

11.8 Go straight at the stoplight in Ripley. A Citgo convenience store is to the left and The Corner Restaurant and Bar is on the right.

13.0 Turn left at stop sign onto New York Highway 5 West. Enjoy a nice shoulder and great Lake Erie views.

15.3 Lakeside Campground is on the right. Just past the campground reenter Pennsylvania.

17.6 Mazza Vineyards is on the left.

(continued)

19.7 Continue straight on PA 5. The Freeport Restaurant is on the right. For a detour to the beach, turn right here and go 0.3 mile. Halli Reid Park has restrooms and picnic areas as well as a nice Lake Erie beach.

20.0 Continue straight on PA 5 West. (*Note:* the ramble route turns left here.)

21.2 The Penn Shore Winery is on the left.

25.4 Turn left onto Highmeyer Road.

26.0 Turn left onto Lewis Road.

27.1 Turn left at stop sign onto unmarked Moorheadville Road, and make the immediate right onto Leet Road.

28.5 Go straight at the stop sign. Road becomes Middle Road.

28.9 Turn left at stop sign onto Brickyard Road.

30.0 Turn right at stop sign onto PA 5 East.

32.2 Turn right onto North Mill Street.

33.7 Turn left onto Gibson Street.

34.2 Go straight at stop sign to cross North Lake Street and enter parking lot.

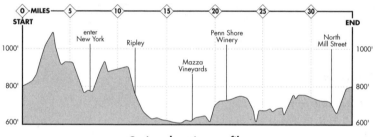

Cruise elevation profile

ACCOMMODATIONS

♦ Lighthouse Keepers B&B, 11934 Seitzinger Road, North East, PA 16428; (814) 725–1817. Treat yourself to the lighthouse room overlooking Lake Erie.

♦ Vineyard B&B, 10757 Sidehill Road, North East, PA 16428, (888) 725–8998. Turn-of-the-twentieth century farmhouse in the heart of the vineyards. Moderate.

BIKE SHOP

♦ Lake Country Bike, 21 East Main Street, North East, PA 16428; (814) 725–1338.

Beautiful view overlooking vineyards and Lake Erie.

RESTROOMS

On the ramble route:
- Mile 7.1: Kelly Hotel and Restaurant
- Mile 11.8: several locations in Ripley
- Mile 17.6: Mazza Vineyards
- Mile 19.7: Freeport Restaurant

On the cruise route:
- Mile 7.1: Kelly Hotel and Restaurant
- Mile 11.8: several locations in Ripley
- Mile 17.6: Mazza Vineyards
- Mile 19.7: Freeport Restaurant
- Mile 21.2: Penn Shore Winery

MAP

- *DeLorme Pennsylvania Atlas & Gazetteer,* map 27

Cambridge Springs Rides

Situated in southern Erie and northern Crawford Counties, the Cambridge Springs ramble and cruise are relatively easy and tranquil tours of the farmlands and woodlands surrounding the meandering French Creek. Pass through the Western State Game Farm on your way to Cambridge Springs, home of the Riverside Inn. Stop for lunch or even the night at this beautiful inn and learn the history of the town and mineral springs that started it all. Finish the ride in Edinboro, a lively college town and home to the Crossroads Diner, where you can dine in an authentic streetcar.

Thanks to Bob Cramer of Country Side Cycling of Edinboro for submitting these fine rides. This well-equipped bike shop is located at the intersection of Lakeside Drive and West Plum Street, and you must pass the shop on your way to the starting point. Stop in to say hello and pick up any supplies you need. Bob is more than willing to help out with other route ideas you may have for cycling this region.

If you are in for just the day, I suggest that you start the ride in Edinboro and plan a rest stop in Cambridge Springs. If you plan to spend a night, consider staying at Riverside Inn or another establishment in Cambridge Springs. You can start the ride from there and use Edinboro and its many eateries as a midride stop. Home to Edinboro University, the borough has an inviting downtown district with plenty of shops and restaurants.

The ramble and cruise share the same route until Cambridge Springs. The ride starts out by skirting downtown Edinboro and soon heads out to fine countryside. The terrain is gentle, and when hilly Mt. Pleasant appears in front of you, the route conveniently turns and circles around it. After an easy spin

Start: From James Haggerty Memorial Park on Lakeside Drive, Edinboro.

Length: 21 miles for the ramble; 34 miles for the cruise.

Terrain: Flat to gently rolling. Beginners will have no problem with the shorter ramble route. A few more rollers and additional miles place the longer ride in the cruise category, but the ride remains one of the easier cruises in this book.

Traffic and hazards: All roads on this route are paved, low traffic, and rural. No particular areas of caution.

Getting there: From Interstate 79, take the U.S. Highway 6N exit and head east in the direction of Edinboro. Go 2.0 miles to Lakeside Drive, located on the left just past a small plaza where Country Side Cycling is situated. Turn left onto Lakeside Drive and go 0.2 mile to the James Haggerty Memorial Park, located on the right along the shoreline of Edinboro Lake. Free parking.

into Cambridge Springs, you have an opportunity to refuel and pay a visit to the Riverside Inn.

The Riverside Inn, on the National Register of Historic Places, sits on the banks of French Creek and has been in continuous operation since 1885. This lovely inn got its start during the Mineral Waters Era and became the first "health spa" of its kind. Of the nearly forty such establishments that sprang up in the Cambridge Springs area, only the Riverside Inn remains today. The inn makes for an enjoyable stay; the resort offers golf as well as a dinner theater. Call (800) 964–5173 for the inn's reasonably priced packages.

The cruise option branches off here to add a 13-mile loop. The additional mileage is similar—rural with gently rolling terrain along twisting French Creek. On Pennsylvania Highway 408, the cruise passes through the Western State Game Farm. The thousands of pheasants raised here make for an amusing sight.

Leaving Cambridge Springs, consider a stop at Campbell Pottery at Mile 27.1. Nationally known Master Potter Bill Campbell showcases his prized porcelain in a restored century-old barn. You can have your purchases shipped or just drive back after your ride. Just 1.5 miles past the Campbell Pottery brings you to Finney's Pumpkinville, a fun autumn stop.

Back in Edinboro, seek out the Crossroads Diner, open daily for breakfast, lunch, and dinner. Some seating is available in an original trolley car that once traversed this college town. Later, cool off in Edinboro Lake, which borders the town and offers numerous recreational activities.

LOCAL INFORMATION

◆ Edinboro Area Chamber of Commerce, 131 Erie Street, Edinboro, PA 16412; (814) 734–6561.

LOCAL EVENTS/ATTRACTIONS

♦ Riverside Inn Dinner Theater. Presentations include murder mysteries, comedies, and Christmas shows. Call the box office for current shows; (800) 964–5173.

RESTAURANTS

♦ Riverside Inn, One Fountain Avenue, Cambridge Springs, PA 16403; (800) 964–5173. Historic 1885 inn serving breakfast, lunch, and dinner.
♦ The Crossroads Diner, 101 Plum Street, Edinboro, PA 16412; (814) 734–1912. Local favorite built around an authentic streetcar. Open daily for breakfast, lunch, and dinner.

ACCOMMODATIONS

♦ Riverside Inn, One Fountain Avenue, Cambridge Springs, PA 16403; (800) 964–5173. Historic 1885 inn with many amenities. Moderate.

BIKE SHOP

♦ Country Side Cycling, 318 West Plum Street, Edinboro, PA 16412; (814) 734–7366.

Cyclists enjoy the gentle terrain near Edinboro.

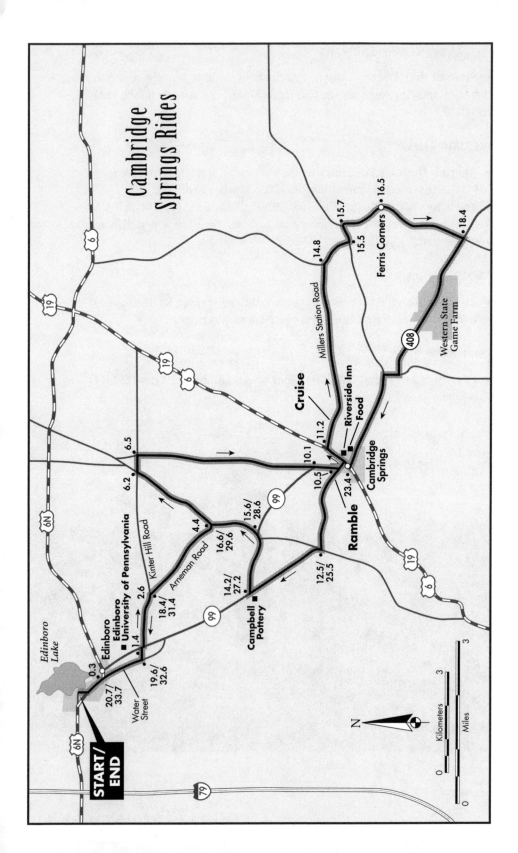

Cambridge Springs Rides

START/END

Edinboro Lake

Water Street
19.6/32.6
20.7/33.7
0.3
Edinboro
Edinboro University of Pennsylvania
1.4
2.6
18.4/31.4
Kinter Hill Road
4.4
Arneman Road
14.2/27.2
16.6/29.6
15.6/28.6
Campbell Pottery
6.2
6.5
12.5/25.5
Ramble
99
Cruise
10.1
10.5
11.2
Riverside Inn
Food
23.4
Cambridge Springs
Millers Station Road
14.8
15.5
15.7
Ferris Corners
16.5
18.4
408
Western State Game Farm

6
19
6N
19
6
79
6N
6
99
19

N
Kilometers   3
Miles   3
0
0

0.0 Go left out of James Haggerty Memorial Park parking lot onto Lakeside Drive and go 0.2 mile to the intersection with West Plum Street. Country Side Cycling is located here on the right, next door to a bagel shop. Turn left onto West Plum Street.

0.3 Turn right onto Maple Drive just past the Edinboro Inn. Just after you turn off West Plum Street, the road splits three ways. Take the left road, which is Maple Drive.

0.7 Cross Chestnut Street at stop sign. Jog slightly to the left and continue straight on Water Street.

1.4 Turn left at the stop sign onto Kinter Hill Road. In 0.2 mile continue straight at the stop sign, crossing Pennsylvania Highway 99.

2.6 Turn right onto Arneman Road.

4.4 Turn left onto Mt. Pleasant Road, which becomes Old Plank Road.

6.2 Turn right at stop sign onto Kinter Hill Road.

6.5 Turn right onto State Route 3022/Edinboro Plank Road,also known as Old Pennsylvania 66.

10.1 Bear left at the stop sign onto PA 99 South.

10.5 Turn left at the stop sign onto McClellan Street.

10.7 Arrive at the stoplight at the intersection with North Main Street in Cambridge Springs. To make a stop at the historic Riverside Inn, head straight through the stoplight into the inn's parking lot. For a convenience store stop, go right 0.1 mile to the Red Apple Kwik Fill Store. To continue the 21-mile ramble, turn around here and follow McClellen Street. (*Note:* The cruise route turns left here.)

10.9 Continue straight onto McClellen Street where PA 99 North goes to the right. This is where you entered town at Mile 10.5.

12.5 Turn right at the stop sign onto Old Plank Road.

13.2 Country Cream Ice Cream is on the right.

14.1 Campbell Pottery is located on the left.

14.2 Turn right at the stop sign onto PA 99 South.

15.6 Finney's Pumpkinville is located on the right. Just past Finney's, turn left onto Mt. Pleasant Road.

15.7 At the stop sign, turn right to stay on Mt. Pleasant Road.

16.6 Turn left onto Arneman Road.

18.4 Turn left onto Kinter Hill Road.

19.4 Continue straight at stop sign onto Kinter Hill Road, crossing PA 99.

19.6 Turn right at stop sign onto Water Street.

20.3 Continue straight at the stop sign onto Maple Drive. You'll need to jog slightly left to do this.

(continued)

RAMBLE MILES AND DIRECTIONS (continued)

20.7 Turn left at the stop sign onto US 6N West/West Plum Street.

20.9 Turn right onto Lakeside Drive.

21.0 End the ride back at James Haggerty Memorial Park.

CRUISE MILES AND DIRECTIONS

0.0 Go left out of James Haggerty Memorial Park parking lot on Lakeside Drive and go 0.2 mile to the intersection with West Plum Street. Country Side Cycling is located here on the right, next door to a bagel shop. Turn left onto West Plum Street.

0.3 Turn right onto Maple Drive just past the Edinboro Inn. Just after you turn off West Plum Street, the road splits three ways. Take the left road, which is Maple Drive.

0.7 Cross Chestnut Street at stop sign. Jog slightly left and continue straight on Water Street.

1.4 Turn left at the stop sign onto Kinter Hill Road. In 0.2 mile continue straight at the stop sign, crossing Pennsylvania Highway 99.

2.6 Turn right onto Arneman Road.

4.4 Turn left onto Mt. Pleasant Road.

6.2 Turn right at stop sign onto Kinter Hill Road.

6.5 Turn right onto State Route 3022/Edinboro Plank Road, also known as Old Pennsylvania Highway 66.

10.1 Bear left at the stop sign onto PA 99 South.

10.5 Turn left at the stop sign onto McClellan Street.

10.7 Turn left at the stoplight onto North Main Street. **Detour:** To stop at the historic Riverside Inn, head straight through the stoplight into the inn's parking lot. For a convenience store stop, go right 0.1 mile to the Red Apple Kwik Fill Store. (*Note:* the ramble turns around here and heads back on McClellen Street.)

11.2 Turn right onto State Route 1016/Miller Station Road.

14.8 Bear right at Y intersection after the one-lane bridge to stay on SR 1016.

15.5 Bear left to stay on SR 1016/Miller Station Road.

15.7 Bear right at Y intersection to stay on SR 1016.

16.5 Continue straight to stay on SR 1016. In 0.1 mile, turn right onto Swamp Road.

18.4 Turn right at the stop sign onto PA 408. Pass through the Western State Game Farm. Follow PA 408 all the way back into Cambridge Springs.

23.4 Turn right at stoplight onto South Main Street. Several restaurants are located here.

(continued)

23.6 The Red Apple Kwik Fill Store is on the right.

23.7 Turn left at the stoplight onto McClellen Street. You have completed the extra loop for the cruise route. To stop at the Riverside Inn, turn right at the stoplight instead of left.

23.9 Continue straight on McClellen Street where PA 99 North goes to the right. This is where you entered town at Mile 10.5.

25.5 Turn right at the stop sign onto Plank Road.

26.2 Country Cream Ice Cream is on the right.

27.1 Campbell Pottery is located on the left.

27.2 Turn right at the stop sign onto PA 99 South.

28.6 Finney's Pumpkinville is located on the right. Just past Finney's, turn left onto Mt. Pleasant Road.

28.7 At the stop sign, turn right to stay on Mt. Pleasant Road.

29.6 Turn left onto Arneman Road.

31.4 Turn left onto Kinter Hill Road.

32.4 Continue straight at stop sign on Kinter Hill Road, crossing PA 99.

32.6 Turn right at stop sign onto Water Street.

33.3 Continue straight at the stop sign on Maple Drive. You'll need to jog slightly left to do this.

33.7 Turn left at the stop sign onto US 6N West/West Plum Street.

33.9 Turn right onto Lakeside Drive.

34.0 End the ride back at the James Haggerty Memorial Park.

RESTROOMS

For both routes:

◆ Mile 0.2: the bagel shop, Country Side Cycling, or other establishments in Edinboro

◆ Mile 10.7: Riverside Inn or the Red Apple Kwik Fill Store in Cambridge Springs

MAP

◆ *DeLorme Pennsylvania Atlas & Gazetteer,* map 29

Pymatuning Rides

The Pymatuning ramble and the longer Pymatuning cruise offer some of the flattest and easiest cycling in Western Pennsylvania. Starting near the dam in Pymatuning State Park, both routes head west and north to follow the shoreline of Pennsylvania's largest reservoir. While the ramble takes the 2-mile-long causeway shortcut, the cruise heads farther north to Linesville, where three exciting rest stops await. Take your pick of a state fish hatchery and aquarium, a wildlife museum, or an opportunity to feed the fish at the spillway, a place so congested with carp that ducks literally walk on the fishes' backs. Stop at one of several restaurants along the route, or plan a picnic at one of many waterfront sites along the lake. Plan to stay at one of the many campgrounds surrounding the lake and spend the evening fishing one of the state's hot spots.

Pymatuning was once a swamp and home to the Erie Nation Indians, who were ruled by a crooked and cunning queen. When the Seneca Nation of the Iroquois defeated the Erie Nation, the land was used as their new hunting ground and called Pymatuning, which means "Crooked-mouthed Man's Dwelling Place" in Iroquois. (The name refers to deceit rather than physical deformity.)

The Pymatuning Reservoir was built in the 1930s, primarily to control flooding in the Shenango and Beaver Rivers. Though it still serves that purpose, most everyone associates the Pymatuning area with the multitude of recreational opportunities available at and around the lake. The 17,000-acre reservoir, largest in the state, is one of Pennsylvania's top fishing hot spots. Boating, camping, hunting, hiking, bird-watching, fish and game commission exhibits, picnicking, and, of course, biking round out the activities enjoyed by the many visitors to the area.

In my opinion, the Pymatuning region is the premier flatland bicycling destination in the state. I recommend that you take the 41-mile cruise option and enjoy some of the attractions near Linesville. Throw in several rest stops, such as lunch at a local restaurant, a picnic along the lake, and an hour of relaxation on a beach, and you'll have one of the best bike outings to be found anywhere.

At Mile 10.8 Pymatuning State Park (Ohio) has a beach facility that makes for a pleasant rest stop, even if you do not plan to swim. Just after the beach at Mile 11.1, you turn right and bike over the causeway if doing the shorter ramble. You can stop anywhere along the causeway to watch the many fishermen, especially on the Ohio side, where the state has built a low-lying wharf for that purpose. At the Pennsylvania shore and Lake Road, the Lil'Bit Restaurant on the corner is popular with locals and visitors alike.

If you're doing the longer cruise route, you'll continue straight at Mile 11.1 and circle around the northern portion of Pymatuning Reservoir. Though you'll rarely see the lake along this section, the riding remains flat, tranquil, and pleasant. There will be several restaurants and stores, even a bike shop, in the small but pleasing town of Linesville. After you turn right onto Mercer Street, you'll have some interesting attractions in the next few miles.

The first stop, at Mile 24.4, is the Linesville Fish Cultural Station. Operated by the Pennsylvania Fish and Boat Commission, the hatchery offers tours from March through September. Also at the hatchery is an exhibit area featuring videos, mounted trophies, and an outstanding multistory aquarium featuring

THE BASICS

Start: From the Pymatuning State Park Office parking lot.

Length: 23 miles for the ramble; 41 miles for the cruise.

Terrain: Both routes are very easy; perhaps (along with Erie/Presque Isle) the easiest ramble and cruise in the entire book.

Traffic and hazards: The only area for caution is on the ramble route, as you cross the causeway over the lake at Mile 11.1. Though there is a shoulder, traffic can be heavy, and cars are usually parked along the shoulder on the Pennsylvania side.

Getting there: From Interstate 79 take the exit for Pennsylvania Highway 358 and follow west to Greenville. Turn right onto Pennsylvania Highway 58 West, which leads to Jamestown. PA 58 runs right into U.S. Highway 322 (no turns) in Jamestown. Follow US 322 for approximately 2 miles to Pymatuning State Park on the right. Take the second entrance (State Route 3003/West Lake Road), go about 100 yards, and turn right into the office parking lot.

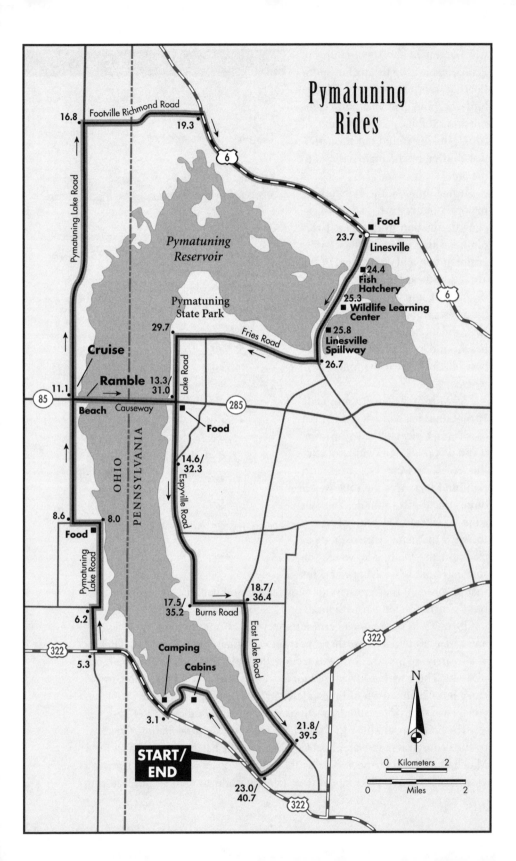

Pymatuning
Rides

Footville Richmond Road

16.8

19.3

6

*Pymatuning
Reservoir*

Food

23.7

Linesville

24.4
Fish
Hatchery

25.3
Wildlife Learning
Center

Pymatuning
State Park

Fries Road

25.8
Linesville
Spillway

26.7

29.7

Cruise

Ramble   13.3/
31.0

Lake Road

11.1

85

Beach   Causeway

285

Pymatuning Lake Road

Food

14.6/
32.3

Espyville Road

8.6

8.0

OHIO

PENNSYLVANIA

Food

Pymatuning
Lake Road

18.7/
36.4

6.2

17.5/
35.2   Burns Road

East Lake Road

322

5.3

Camping

Cabins

3.1

21.8/
39.5

N

**START/
END**

0   Kilometers   2

23.0/
40.7

0   Miles   2

322

0.0 Leave the park office parking lot and go left up to the stop sign at West Lake Road. Turn right onto SR 3003/West Lake Road.
2.1 Jamestown Beach and picnic area is on the right.
2.5 Cabins are scattered around here, administered by the state park.
3.1 Turn right at the stop sign onto US 322 West.
4.6 Enter Ohio.
5.3 Turn right onto Pymatuning Lake Road.
6.2 Bear right to remain on Pymatuning Lake Road.
6.5 Pymatuning Campground and store are on the right.
7.7 Picnic area and restrooms on the right.
8.0 Bear left to remain on Pymatuning Lake Road. The Duck-N-Drake Country Store is on the left at this turn.
8.6 Bear right to remain on Pymatuning Lake Road.
9.6 Pymatuning State Park (Ohio) park office is on the right.
10.8 Pymatuning State Park Beach and picnic area is on the right.
11.1 Turn right at the stoplight onto Ohio Highway 85 to cross the causeway. Road becomes Pennsylvania Highway 285 in Pennsylvania. (*Note:* The cruise option goes straight at the light.)
13.3 Turn right onto State Route 3007/South Lake Road. The cruise option rejoins the ramble route here. Lil'Bit Restaurant is at this corner.
14.6 Continue straight on State Route 3010.
15.3 Green's Grocery Store is on the right.
17.5 Bear left onto Burns Road.
18.7 Turn right at the stop sign onto State Route 3005/East Lake Road.
21.8 Turn right onto the Pymatuning State Park entrance road.
23.0 Turn right at the stop sign onto a park road.
23.1 Turn left into the park office parking lot.

0.0 Leave the park office parking lot and go left up to the stop sign at West Lake Road. Turn right onto SR 3003/West Lake Road.
2.1 Jamestown Beach and picnic area is on the right.
2.5 Cabins are scattered around here, administered by the state park.
3.1 Turn right at the stop sign onto US 322 West.
4.6 Enter Ohio.

(continued)

5.3 Turn right onto Pymatuning Lake Road.

6.2 Bear right to remain on Pymatuning Lake Road.

6.5 Pymatuning Campground and store are on the right.

7.7 Picnic area and restrooms on the right.

8.0 Bear left to remain on Pymatuning Lake Road. The Duck-N-Drake Country Store is on the left at this turn.

8.6 Bear right to remain on Pymatuning Lake Road.

9.6 Pymatuning State Park (Ohio) park office is on the right.

10.8 Pymatuning State Park Beach and picnic area is on the right.

11.1 Continue straight at the stoplight on Pymatuning Lake Road. (*Note:* The ramble turns right at the light to cross the causeway.)

16.8 Turn right onto Footville Richmond Road, which becomes SR 4002/Findley Bridge Road in Pennsylvania.

19.3 Turn right at the stop sign onto U.S. Highway 6 East.

23.7 Bear left at the stop sign onto US 6/Erie Street in Linesville. There are several stores and restaurants scattered throughout town.

23.8 Turn right at the stoplight onto SR 3011/Mercer Street.

24.3 The Spill Way Inn restaurant is on the left.

24.4 The Pennsylvania Fish Cultural Station is on the left.

25.3 The Pymatuning Wildlife Learning Center is on the left.

25.8 The Linesville Spillway is on the left.

26.7 Turn right onto Fries Road.

29.7 Turn left at the stop sign onto North Lake Road. (*Note:* to the right is Tuttle Point camping and picnicking area.)

30.9 The Espyville Marina, with store and restrooms, is on the right.

31.0 Continue straight at the stop sign onto State Route 3007/South Lake Road. The Lil'Bit Restaurant is at this corner. (*Note:* The ramble rejoins the cruise route here.)

32.3 Continue straight on State Route 3010.

33.0 Green's Grocery Store is on the right.

35.2 Bear left onto Burns Road.

36.4 Turn right at the stop sign onto State Route 3005/East Lake Road.

39.5 Turn right onto the Pymatuning State Park entrance road.

40.7 Turn right at the stop sign onto a park road.

40.8 Turn left into the park office parking lot.

Visitors feed the ducks and fish at the Linesville Spillway.

all Pennsylvania's game fishes. These exhibits are open year-round.

The next stop, at mile 25.3, is the Pymatuning Wildlife Learning Center and Visitor Center, operated by the Pennsylvania Game Commission. Open Wednesday through Sunday, the Learning Center is actually a small museum exhibiting more than 300 mounted specimens of native birds and mammals, showcased in their natural surroundings in detailed exhibits. Having educated thousands of visitors for the past sixty-five years, the center also offers many activities and programs that reflect the importance of Pennsylvania's wildlife. In close proximity to the center are wildlife-viewing areas, such as bluebird boxes, a bat condominium, and eagle nesting areas. Before the trees leaf out completely, eagles can be viewed practically every day.

At Mile 25.8 is the Linesville Spillway, where ducks walk on the fishes' backs. Of all Pymatuning's attractions, the spillway may leave the longest impression. Carp swarm in the waters near the spillway, aggressively gobbling up the bread thrown to them by visitors. Ducks and geese compete for the bread and often walk right on top of the massive schools of fish underneath. It's an amusing sight and a lot of fun. You can pick up inexpensive stale bread at a concession right at the spillway. Take it from me; the bread is not very tasty.

The cruise rejoins the ramble route at the causeway and follows South Lake Road along Pymatuning's eastern shore. It's fun to cycle by the countless and far-ranging variety of summer camps and cabins in this region. Don't miss the turn to take you over the dam—it's easy to miss. Since hotel options close to Pymatuning Reservoir are limited, I recommend that you make plans to stay at Jamestown Campground, offering modern and primitive sites, sunny or shaded. Or look into the rental cabins that are located along the both routes just 2.5 miles from the park office.

LOCAL INFORMATION

♦ Crawford County Convention & Visitors Bureau, 211 Chestnut Street, Meadville, PA 16335; (814) 333–1258 or (800) 332–2338.
♦ Pymatuning State Park, 2600 Williams Field Road, Jamestown, PA 16134; (724) 932–3141.

LOCAL EVENTS/ATTRACTIONS

♦ The Linesville Fish Cultural Station, 13300 Hartstown Road, Linesville, PA 16424; (814) 683–4451. Offers tours of the hatchery in season in addition to year-round exhibits, including multistory aquarium. Free.
♦ Pymatuning Wildlife Learning Center, 12590 Hartstown Road, Linesville, PA 16424; (814) 683–5545. Open 9:00 A.M. to 4:00 P.M. from early April through September; closed Monday and Tuesday. Offers exhibits of native birds and mammals; wildlife viewing areas. Free.

RESTAURANTS

♦ Lil'Bit Restaurant, 1255 U.S. Highway 285, Espyville, PA 16424; (724) 927–6977. Popular spot conveniently located on both routes.
♦ The Spill Way Inn, 493 South Mercer Street, Linesville, PA 16424; (814) 683–2304. Casual pub along the cruise route near the hatchery.

ACCOMMODATIONS

♦ Pymatuning State Park, 2660 Willaims Field Road, Jamestown, PA 16134. Cabins and campground; hundreds of campsites and more than fifty cabins. Very reasonable. Reserve by calling (888) PA–PARKS (888–727–2757).
♦ For hotels check Conneaut Lake or Meadville.

BIKE SHOP

♦ Linesville Bicycle Shop, 156 Erie Street, Linesville, PA 16424; (814) 683–2365.

On the ramble route:

♦ Mile 0.0: in the park office
♦ Mile 7.7: picnic area
♦ Mile 10.8: state park beach
♦ Mile 13.3: Lil'Bit Restaurant

On the cruise route:

♦ Mile 0.0: in the park office
♦ Mile 7.7: picnic area
♦ Mile 10.8: state park beach
♦ Mile 23.7: various locations in Linesville
♦ Mile 25.8: Linesville Spillway
♦ Mile 30.9: Espyville Marina
♦ Mile 31.0: Lil'Bit Restaurant

MAPS

♦ *DeLorme Pennsylvania Atlas & Gazetteer,* maps 28 and 42

Oil Creek Rides

T he Titusville area offers two very different cycling opportunities. The ramble takes cyclists along the Oil Creek Bicycle Trail for a relaxing out-and-back ride to the Drake Well Museum. Visit the full-scale replica of the Drake Well and learn how this valley "changed the world" in 1859. For the energetic, the challenge route climbs out of the Oil Creek gorge and visits Pithole City, one of America's largest oil boomtowns, whose fame lasted all of two years. More climbing brings the cyclist to Pleasantville, where several inviting restaurants await. After a long, gradual descent into Titusville, pick up the paved Oil Creek Bicycle Trail at the Drake Museum site and be rewarded with a relaxing ride all the way back to Petroleum Center.

On August 27, 1859, Edwin Drake struck oil along Oil Creek, an event that changed the world. Within several years, numerous wells lined the banks of Oil Creek, producing thousands of barrels a day. Although competition eventually forced Drake and his partners out of business, the petroleum industry was launched and the boom continued.

By 1875 many of the wells began to dry up, and most of the towns in the region started to die. Pithole, America's largest oil boomtown, about 7 miles southeast of Drake's Well, is a prime example. Exhibits detail the rise and fall of the former town, now just rolling meadows of wildflowers. Pithole City ghost town is located on the challenge route and is a must stop. More about it later.

If you are doing just the Oil Creek Trail, plan on an out-and-back ride totaling 20 miles with a break at the Drake Well Museum, located at the ride's midpoint. The Drake Well Museum contains replicas of the engine and derrick over the early oil well and has more than seventy exhibits pertaining to the region's oil industry. It is a fitting tribute to the pioneering spirit of Drake and ensures that the man's perseverance will never be forgotten.

In season, concessions as well as bike rentals are available at the start of the rides in Petroleum Center. Along the route you will encounter various picnic sites as well as restrooms, rain shelters, and historical markers. The trail is paved but is open to two-way travel. The entire trail is within the Oil Creek State Park and follows twisting Oil Creek as it cuts through this historic gorge. The trail offers a unique combination of natural beauty and historical significance.

If you're doing the challenge route, I recommend riding the loop counterclockwise, getting the hillier segments over with first, then finishing with the easy run down the Oil Creek Trail. Though a short challenge, the terrain in these parts is harsh; when you pull into Pithole, you'll wish there were some saloons left over from its glory days.

Oil was discovered in Pithole in January 1865, and by September

1865 the population exploded to 15,000. More than fifty hotels sprouted in Pithole, which boasted a daily newspaper and the third-busiest post office in the state at that time. The wells soon dried up, and within two years Pithole was deserted. Very little remains today, but a small museum offers a glimpse of the past with a scale model and many pictures of the boomtown at its peak. I guess if I lived in a town called Pithole, I'd leave, too. There is a small admission charge ($2.00) to the museum.

Expect more hills once you leave Pithole. When you reach Pleasantville, you can refuel at one of several restaurants and convenience stores. Then it's a long, gradual descent to Titusville, another city whose growth is attributed to the oil

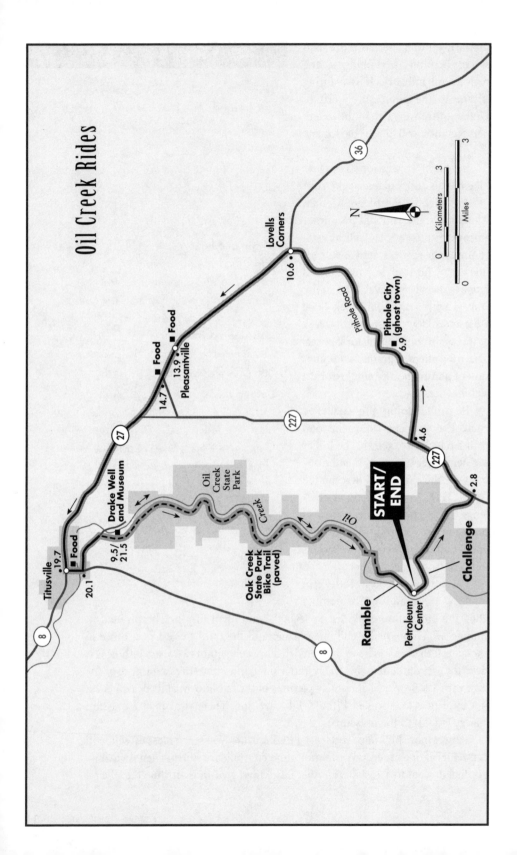

Oil Creek Rides

N

Kilometers   3

Miles   3

8

Titusville
19.7 Food
20.1

27
Drake Well
and Museum
9.5/ 21.5

Oak Creek State Park
Bike Trail (paved)

Oil Creek State Park

Creek

Pleasantville
13.9 Food
14.7 Food

Lovells Corners
10.6

Pithole Road

Pithole City (ghost town)
6.9

227

4.6

227

2.8

START/ END

Petroleum Center

O!O

Ramble

Challenge

8

36

0.0 Follow signs for the Oil Creek Bicycle Trail, located just next to the bridge spanning Oil Creek.

9.5 At the end of the trail, cycle through the parking lot, exit, and turn right. Stay to the right to enter the Drake Well Museum. After your visit, turn around and retrace the route on the Oil Creek Trail. Your mileage may vary depending on how much riding you do around the Drake Museum site.

20.0 End the ride back at the Petroleum Center parking lot.

C H A L L E N G E   M I L E S   A N D   D I R E C T I O N S

0.0 Follow SR 1004 away from Oil Creek and the bike trail. Begin a tough 1-mile climb that will take you out of the state park.

2.8 Turn left at the stop sign onto Pennsylvania Highway 227 East.

4.6 Turn right onto State Route 1006/Pithole Road.

6.9 Pithole City ghost town site is located on the right. Continue on SR 1006 all the way to Pennsylvania Highway 36.

10.6 Turn left onto PA 36.

13.9 Continue straight on PA 227/27 at the flashing light. There are several restaurants located at this intersection in Pleasantville.

14.7 Continue straight on PA 27 West. The Keystone Restaurant is on the left. Road becomes East Main Street in Titusville; follow to Franklin Street in the center of town.

19.7 Turn left on PA 8 South/Franklin Street.

20.0 There is a McDonald's located here.

20.1 Turn left at the stoplight on East Bloss Street.

21.1 Turn right into parking lot for the northern trailhead of the Oil Creek Bicycle Trail. Head south on the trail back to Petroleum Center. To visit the Drake Well Museum, pass the parking lot, cross the bridge, then bear right into the museum.

30.6 End the ride back at Petroleum Center.

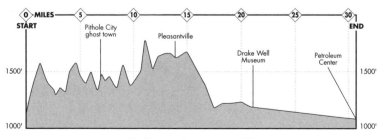

Challenge elevation profile

boom of the 1860s. Several restaurants are located along the route in the city. Continue to the Drake Well Museum and pick up the Oil Creek Trail for an easy spin back to Petroleum Center.

LOCAL INFORMATION

♦ Titusville Area Chamber of Commerce, 202 West Central Avenue, Titusville, PA 16354; (814) 827–2941.

LOCAL EVENTS/ATTRACTIONS

♦ Drake Well Museum, 205 Museum Lane, Titusville, PA 16354; (814) 827–2797. Outstanding exhibits portray the birthplace of the petroleum industry. Closed Monday. Admission charges vary according to season; adults about $4.00 to $5.00.
♦ Titusville Oil Festival. Held in mid-August, this festival celebrates Titusville's history as the birthplace of the oil industry. Features arts and crafts, food, entertainment, games, and a parade. Call the chamber of commerce for info; (814) 827–2941.

RESTAURANTS

♦ Coal Oil Johnny's Eatery, 117 East State Street, Pleasantville, PA 16341; (814) 589–5500. Local favorite along the challenge route in Pleasantville.

Now, this sure looks like fun! Photo courtesy of Northwest Pennsylvania Great Outdoors Visitors Bureau

ACCOMMODATIONS

♦ Knapping Knapp Farm B&B, 43778 Thompson Run Road, Titusville, PA 16354; (814) 827–1092. Country farmhouse on 1,000 acres. Horseback riding, guided hunting. Moderate.
♦ Oil Creek Family Campground, RD 3, Box 217, Titusville, PA 16354; (814) 827–1023. Cabins also available at this campground located adjacent to Oil Creek State Park.

BIKE SHOP

♦ Country Pedalers, Inc., U.S. Highway 322 East, Franklin, PA 16323; (814) 432–8055.

At the Drake Well Museum along the historic Oil Creek Trail.

On the ramble route:
- Mile 0.0: Petroleum Center
- Various places along Oil Creek Bicycle Trail
- Mile 9.5: Drake Well Museum

On the challenge route:
- Mile 6.9: Pithole Museum site
- Mile 13.9: various restaurants in Pleasantville
- Mile 14.7: Keystone Restaurant
- Mile 19.7: various places in Titusville; McDonald's
- Mile 21.1: Drake Well Museum
- Various places along the Oil Creek Bicycle Trail

MAP

- *DeLorme Pennsylvania Atlas & Gazetteer,* map 30

Kinzua Cruise

*L*ocated almost entirely within the Allegheny National Forest, the Kinzua Cruise is a picturesque tour of the Allegheny Reservoir and surrounding woodlands. Following the popular Longhouse Scenic Byway driving tour, the cruise climbs out of the lakebed for a tough 2.5-mile warm-up. Plan a visit to the Old Powerhouse and learn how oil wells from miles around were powered from this one central building. Enjoy a long, gradual descent back to the banks of this unspoiled reservoir. Follow the roller-coaster Forest Road as you wind your way along the reservoir's rugged western shore. Enjoy the region's panoramic splendor from one of several overlooks. Complete your bike outing to Kinzua territory with a stop at Docksiders Cafe, where you can enjoy a celebratory dinner overlooking the reservoir.

About 60 percent of Pennsylvania is forested land, and a significant portion lies within the magnificent Allegheny National Forest. Comprising more than 500,000 acres, the Allegheny National Forest offers four seasons of outdoor recreation highlighted by the 25-mile long Allegheny Reservoir. The Kinzua Cruise is a postcard-pretty tour of the Seneca Highlands Region of the forest in addition to the Kinzua Bay arm of the reservoir.

Completed in 1965, the 1,900-foot-long Kinzua Dam captures the Allegheny River, creating the 12,000-acre reservoir. Built for hydroelectric power and flood control, the Allegheny Reservoir's fishing is legendary, with walleye, muskellunge, and bass topping the list (*Kinzua* is a Seneca Indian word meaning "place of many big fishes"). Strap your collapsible rod to your bike, as many inviting opportunities to test your luck await you.

You will notice road signs marking the route as LONGHOUSE SCENIC BYWAY. Indeed, the Kinzua Cruise is synonymous with the automobile scenic drive. Longhouse refers to the long, communal dwellings in which Seneca Indians lived centuries ago. Mostly because of its views of the pristine Allegheny Reservoir, the route was designated a National Scenic Byway in 1990. To lengthen the cruise, consider taking an out-and-back detour to one of several scenic overlooks on the route, particularly Rimrock and Jakes Rocks.

Leaving the information center, you'll cross Casey Bridge, often called Cornplanter Bridge. On the east bank are a marina, restaurant, and swimming beach. If you haven't picked up supplies, do so here; your next opportunity is 18 miles down the road. The biggest climb of the tour starts just after the bridge and continues for about 2.5 miles. PA 59

The Powerhouse Historic Site in Kinzua Country.

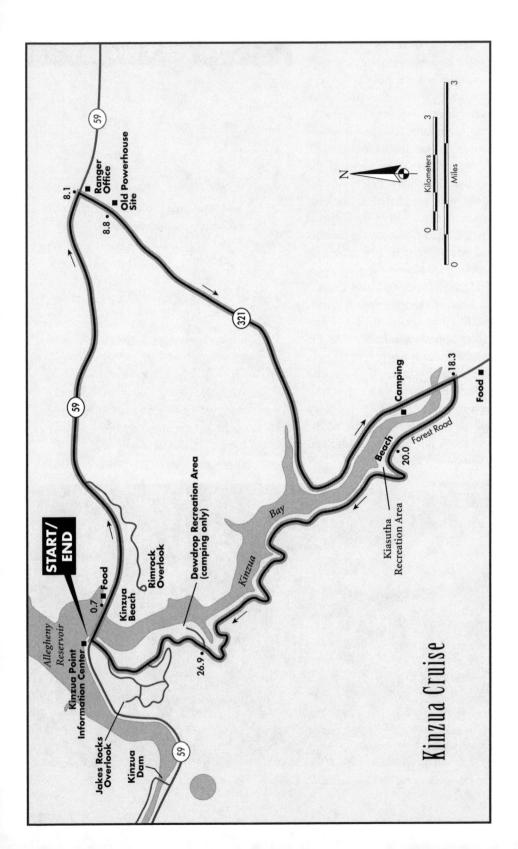

Kinzua Cruise

0.0 Turn left from the information center onto PA 59 East.

0.7 On the right is a picnic area and a sandy beach. In another 0.1 mile, the Kinzua–Wolf Run Marina will be on your left. Docksiders Cafe restaurant is located here.

8.1 Turn right onto PA 321 South. Immediately after the turn, the Bradford Ranger District Office will be on the left.

8.8 On the left is the Old Powerhouse Historic Site. Check with the ranger office for operating times.

17.4 Red Bridge Campground is on the right.

18.3 Turn right onto PA 262/Forest Road to stay on the route. If you're looking for food, continue south on PA 321 for 0.7 mile. Paul's Trading Post (groceries) will be on your left. Continuing another 0.2 mile will bring you to Bob's Trading Post, where there is a restaurant and a Hershey's ice cream stand.

20.0 Kiasutha Recreation Area is on the right. Nice beach and picnic areas.

26.9 Dewdrop Recreation Area is on the right and is strictly a camping area.

29.7 Turn left onto PA 59 West and make the immediate right back into the information center and the end of the cruise.

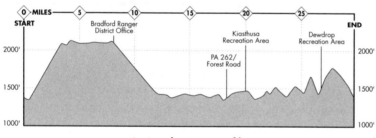

Cruise elevation profile

has fast traffic, but a wide shoulder makes cycling comfortable. Once you're on top of the ridge, cycling is pretty much effortless for the next 15 miles or so. When you make the right turn onto PA 321 South, plan a rest stop at the ranger station, where you'll find restrooms, water, and a very helpful staff.

Three-quarters of a mile past the ranger station is the historic Old Powerhouse. The 22.5 horsepower Cooper Bessemer engine, band wheel, belts, and other equipment supplied the power to numerous rod lines connected to gas and oil pump jacks in neighboring oil fields. Demonstrations of this "central power system" are provided during special events and by appointment.

After the powerhouse, a long, gradual descent brings you back to the Kinzua shoreline. Before you make the turn onto Pennsylvania Highway

View of the Allegheny Reservoir from Rimrock Overlook. Photo courtesy of the Allegheny National Forest Vacation Bureau

262/Forest Road, consider detouring 0.75 mile south on PA 321. Paul's Trading Post has groceries. Bob's Trading Post, 0.25 mile farther, has a restaurant and Hershey's ice cream for dessert. Otherwise, turn right onto Forest Road and finish the tour with one of the most scenic forest drives in Pennsylvania.

The two-lane, 35-mph Forest Road is extremely picturesque, and you'll be reaching for that camera at many of the scenic pullouts and picnic areas along the reservoir. An autumn cycle tour would be the most colorful time to do this cruise, but mid-June to July you will enjoy the pale-pink blooms of laurel and continuous embankments of wildflowers. Several state-run campgrounds located along Forest Road would make a delightful overnight stay and a convenient ride starting point. The hilliest segment of the triangular-shaped route, Forest Road also offers the Kiasutha recreational area, where an inviting beach will invigorate any tired cyclist.

LOCAL INFORMATION

♦ Allegheny National Forest, Bradford Ranger District Office, HC 1, Box 88, Bradford, PA 16701; (814) 362–4613.

LOCAL EVENTS/ATTRACTIONS

♦ Kinzua Classic Bike Race. Usually held the second Sunday in August, this 30-
or 60-mile road race uses the same roads as this cruise. Benefits Family Services
of Warren County. Web site: www.kinzuaclassic.com.

RESTAURANTS

♦ Docksiders Cafe, 203 Route 59, Warren, PA 16365; (814) 726–9645. Seasonal
restaurant overlooking Allegheny Reservoir.

ACCOMMODATIONS

♦ Horton House Bed & Breakfast, 504 Market Street, Warren, PA 16365; (888)
723–7472. Historic twenty-two-room Victorian mansion. Moderate to high-
end.
♦ The three campgrounds on the Kinzua Cruise—Dewdrop, Kiasutha, and
Red Bridge—are all within the Allegheny National Forest. Reserve by calling
the National Recreation Reservation System; (877) 444–6777.

BIKE SHOP

♦ Bike World of Warren, 2025 Pennsylvania Avenue East, Warren, PA 16365;
(814) 723–1758.

RESTROOMS

♦ Mile 0.0: visitor center
♦ Mile 0.7: Kinzua–Wolf Run Marina
♦ Mile 8.1: Bradford Ranger District Office
♦ Mile 18.3: Bob's Trading Post, just 0.9 mile off the route
♦ Mile 20.0: Kiasutha Recreation Area

MAPS

♦ *DeLorme Pennsylvania Atlas & Gazetteer,* maps 31 and 32

Cook Forest Ramble

T he Cook Forest Ramble is a delightful spin through a deep, dark forest of old-growth timber. Combine your tour with a short hike on one of the many trails in the state park. Plan a picnic along the scenic and gentle Clarion River and take a refreshing dip in its invigorating waters. After your ramble, rent a canoe or inner tube and enjoy the river as hundreds of Clarion University students do. Spend the night at the Gateway Lodge, one of the top country inns in the United States.

Originally the hunting ground of the Seneca Nation of the Iroquois, Cook Forest was first settled permanently in the 1820s by John Cook. Cook set up sawmills and rafted his logs downriver to Pittsburgh. A century later, the Cook Forest Foundation was formed to save the few areas of surviving old-growth timber. Today Cook Forest encompasses more than 7,000 acres and is renowned for its natural resources and recreational opportunities.

The ramble starts at the park office, which is also the best place for information on the area. There are restrooms and water available, as well as useful maps of the park, highlighting more than 30 miles of hiking trails in addition to unpaved roads for the more adventurous cyclist. A cycling map can be obtained there, but be aware that the park's suggested loop utilizes several unpaved roads. You should have mountain bike–sized tires to ride it.

For an easy 16-mile ramble, simply turn left out of the park office parking lot on River Road. In 0.25 mile there's a small restaurant and grocery store on the left to pick up what you need. There are numerous picnic sites along River Road, so be sure to pack something for a rest stop. You're always in sight of the Clarion River, and watching the canoeists and rafters is always a delight. You can take River Road for about 8.2 miles until its intersection with Pennsylvania Highway 899. Since PA 899 carries lots of truck traffic, I'd recommend that you turn around here and follow River Road back the way you came. The ride back, now following the Clarion River downstream, is just a bit easier.

For a ramble requiring a little more effort (detailed in the directions below), turn right out of the park office parking lot. You'll cycle right through the heart of Cook Forest and pass the Log Cabin Inn Nature Center on the right. From here you can easily hike the 1.2 miles to the Forest Cathedral, one of the largest stands of virgin white pine and eastern hemlock in the eastern United States. The stand is often called "William Penn Trees" because they date about 300 years, to the era when William Penn was the first governor of "Penn's Woods."

Just after the nature center, you'll begin gaining elevation. And though you'll be climbing for several miles, only about 0.5 mile is difficult. At the top of this grade on the right is the Sawmill Center for the Arts. Here you will find a small 180-seat intimate theater with locally staged productions in season. Just past the theater is an inviting swimming pool operated by the state park.

Turn off Forest Drive onto Greenwood Road and enjoy some gentler cycling. One more manageable climb sets you up for a thrilling descent back down to the Clarion River. Use caution here. At the bottom of the hill you'll need to make a sharp right onto River Road. I recommend bearing left here to ride out the hill safely. Those coming down the hill have no stop sign; those from the other two directions of this three-way intersection do have a stop sign. Be careful, and make sure other drivers do indeed stop.

The rest of the ramble is a breeze. River Road is lined with attractive cottages on one side and the rippling, boulder-strewn Clarion River on the other.

THE BASICS

Start: From the Cook Forest State Park Office, River Road, Cooksburg.

Length: 16 or 18 miles.

Terrain: For the out-and-back 16-mile ride, the terrain is very gentle and suitable for anyone. The 18-mile ride introduces several hills that will challenge beginners.

Traffic and hazards: All roads on this route are paved, low traffic, and rural. River Road is a delight to cycle, though you must share the road with slow-moving touring motorists and 1960-vintage canoe-toting trucks. On the 18-mile route, use caution on the descent on Greenwood Road/State Route 2001.

Getting there: Traveling east on Interstate 80, take the exit for Pennsylvania Highway 66 North, near Clarion. Follow for 15 miles to Leeper. Turn right onto Pennsylvania Highway 36 South and go 6.6 miles to River Road/State Route 2002. Turn left and go 1 block to the state park office on the left. If traveling west on I–80, take the PA 36 North exit near Brookville. Go 16 miles to River Road/SR 2002. Turn right and go 1 block to the state park office on the left. Plenty of free parking, restrooms, and water and information are available here.

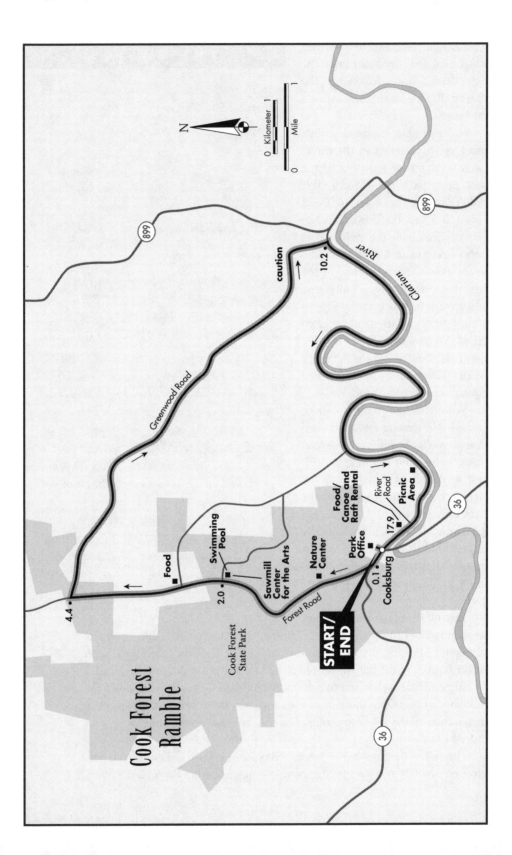

Cook Forest Ramble

Cook Forest State Park

Food 4.4

Greenwood Road

caution

899

899

Clarion River

Food

Swimming Pool

2.0

Sawmill Center for the Arts

Nature Center

Forest Road

Food/ Canoe and Raft Rental

River Road

Park Office

17.9

Picnic Area

10.2

0.1

Cooksburg

36

36

START/ END

N

0 Kilometer 1

0 Mile 1

0.0 For the 16-mile out-and-back ramble, turn left out of the park office parking lot onto SR 2002/River Road. In 0.25 mile, Cooksburg Cafe and Cooksburg Dry Goods Store will be on the left. Follow River Road all the way to PA 899. Turn around and return by the same route.

For the 18-mile ramble, turn right out of the park office parking lot and proceed 1 block to the stop sign at PA 36. Turn right onto PA 36 North. Just before this turn, Cook Homestead B&B will be on the right.

0.1 Bear right onto State Route 1015/Forest Road.

1.1 The Log Cabin Inn Nature Center is on the right. Plenty of picnic areas and restrooms in this area. An easy hike to the Forest Cathedral could start here.

2.0 Sawmill Center for the Arts is on the right. State park swimming pool also located here. The Center for the Arts includes a performing theater as well as display areas for various fairs and demonstrations.

2.9 Trail's End Restaurant & Bar is on the right.

3.3 Americo's Restaurant is on the left.

4.4 Turn right onto State Route 1012/Greenwood Road. Road becomes State Route 2001.

9.5 Use caution on the upcoming descent; need to turn right at bottom of hill.

10.2 Turn right onto SR 2002/River Road.

13.0 Clarion River Lodge and Restaurant is on the right.

16.8 Major picnic area here. Plenty of tables, barbecue grills, and restrooms available.

17.9 Cooksburg Cafe and Cooksburg Dry Goods Store are on the right. Also located here is the Pale Whale, a popular place to rent canoes, rafts, and floats.

18.2 Turn right to end the ride at the park office.

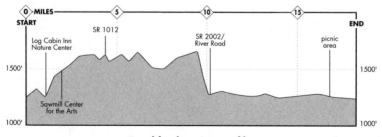

Ramble elevation profile

Though there are lots of nice picnicking spots, seek out a nice flat rock (there are many) in the river, and soak up the warming sun after a refreshing dip in the Clarion.

LOCAL INFORMATION

♦ Cook Forest State Park Office, P.O. Box 120, River Road, Cooksburg, PA 16217; (814) 744–8407.

LOCAL EVENTS/ATTRACTIONS

♦ Autumn Leaf Festival. Running for fifty years in nearby Clarion, this celebration was voted the number-one small-town festival in the world by the International Festivals Committee. Runs for nine days in early October. Call (814) 226–9161.

RESTAURANTS

♦ Gateway Lodge, Box 125, Route 36, Cooksburg, PA 16217; (800) 843–6862. No better place for a country breakfast to start your day.
♦ Trail's End, Star Route, Cooksburg, PA 16217; (814) 927–8400. Casual dining located on the route.

The Clarion River winds through scenic Cook Forest. Photo courtesy of Northwest Pennsylvania Great Outdoors Visitors Bureau

ACCOMMODATIONS

♦ Gateway Lodge, Box 125, PA 36, Cooksburg, PA 16217; (800) 843–6862. Internationally acclaimed country inn; also cottages with river views. Moderate.

♦ Cook Homestead B&B, PA 36 and River Road, Cooksburg, PA 16217; (814) 744–8869. Conveniently located at start of ride.

BIKE SHOP

♦ High Gear, 623 Main Street, Clarion, PA 16214; (814) 226–4763.

RESTROOMS

♦ Mile 0.0: in the park office
♦ Mile 1.1: Log Cabin Nature Center picnic area
♦ Mile 2.0: Sawmill Center for the Arts
♦ Mile 2.9: Trail's End Restaurant & Bar
♦ Mile 16.8: various locations in the state park's picnic areas

MAP

♦ *DeLorme Pennsylvania Atlas & Gazetteer*, map 45

Ridgway Rides

A visit to Ridgway offers several wilderness rides of varying difficulties. Take a relaxing ramble on the flat Clarion/Little Toby Creek Rail-Trail; sample the Allegheny National Forest and more rugged terrain on a longer 24-mile cruise; or face the challenge of a 45-mile tour that includes more hills but also one of the premier biking roads in the state. Enjoy 10 heavenly miles of cycling along the wild Clarion River as it winds its way through the deep and dark Allegheny National Forest. Use Ridgway as your base for exploring the region, and spend the night in an authentic lumber baron's mansion. Walk Ridgway's friendly streets and relish its small-town charm.

Ridgway is located on the eastern edge of the half-million-acre Allegheny National Forest and is a perfect base from which to explore its splendor. Built in the late 1800s, Ridgway was named for Jacob Ridgway, a local landowner, and is now the Elk County seat. The borough, displaying much architecture of the Victorian era, maintains a friendly, small-town atmosphere. It's a delight to stroll or bike around, and unique boutiques, restaurants, and B&Bs abound.

The County Courthouse dominates the town center; directly across from it on Main Street is the chamber of commerce. This is your best bet for information on the region. Adjacent to the courthouse across South Broad Street is a Sheetz convenience store. Stores along the route are nonexistent once you leave town, so get what you need before you start out.

For those looking for a vehicle-free, hill-free route, consider the Clarion/Little Toby Rail-Trail. The crushed limestone trail runs 18 miles from Ridgway to Brockway. For the first 8 miles, the trail follows the Clarion River,

Autumn comes to the Allegheny National Forest near Ridgway. Photo courtesy of the Allegheny National Forest Vacation Bureau

Start: From the Clarion/Little Toby Rail-Trail parking lot.

Length: 24 miles for the cruise; 45 miles for the challenge.

Terrain: Moderate to hilly. Some long, easy stretches between hills. The longer challenge route adds several climbs.

Traffic and hazards: All roads on this route are paved, low traffic, and rural. Use caution at Mile 10.1 on the challenge route; the descent is steep and leads to a one-lane bridge at the bottom.

Getting there: From Interstate 80, follow U.S. Highway 219 North to Ridgway. PA 219 becomes Main Street in town. At the stoplight in the center of town (where US 219 goes right), continue straight on Main Street/Pennsylvania Highway 948. (The Ridgway–Elk County Chamber of Commerce is located on the right just after this stoplight.) Go 0.3 mile and turn left onto Water Street. Go 1 block to the Clarion/Little Toby Rail-Trail parking lot. Free parking.

designated by Congress as a Wild and Scenic River. The trail then turns south and follows Little Toby Creek for 10 miles to Brockway. The trail traverses state game lands, and the entire trail can be cycled without crossing a highway. As with all unpaved trails, I recommend using 2-inch mountain bike–sized tires or hybrids sized 700 × 28 or wider. Pavilions at both the Ridgway and Brockway trailheads make good rest stops.

The challenge and cruise road routes share the same start from town. After a hilly but gorgeous 9 miles through Allegheny Forest, the shorter cruise branches off to cross the Clarion River at Arroyo. The cruise reenters the challenge route on Pennsylvania Highway 949 and follows that road east all the way back into Ridgway. Though short at 24 miles, the cruise will definitely provide fine scenery and a good workout but unfortunately misses out on one of Pennsylvania's premier cycling roads. If you can muster it, leave early in the day, pack energy foods, and attempt the longer challenge route.

Those on the challenge route will drop down to the Clarion River right after the shorter cruise option leaves to the left. Once down to the river, you will experience 10 miles of cycling heaven. Follow River Road downstream, with nothing but the Allegheny Forest on your right and the unspoiled Clarion River on your left. Throw in lots of wildlife and remove all traffic and civilization— well, it really doesn't get any better than this.

If you don't plan on spending time in Ridgway, consider fashioning a different cruise by starting at Mile 20.4, near Belltown. Visualizing the route as a flat figure eight, try the left side of the figure-eight route for a magnificent 28-mile cruise. Follow the route counterclockwise to tackle the hills on the first half of the cruise. Take the left on Arroyo Road and pick up the challenge route again at Mile 9.1. You'll then finish with the wonderful 10-mile spin along the Clarion to Belltown.

From Belltown back to Ridgway, the route follows PA 949 through miles of state game lands. Expect to spot white-tailed deer and, if you're lucky, the elusive black bear. At Mile 32.3 you're guaranteed to see elk—fenced in, that is, at the Elk County Elk Farm. A little farther down the road is an entrance to the Clarion/Little Toby Rail-Trail. If you're looking to add a few miles, consider riding south along Little Toby Creek. Otherwise, remain on the route for

Typical scenery throughout the wonderful Allegheny National Forest. Photo courtesy of Northwest Pennsylvania Great Outdoors Visitors Bureau/Carla Wehler

a gentle 8 miles back into Ridgway. After the ride, walk back to Main Street and refuel at Susan's Family Restaurant. Enjoy your family-style dinners at family-style prices with the friendly locals.

Thanks to Dave Love, owner of Love's Canoe Rentals and Sales, for submitting this ride. You will see Dave's business as you leave Water Street at the beginning of your ride. He is located on the right at 3 Main Street at about Mile 0.1. If you're looking to canoe any part of the Clarion River during your visit, look up Dave. He's not only knowledgeable about river conditions but also the best road and off-road bike routes in the area.

LOCAL INFORMATION

♦ Ridgway–Elk County Chamber of Commerce, 231 Main Street, Ridgway, PA 15853; (814) 776–1424.

LOCAL EVENTS/ATTRACTIONS

♦ Ridgway Independence Festival. Held on a Friday and Saturday in late June; (814) 773–3131. Entertainment, food, crafts, car show, and running road races.

RESTAURANTS

♦ Susan's Family Restaurant, 102 Main Street, Ridgway, PA 15853; (814) 776–6064. Friendly, family-style eatery located on the route in town.

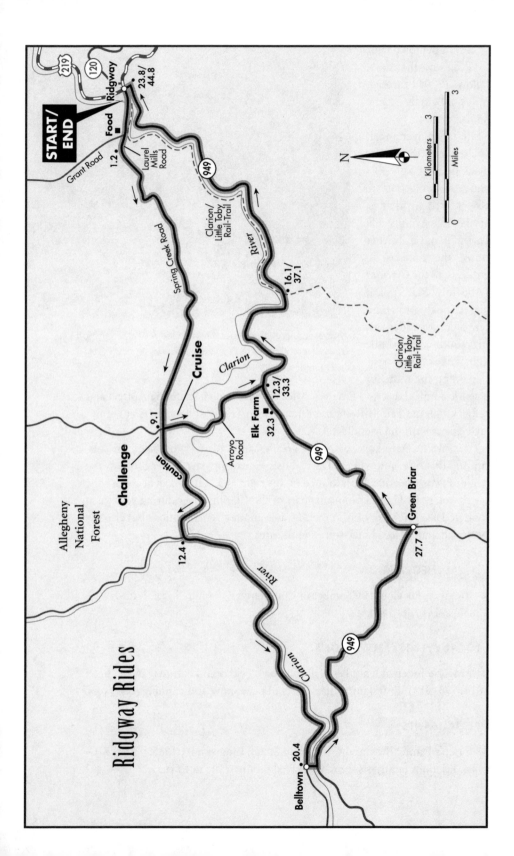

Ridgway Rides

START/END

Food

Ridgway

219

120

23.8/
44.8

Grant Road

1.2

Laurel Mills Road

Clarion/
Little Toby
Rail-Trail

949

River

16.1/
37.1

Clarion/
Little Toby
Rail-Trail

Spring Creek Road

Cruise

Clarion

9.1

Arroyo Road

12.3/
33.3

Elk Farm

32.3

Challenge

caution

Clarion

949

Allegheny
National
Forest

12.4

River

Green Briar

27.7

949

Clarion

Belltown

20.4

949

N

Kilometers   3

0   Miles   3

0   3

CRUISE MILES AND DIRECTIONS

0.0 Follow Water Street back to Main Street and turn left. Follow Main Street/ PA 948 for 0.25 mile. When PA 948 goes off to the right at the stoplight, stay straight on Main Street.

0.7 The West End Superette is on the right; last chance for food.

1.2 Bear left onto Laurel Mills Road, which becomes Spring Creek Road.

9.1 Turn left onto Arroyo Road. In 1.5 miles, cross the Arroyo Bridge over the Clarion River.

12.3 Turn left at the stop sign onto PA 949.

16.1 On the right is the access to Clarion/Little Toby Rail Trail (Carmen trailhead).

23.8 Turn left onto South Broad Street.

23.9 Turn left at the stoplight onto Main Street/PA 948.

24.1 Susan's Family Restaurant is on the left.

24.2 Turn left onto Water Street to finish the ride.

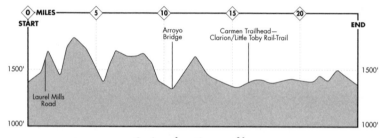

Cruise elevation profile

CHALLENGE MILES AND DIRECTIONS

0.0 Follow Water Street back to Main Street and turn left. Follow Main Street/ PA 948 for 0.25 mile. When PA 948 goes off to the right at the stoplight, stay straight on Main Street.

0.7 The West End Superette is on the right; last chance for food.

1.2 Bear left onto Laurel Mills Road, which becomes Spring Creek Road.

9.1 The shorter cruise option turns left here. For the challenge route, continue straight. Road name changes back to Laurel Mills Road.

10.1 Use caution on upcoming descent; steep with one-lane bridge at the bottom.

12.4 Turn left onto River Road. After bridge, bear left to stay on River Road.

20.4 Turn left at stop sign onto Pennsylvania Highway 3001 to cross bridge over the Clarion River. After the bridge, turn left onto PA 949 North.

(continued)

27.7 Turn left at stop sign to stay on PA 949.

32.3 The Elk County Elk Farm is on the left.

33.3 Continue straight on PA 949. Arroyo Road and the shorter cruise route join here from the left.

37.1 On the right is the access to Clarion/Little Toby Rail-Trail (Carmen trailhead).

44.8 Turn left onto South Broad Street.

44.9 Turn left at the stoplight on Main Street/PA 948.

45.1 Susan's Family Restaurant is on the left.

45.2 Turn left onto Water Street to finish the ride.

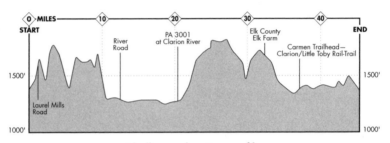

Challenge elevation profile

ACCOMMODATIONS

♦ The Towers Victorian Inn, 330 South Street, Ridgway, PA 15853; (814) 772–7657. Authentic 1865 lumber baron's mansion. Within walking distance of town and ride's start. Moderate.

BIKE SHOP

♦ Love's Canoe Rentals and Sales, 3 Main Street, Ridgway, PA 15853; (814) 776–6285. Besides canoes, Love's also carries bikes and supplies and offers bike rentals.

RESTROOMS

For both routes:
♦ Mile 0.0: various establishments in town

MAPS

♦ *DeLorme Pennsylvania Atlas & Gazetteer,* maps 45 and 46

9

Elk View Challenge

The Elk View Challenge takes cyclists through one of Pennsylvania's most remote regions. Leaving tiny Benezette, the route follows a branch of Sinnemahoning Creek downstream for a pleasant warm-up. Face the uphill challenge of renowned Wykoff Run Road, and savor the solitude of the Quehanna Wild Area. Follow the Quehanna Highway through Elk and Moshannon State Forests atop the Allegheny Plateau, before dropping back down to the streambed at Medix Run. At all times, keep your eyes and ears open for the region's free-roaming elk herd. Seeing and hearing these magnificent creatures will highlight any visit to Pennsylvania's "wild" country.

Elk County was formed in 1843 and was named for the noble animal that once abounded in this region. After complete elimination from the state, elk were reintroduced from the Rockies; the region is now home to approximately 500 free-roaming animals. Cyclists starting out early in the morning in Benezette have an excellent chance of viewing these majestic creatures.

Benezette makes an ideal starting point for the challenge. Within walking distance of the start are a hotel, post office, restaurant, campground, and small grocery/gift store. Be sure to pack necessary food and supplies. Most of the challenge lies within Elk and Moshannon State Forests, and facilities are practically nonexistent.

The challenge leaves Benezette and follows the Bennett Branch of Sinnemahoning Creek. Though there are some rollers, the terrain is fairly mild as the tour follows the large creek downstream. In Driftwood, Weebull's

Start: From the Benezette Post Office on Pennsylvania Highway 555.

Length: 48 miles.

Terrain: One long ascent (approximately 10 miles) up Wykoff Run Road. Gentle to moderate terrain the rest of the challenge.

Traffic and hazards: All roads on this route are low traffic and rural. Traffic can be fast on PA 555 and on Quehanna Highway, but if you have a collision, it would more likely be with an elk than an automobile.

Getting there: From Interstate 80 take the exit for Pennsylvania Highway 255 North near Dubois. Follow PA 255 for 16 miles, and then bear right onto PA 555 East in Weedville. Follow PA 555 for 9.5 miles to the Benezette Post Office on the left. Plenty of parking; just across the street is a small visitor center for Elk County.

Steakhouse and Pub is one of the few places for a pit stop along the route.

At Mile 20.4 make the right turn onto Wykoff Run Road and enjoy one of prettiest stretches of road in the state. This segment is also the reason this ride is classified as a challenge and not a cruise. Expect a long gradual pull, nearly 10 miles, as you wind your way up Wykoff Run. You will enter a 50,000-acre tract of land designated the Quehanna Wild Area. Traffic is extremely light and scenery extremely spectacular in this part of Quehanna. Look for the occasional waterfall, take a break from the climb, and cherish your time along Wykoff Run. It's Pennsylvania at its finest.

At the end of Wykoff Run Road, the challenge turns onto Quehanna Highway and directly through the Moshannon State Forest. Once again, facilities are nonexistent and the scenery impressive along this 14-mile segment. This stretch of highway runs atop the Allegheny Plateau and hovers around 2,000 feet above sea level for the entire stretch. Around Mile 41, begin your descent back down to the Sinnemahoning at Medix Run. It's a thrilling 3.5-mile descent with no tight turns or sudden stops. Enjoy.

At the junction of Quehanna Highway and PA 555 are the Medix Run Hotel and Restaurant and the Elk Country Store. As there is some parking in this general area, consider starting the challenge here, especially if you decide to stay at the hotel. Otherwise, turn right onto PA 555, where the challenge ends in just 3 miles.

After the challenge, consider driving up Winslow Hill Road, which runs north from PA 555 from the Benezette Post Office. About 4 miles up the road is a fine elk viewing area where your chances of a sighting are high. September and October is elk breeding season—and a time when people come not only to see the elk but also to hear them. During autumn mating, the stately bulls bugle a piercing call to attract cows to their harem. I hope you not only succeed in completing the cycling challenge but also the challenge of seeing and hearing Pennsylvania's largest game animal.

LOCAL INFORMATION

♦ Small visitor center located adjacent to Benezette Restaurant, Route 555, Benezette, PA 15821; (814) 787–7456. Elk sighting information available here.

LOCAL EVENTS/ATTRACTIONS

♦ Elk Fest. Late July at the Benezette Community Hall, Benezette, PA 15821; (814) 787–5567. Vendors, food, and entertainment in honor of the region's prized animal.

RESTAURANTS

♦ Medix Hotel and Restaurant, 23155 Quehanny Highway, Weedville, PA 15868; (814) 787–5920. Along the challenge route.
♦ Benezette Store and Restaurant, PA 555, Benezette, PA 15821; (814) 787–7456. Conveniently located at the start of the ride.

ACCOMMODATIONS

♦ Medix Hotel and Restaurant, 23155 Quehanny Highway, Weedville, PA 15868; (814) 787–5920. Along the challenge route.
♦ Benezette Hotel, Winslow Hill Road, Benezette, PA 15821; (814) 787–4355. Conveniently located at the start of the ride.

A free-roaming elk herd near Benezette. Photo courtesy of Northwest Pennsylvania Great Outdoors Visitors Bureau/Larry Holjencin

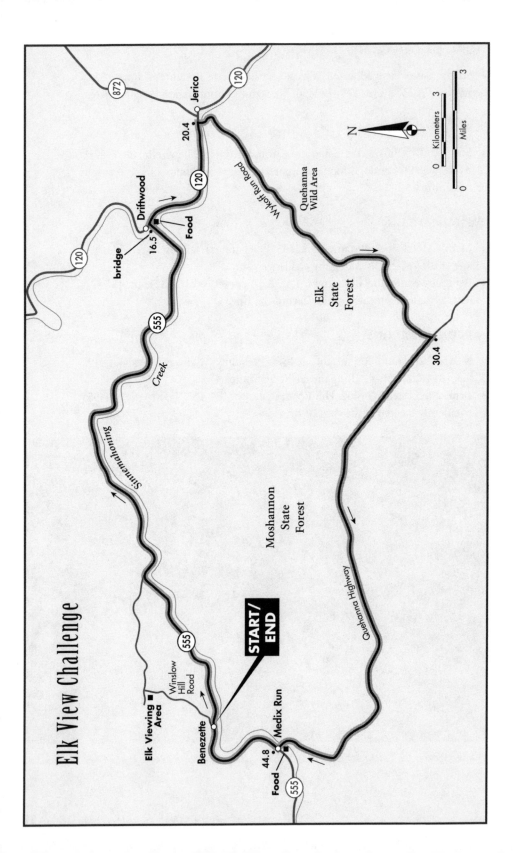

Elk View Challenge

0.0 Turn left out of the Benezette Post Office parking area on PA 555 East. Just across the street are a restaurant and a small grocery store.

16.5 After the one-lane bridge, turn right to stay on PA 555. Weebull's Steakhouse and Restaurant is on the left after the turn.

16.7 Turn right at the stop sign on Pennsylvania Highway 120 East in Driftwood.

20.4 Turn right onto State Route 2001/Wykoff Run Road. Just before the turn, Willows Restaurant is on the left.

23.7 Enter the Quehanna Wild Area.

30.4 Turn right onto State Route 2004/Quehanna Highway.

37.2 Look for the Moshannon State Forest Park Office on the right. No facilities here, but help could be sought here in an emergency.

41.0 Begin descent from the plateau; fast but manageable downhill.

44.8 Turn right at stop sign onto PA 555 East. At this intersection are the Medix Hotel and Restaurant and the Elk Country Store.

46.9 Elk Path Food and Snack Bar is on the left.

47.7 End the challenge at the Benezette Post Office.

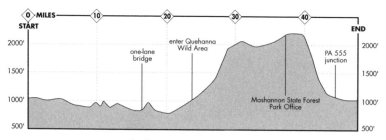

Challenge elevation profile

BIKE SHOP

♦ None in the area.

RESTROOMS

♦ Mile 0.0: Benezette Store restaurant and the Elk County Visitor Center
♦ Mile 16.5: Weebuls's Restaurant
♦ Mile 20.4: Willows Restaurant
♦ Mile 44.8: Medix Hotel and Restaurant

MAP

♦ *DeLorme Pennsylvania Atlas & Gazetteer,* map 47

Volant Classic

The Volant Classic traverses the farmlands and unique small villages of Mercer, Butler, and Lawrence Counties. Although experienced cyclists can complete this classic in one day, consider taking two and overnighting in the charming town of Volant. Stroll its popular Main Street and browse its specialty shops, some housed in train cars. Cycle through New Wilmington and out among the Old Order Amish farms that surround the peaceful college community. Relax after the ride in the town square of Mercer under the historic courthouse and famous dome.

The Volant Classic can be done several ways. For those accustomed to riding 60 miles in a day, you could start the ride in Mercer as written or near the midpoint in Volant. Others may want to begin their ride in Slippery Rock Community Park at Mile 17.9, which happens to be the starting point for Rides in the Slippery Rock area (see Chapter 11). For intermediate cyclists, consider starting in Mercer and spend the night at a B&B in Volant. It's a small but popular town with a number of interesting shops, several restaurants, and a trout stream running through it. Your two-day adventure would require cycling 33 miles the first day and 27 miles the second. Intermediate cyclists should not have a problem completing the ride in this manner.

You can pick up breakfast or supplies at a number of locations in Mercer, particularly around the town square. Within a mile you'll already be out of town and enjoying the rolling hills of Mercer, Butler, and Lawrence Counties. Keep an eye out for the Amish working their fields or traveling in their horse-drawn buggies. There are quite a few in this region, particularly around New Wilmington.

However you configure your classic route, be sure to plan a stop in Volant. The town was a bustling commercial community in the late 1800s, thanks to a successful grist-mill and a popular railroad line. When the mill closed in the 1960s and the railroad ended its runs through the town in 1975, Volant became a forgotten community. Using its old mill as a centerpiece, Volant began a renaissance in 1984 that turned the sleepy village into a top Western Pennsylvania tourist attraction. More than forty stores and restaurants line Main Street, and weekends find the town extremely busy.

Another interesting small town lies 4 miles west. New Wilmington is home to Westminster College, founded in 1852 by the United Presbyterian Church. Several buildings dating to the mid-1800s still stand and house a handful of specialty shops and restaurants. If Volant was too crowded for your taste, New Wilmington should suit just fine.

The rest of the classic runs through western Mercer County without any stops of major interest. After the ride, stroll the historic Courthouse Square in Mercer and check out one of Pennsylvania's most impressive courthouses, featuring its 160-foot dome, a replica of St. Peter's Basilica in Rome. Seek out the Magoffin House, an 1884 Queen Ann Victorian that now serves as a fine restaurant and country inn. Adjacent is the Magoffin House Museum, home of the Mercer County Historical Society.

LOCAL INFORMATION

♦ Mercer County Convention & Visitors Bureau, 50 North Water Avenue, Sharon, PA 16146; (800) 637–2370.

♦ Lawrence County Tourism, 229 South Jefferson Street, New Castle, PA 16101; (724) 654–8408.

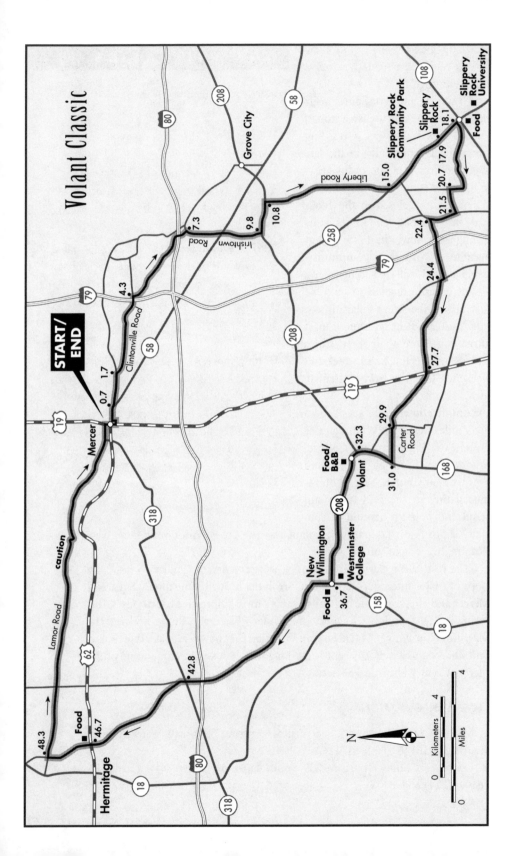

Volant Classic

0.0 From the public parking lots, go west on Venango Street (toward US 19/ North Erie Street). At the stoplight, turn left onto US 19/North Erie Street.

0.2 Just after the courthouse on the left, turn left onto South Diamond Street.

0.3 Turn left at the stop sign onto South Pitt Street, then make the immediate right onto Pennsylvania Highway 58 East/East Market Street at the stoplight.

0.7 Continue straight on State Route 2014/East Market Street. (PA 58 goes to the right).

1.7 Turn right on Clintonville Road.

4.3 Turn right to remain onto Clintonville Road.

7.3 Turn right at the stop sign onto State Route 2005/Irishtown Road.

9.8 Turn left at the stop sign onto Pennsylvania Highway 208 East.

10.8 Turn right onto State Route 2025/North Liberty Road.

15.0 Turn left at the stop sign onto Pennsylvania Highway 258 South.

17.9 Slippery Rock Community Park is located on the left; restrooms. (Alternative starting location.)

18.1 Turn right onto West Water Street, which becomes State Route 4004/Miller Road. (*Note:* Before the turn, several convenience stores are just ahead in downtown Slippery Rock.)

20.7 Bear left to remain on SR 4004. Once you enter Lawrence County, the road becomes State Route 1020.

21.5 Turn right at the stop sign onto State Route 1015/Moores Corner Road.

22.4 Turn left at the yield sign onto State Route 1016.

24.4 Turn right at the stop sign; in 0.1 mile, turn left to remain on SR 1016.

27.7 Continue straight at the stop sign on Lake Road. Cross US 19.

29.9 Turn left onto Gerber Lake Road. *Caution:* Don't be confused by Carter Road, to the left just before this turn.

31.0 Turn right onto Pennsylvania Highway 168 North.

32.3 Turn left at the stop sign onto PA 208 West.

32.4 Enter Volant. There are lots of stores and a few restaurants in town.

(continued)

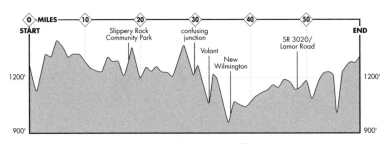

Classic elevation profile

32.5 Continue straight on PA 208. If you're looking for a B&B, to the right about 100 yards down Mercer Street is the Candleford Inn.

36.3 Enter New Wilmington. Several stores and restaurants are located in town.

36.7 Turn right onto State Route 1001/High Street. When you reenter Mercer County, the road becomes State Route 3011.

42.8 Continue straight at the stop sign on SR 3011. In 0.1 mile, bear left to remain on SR 3011.

46.7 Continue straight at the stoplight on SR 3011. Cross U.S. Highway 62. A Tic Toc Food Mart is at this intersection.

48.3 Turn right at the stop sign onto State Route 3020/Lamor Road.

55.0 Caution, some tight turns ahead.

59.4 Turn right onto North Shenango Street.

59.5 Turn left at the stop sign onto West Venango Street.

59.6 End the ride back at the public lots.

LOCAL EVENTS/ATTRACTIONS

♦ Victorian Weekend. Held at the historic County Courthouse Square in downtown Mercer in mid-July. Concerts, crafts, grand Victorian parade, house tours, auto show, and fireworks. Call the Mercer Chamber of Commerce at (724) 662–4185.

RESTAURANTS

♦ Neshannock Creek Inn Restaurant, 1 West Main Street, Volant, PA 16156; (724) 533–2233. Volant's largest and most popular restaurant. Located on the route.

♦ Dumplin' Haus, 1 Main Street, Volant, PA 16156; (724) 533–3732. On the route in Volant. Quaint restaurant featuring soups and sandwiches and their specialty, apple dumplings.

ACCOMMODATIONS

♦ Candleford Inn B&B, 225 Mercer Street, Volant, PA 16156; (724) 533–4497. Moderate inn in the heart of Volant.

♦ The Magoffin Inn B&B, 129 South Pitt Street, Mercer, PA 16137; (800) 841–0824 or (724) 662–4611. Upscale 1884 Queen Ann Victorian inn with fine restaurant in the heart of Mercer.

A restored gristmill in popular Volant.

BIKE SHOP

♦ Bicycles & Fitness World, 1779 East State Street, Hermitage, PA 16148; (724) 342–2031.

RESTROOMS

♦ Mile 0.0: various locations in Mercer
♦ Mile 17.9: Slippery Rock Community Park
♦ Mile 18.1: several locations in Slippery Rock
♦ Mile 32.4: various locations in Volant
♦ Mile 36.3: various locations in New Wilmington
♦ Mile 46.7: Tic Toc Food Mart

MAPS

♦ *DeLorme Pennsylvania Atlas & Gazetteer,* maps 42 and 43

Slippery Rock Rides

*L*eaving from the university town of Slippery Rock, a cruise and a challenge offer two moderately difficult rides through the woodlands and pastures of northern Butler County. Cycle through Moraine State Park's canopied forest as you make your way to the Old Stone House. Take a short tour of this pioneer wayside inn and learn about its interesting history. Branch off the shorter cruise route if you desire more hills to climb, while getting the chance to explore some of Butler County's charming country villages. Spend the night in a restored 1844 farmhouse and recover in the inn's spa and massage room.

Thanks to the Western Pennsylvania Wheelmen for submitting these tours of northern Butler County. One of the largest bike clubs in Pennsylvania, the WPW hosts hundreds of weekend rides each year, as well as standing rides on weekdays. They also publish the WPW Ride Package, an assembly of 171 cue sheets and maps for rides throughout southwest Pennsylvania. If you live in the region and don't belong to the WPW, join now.

The cruise is WPW Ride 39 and the challenge is WPW Ride 45. The only change I made was the starting location, which I moved from the Slippery Rock University campus to the Slippery Rock Community Park. By starting at the park, you don't need to worry about disgruntled parking enforcement on campus. In addition, you can use the restrooms and pick up water at the park. Within 0.5 mile of the start, you'll pass several convenience stores in Slippery Rock if you need energy foods to take along.

Northern Butler County is a prime and popular area to bike. You'll have quite a variety of cycling conditions, from several flat, relaxing country roads to some heart-thumping hills. A particularly pleasant stretch comes on Pennsylvania Highway 528 just after West Liberty, when you're actually cycling within Moraine State Park. The deep, cool forest is a refreshing change of pace from the pastures and farmlands that dominate the rest of the route. You exit the state park on PA 8, where you should plan a short stop at the Old Stone House.

The Old Stone House is at the approximate location of an old Native American path, the Venango Trail. During the French and Indian War, the trail was used by both the French and British armies—the French using the trail to retreat to Canada. A stagecoach road was later built along the trail, creating a need for a tavern/lodging house/stagecoach stop. The Old Stone House

was built in 1822 to replace a smaller cabin used for the same purpose. The house has an unusual and very interesting history, which you can learn about on a free Slippery Rock University–conducted tour.

At Mile 15.7, just after West Sunbury, you'll need to decide which of the two routes you want to do. The longer challenge route basically adds a long loop of about 20 miles and takes in the small village of Eau Clair before rejoining the cruise route at Five Points. Eau Clair has a small market where you can reenergize.

After the ride you can recover at several restaurants in Slippery Rock, though most cater to the 6,000-plus university crowd. You might consider heading south to Butler or Pittsburgh if you're looking for something special.

LOCAL INFORMATION

♦ Butler County Chamber of Commerce, 112 Woody Drive, Butler, PA 16003; (724) 283–2222.

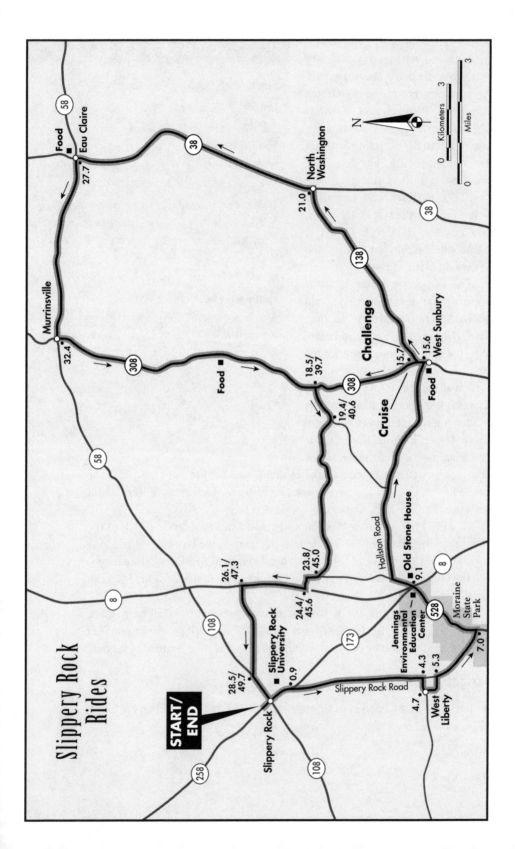

Slippery Rock Rides

START/END

Slippery Rock

Slippery Rock University ■ 0.9

Food ■

Eau Claire ● 27.7
Food ■

58

38

North Washington ● 21.0

38

138

Murrinsville ● 32.4

308

West Sunbury ● 15.6
15.7

Food ■

Challenge

Cruise

308

18.5/39.7 ●

19.4/40.6 ●

28.5/49.7 ●

108

26.1/47.3 ●

24.4/45.6 ●

23.8/45.0 ●

173

Hallston Road

Old Stone House ■ 9.1

8

Jennings Environmental Education Center ■

528
● 4.3
● 5.3

Moraine State Park

West Liberty ● 4.7
7.0 ●

Slippery Rock Road

108

258

8

58

N

Kilometers
0   3
Miles
0   3

0.0 Turn left out of the community park onto PA 258/North Main Street.

0.3 Continue straight at the stoplight on Pennsylvania Highway 173 South/ South Main Street. There are several service station stores at this intersection.

0.5 A Sheetz and a McDonald's are on the right, in addition to several other fast-food outlets.

0.9 Bear right onto Route 4008/West Liberty Street.

4.3 Bear right to remain on State Route 4008.

4.7 Turn left at the stop sign onto State Route 4011, and in 0.2 mile bear left to remain on PA 4011.

5.3 Turn right at the stop sign onto SR 4011/West Liberty Road.

7.0 Turn left at the stop sign onto PA 528.

8.9 Jennings Environmental Education Center and picnic areas/restrooms are located on both sides of PA 528.

9.1 Turn left at the stop sign onto PA 8 North. The Old Stone House is on the right. Just past the house, turn right onto State Route 1010.

15.6 Turn left onto Pennsylvania Highway 308 North/Main Street in West Sunbury. If you need a store, turn right onto Main Street; a market will be 0.1 mile on your right.

15.7 Continue straight on PA 308 North. (*Note:* The challenge route goes to the right at this point.)

18.5 Turn left onto State Route 4006/Keister Road.

19.4 Bear right to remain on SR 4006.

23.8 Turn right to remain on SR 4006.

24.4 Turn right at the stop sign onto PA 8 North.

26.1 Turn left onto State Route 4010/Branchton Road.

28.5 Turn left at the stop sign onto Pennsylvania Highway 108 West.

29.3 Turn right at the stoplight onto PA 258 North/North Main Street.

29.6 Turn right into Slippery Rock Community Park.

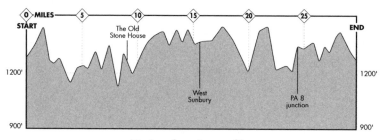

Cruise elevation profile

0.0 Turn left out of the community park onto PA 258/North Main Street.

0.3 Continue straight at the stoplight on Pennsylvania Highway 173 South/ South Main Street. There are several service station stores at this intersection.

0.5 A Sheetz and a McDonald's are on the right, in addition to several other fast-food outlets.

0.9 Bear right onto State Route 4008/West Liberty Street.

4.3 Bear right to remain on SR 4008.

4.7 Turn left at the stop sign onto State Route 4011, and in 0.2 mile bear left to remain on SR 4011.

5.3 Turn right at the stop sign onto SR 4011/West Liberty Road.

7.0 Turn left at the stop sign onto PA 528.

8.9 Jennings Environmental Education Center and picnic areas/restrooms are located on both sides of PA 528.

9.1 Turn left at the stop sign onto PA 8 North. The Old Stone House is on the right. Just past the house, turn right onto State Route 1010.

15.6 Turn left onto Pennsylvania Highway 308 North/Main Street in West Sunbury. If you need a store, turn right onto Main Street, where a market will be 0.1 mile on your right.

15.7 Bear right onto Pennsylvania Highway 138 North.

21.0 Turn left at the flashing light onto Pennsylvania Highway 38 North.

27.7 Turn left onto Pennsylvania Highway 58 West in Eau Clair. Thompson's Market is on the left at this intersection.

32.4 Turn left at the stop sign onto PA 308 South.

36.4 The Annandale Country Station is on the right.

39.7 Turn right onto State Route 4006/Keister Road. (*Note:* The challenge rejoins the cruise route here.)

40.6 Bear right to remain on SR 4006.

45.0 Turn right to remain on SR 4006.

(continued)

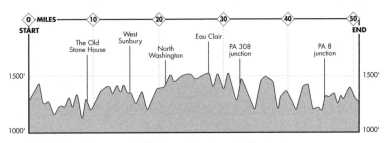

Challenge elevation profile

45.6 Turn right at the stop sign onto PA 8 North.

47.3 Turn left onto State Route 4010/Branchton Road.

49.7 Turn left at the stop sign onto Pennsylvania Highway 108 West.

50.5 Turn right at the stoplight onto PA 258 North/North Main Street.

50.8 Turn right into Slippery Rock Community Park.

LOCAL EVENTS/ATTRACTIONS

♦ The Old Stone House, intersection of Pennsylvania Highways 8 and 173 in Butler County. Open May 1 through October 31, 10:00 A.M. to 5:00 P.M. Saturday and Noon to 5:00 P.M. Sunday. Tours conducted by Slippery Rock University, which owns and administers the house. Free; (724) 794–4296.

RESTAURANTS

♦ Luigi's Pizza House and Family Restaurant, 354 South Main Street, Slippery Rock, PA 16057; (724) 794–5213.

The Old Stone House near Slippery Rock once served as a pioneer wayside inn.

ACCOMMODATIONS

♦ Applebutter Inn, 666 Centreville Pike, Slippery Rock, PA 16057, (888) 275–3466 or (724) 794–1844. An 1844 farmhouse located about 1 mile south of town. Moderate. Also has a spa and massage room.

BIKE SHOP

♦ Ultimate Sports, 627 East Main Street Extension, Grove City, PA 16127; (724) 458–8657.

RESTROOMS

On the cruise route:
♦ Mile 0.0: in the community park
♦ Mile 0.5: various locations in Slippery Rock
♦ Mile 8.9: Jennings Environmental Education Center

On the challenge route:
♦ Mile 0.0: in the community park
♦ Mile 0.5: various locations in Slippery Rock
♦ Mile 8.9: Jennings Environmental Education Center
♦ Mile 36.4: Annandale Country Station

MAPS

♦ *DeLorme Pennsylvania Atlas & Gazetteer,* maps 43 and 57

Lake Arthur Rides

The Lake Arthur cruise and challenge are two hilly rides over the rugged and once glacier-covered terrain of Butler and Lawrence Counties. Both routes constantly roll through the region's picturesque countryside before dropping down to McConnell's Mill, located in the gorgeous Slippery Rock gorge. Ride through a covered bridge spanning the gushing Slippery Rock Creek and tour the historic gristmill, one of the country's first "rolling mills." The challenge veers off to encircle Lake Arthur, Pennsylvania's largest man-made lake, which is extremely popular with sailing enthusiasts. Finish off the challenge with a delightful spin along the lake's northern shoreline, or hop on the 7-mile paved bike path for an effortless ending to a rather demanding ride.

The cruise and the challenge are two moderately difficult tours of northwest Butler and eastern Lawrence Counties. Both routes share the same roads for the first 19.5 miles, where the challenge then peels off for a tour of Moraine State Park and Lake Arthur.

The bike concession area makes a perfect starting point for both routes. There is plenty of free parking available, as well as restrooms, water, and a vending area. It's also the starting point for the 7-mile paved bike path that runs along Lake Arthur's north shore. Although the concession rents bikes, many of the rentals are for those cycling the very easy bike path. Most rental bikes are not suitable for tackling the terrain that you're going to encounter once you leave the state park boundary.

The hilly terrain begins as soon as you leave the park and pretty much continues all the way to McConnell's Mill. The scenery is fairly typical for Butler

The historic McConnell's Mill along Slippery Rock Creek.

and Lawrence Counties—a nice mixture of hardwood forests, cattle pastures and horse farms. More interesting geology will be found when you glide down the steep gorge into McConnells Mill State Park.

About 140,000 years ago, this region was on the edge of a great continental glacier. As the glacier retreated, rushing water from draining lakes flowed into this channel and scoured the gorge to more than 400 feet deep. Giant boulders now lie in swift-moving Slippery Rock Creek and provide a tough test for the many white-water enthusiasts who flock here. The gorge also presents a challenge to another group of adventurers. Two areas are designated for climbing and rappelling, one area for beginners and another that requires advanced skills. Perhaps due to the slippery rock?

Spanning Slippery Rock Creek at the bottom of the gorge is one of Lawrence County's two remaining covered bridges. The McConnells Mill Covered Bridge was built in 1874 and uses a Howe Truss. Just after the bridge is McConnell's Mill, built by Daniel Kennedy in 1852. The mill was modernized in 1875, when its grinding stones were replaced with rolling mills. The upgrades enabled the mill to process corn, oats, and wheat more efficiently until sagging profits closed the mill in 1928. Guided tours of the gristmill are conducted daily from Memorial Day through Labor Day and at other times by appointment.

At Mile 19.5 the cruise route turns left for a quick return to Moraine State Park, while the challenge route turns right to extend the tour by encircling 3,225-acre Lake Arthur. You can stop along the Pennsylvania Highway 528 bridge for fantastic views of the lake, which is often filled with bass fishermen and sailboats. Some of the toughest hills in the region must be traversed on you way back to the lake's north shore. You can remain on the road or hop on the paved bike path at several locations for the last few miles. Many picnic areas line the lake's shoreline, and a popular beach is located at Lakeview. If you have energy left after these rides, seek out the rigorous 6-mile mountain bike loop or one of several hiking trails within the park.

LOCAL INFORMATION

♦ Butler County Chamber of Commerce, 112 Woody Drive, Butler, PA 16003; (724) 283–2222.
♦ Moraine State Park, 225 Pleasant Valley Road, Portersville, PA 16051; (724) 368–8811.

THE BASICS

Start: From the Lake Arthur Bike Concession Area.

Length: 21 miles for the cruise; 46 miles for the challenge.

Terrain: Hilly. The cruise route includes many short, steep climbs, but the overall effort is manageable due to its short length. The challenge route more than doubles the cruise route climbing and is designed for the experienced cyclist.

Traffic and hazards: On both routes, use caution at Mile 6.0 on the twisting descent; at mile 9.6 when crossing U.S. Highway 422; and at Mile 16.2 as you encounter a dangerous descent to McConnells Mill State Park. On the challenge route, also use caution at Mile 41.4, where there is a stop sign at the bottom of a steep hill.

Getting there: From Interstate 79, take the exit for Pennsylvania Highway 488. Head west for 0.5 mile and turn right onto U.S. Highway 19 North. Continue 0.5 mile and turn right onto West Park Road. Go 2.7 miles and turn right on North Shore Drive at the MORAINE STATE PARK NORTH SHORE sign. Continue for 0.7 mile to the bike concession area on the right. Plenty of free parking is available.

LOCAL EVENTS/ATTRACTIONS

♦ McConnells Mill State Park. Guided tours of the gristmill are conducted daily from 10:15 A.M. to 5:45 P.M. Memorial Day through Labor Day.
♦ The Regatta at Lake Arthur. Sponsored by the Butler County Chamber of Commerce in late August; (724) 283–2222. Canoe, kayak, and sailboat races; photography show; entertainment; hot air balloon launch; skydivers; fireworks.

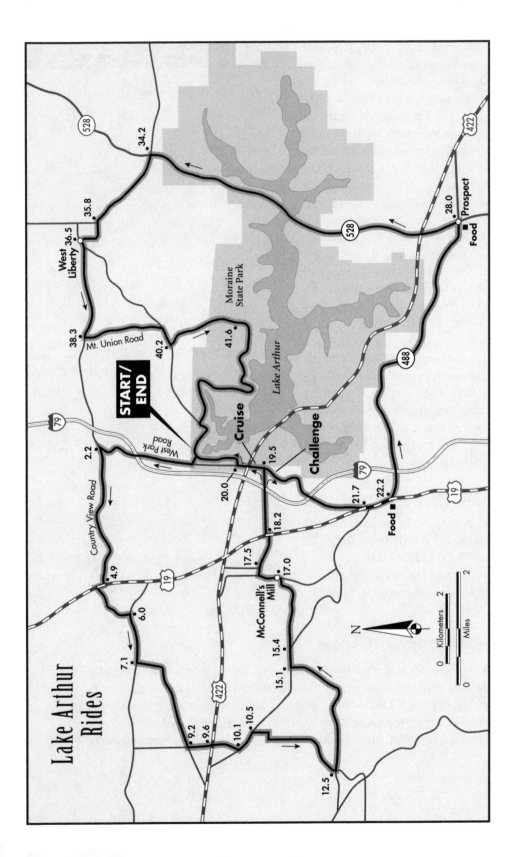

Lake Arthur Rides

Moraine State Park

Lake Arthur

START/END

West Park Road

Cruise

Challenge

Country View Road

Mt. Union Road

West Liberty

McConnell's Mill

Food

Prospect

Food

528
422
528
488
79
79
19
19
422

2.2
4.9
6.0
7.1
9.2
9.6
10.1
10.5
12.5
15.1
15.4
17.0
17.5
18.2
19.5
20.0
21.7
22.2
28.0
34.2
35.8
36.5
38.3
40.2
41.6

N

Kilometers   0   2
Miles   0   2

RESTAURANTS

♦ Moraine North Shore Restaurant, 440 North Shore Drive, Portersville, PA 16051; (724) 368–3656. Open daily Memorial Day through Labor Day and on weekends during May, September, and October. Located within the Moraine State Park on the north shore.

ACCOMMODATIONS

♦ The Porter House Gallery & Guest Rooms, 1284 Perry Highway, Portersville, PA 16051; (724) 368–9715.
♦ Moraine State Park, 225 Pleasant Valley Road, Portersville, PA 16051. Modern cabins available. Call the Pennsylvania reservations system at (888) PA-PARKS (888–727–2757).

BIKE SHOP

♦ Rapp's Bicycle Center, 179 New Castle Road, Butler, PA 16001; (724) 287–8048.

RESTROOMS

On the cruise route:
♦ Mile 0.0: bike concession area
♦ Mile 17.0: McConnell's Mill
On the challenge route:
♦ Mile 0.0: bike concession area
♦ Mile 17.0: McConnell's Mill
♦ Mile 22.2: convenience store on the right

MAPS

♦ *DeLorme Pennsylvania Atlas & Gazetteer,* maps 43, 56, and 57

CRUISE MILES AND DIRECTIONS

0.0 Turn left out of the parking lot onto North Shore Drive. After several hundred yards, bear right and continue to the stop sign. Turn right onto State Route 4007/West Park Road.

2.2 Turn left onto Country View Road.

4.9 Turn right at the stop sign onto US 19 North, and in 0.1 mile turn left onto State Route 1012/Frew Mill Road.

6.0 Bear right to remain on SR 1012. Use caution on the upcoming descent; there is a tight turn leading to a one-lane bridge.

(continued)

7.1 Turn left onto Princeton–Station Road.

9.2 Turn left at the stop sign onto State Route 2013.

9.6 Continue straight on SR 2013 at the stop sign. Use caution crossing US 422.

10.1 Turn left to remain on SR 2013.

10.5 Turn right onto Shaffer Road.

12.5 Turn left at the stop sign onto State Route 2028/Fairview School Road.

15.1 Turn right at the stop sign onto SR 2013/McConnell's Mill–Eckert Bridge Road.

15.4 Bear left onto McConnell's Mill Road.

16.2 Use caution on this descent; tight turn leading to a one-lane covered bridge.

17.0 Continue through the bridge and past McConnell's Mill on the left.

17.5 Continue straight at the stop sign on Johnson Road.

18.2 Turn left at the stop sign onto US 19 North, then make the immediate right onto Burnside Road.

19.5 Turn left at the stop sign onto West Park Road. (*Note:* the challenge route turns right here.)

20.0 Turn right onto North Shore Drive, signed MORAINE STATE PARK NORTH SHORE.

20.7 End the ride back at the bike concession area.

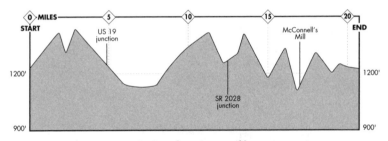

Cruise elevation profile

0.0 Turn left out of the parking lot onto North Shore Drive. After several hundred yards, bear right and continue to the stop sign. Turn right onto State Route 4007/West Park Road.

2.2 Turn left onto Country View Road.

4.9 Turn right at the stop sign onto US 19 North, and in 0.1 mile turn left onto State Route 1012/Frew Mill Road.

6.0 Bear right to remain on SR 1012. Use caution on the upcoming descent; there is a tight turn leading to a one-lane bridge.

(continued)

7.1 Turn left onto Princeton–Station Road.

9.2 Turn left at the stop sign onto State Route 2013.

9.6 Continue straight onto SR 2013 at the stop sign. Use caution crossing US 422.

10.1 Turn left to remain on SR 2013.

10.5 Turn right onto Shaffer Road.

12.5 Turn left at the stop sign onto State Route 2028/Fairview School Road.

15.1 Turn right at the stop sign onto SR 2013/McConnell's Mill–Eckert Bridge Road.

15.4 Bear left onto McConnells Mill Road.

16.2 Use caution on this descent; tight turn leading to a one-lane covered bridge.

17.0 Continue through the bridge and past McConnell's Mill on the left.

17.5 Continue straight at the stop sign onto Johnson Road.

18.2 Turn left at the stop sign onto US 19 North, then make the immediate right onto Burnside Road.

19.5 Turn right at the stop sign onto West Park Road. (*Note:* The cruise route turns left here.)

21.7 Turn left at the stop sign onto US 19 South.

22.2 Turn left onto PA 488 East. Cal's Groceries and a convenience store are on the right before the turn.

28.0 Turn left at the flashing light onto PA 528 North. The Corner Store is on the right before the turn.

34.2 Turn left onto State Route 4011.

35.8 Bear left to remain on SR 4011.

36.5 Turn left onto State Route 4008/Slippery Rock Road. In 0.1 mile bear right to remain on SR 4008/Slippery Rock Road, which becomes West Liberty Road outside township.

38.3 Turn left onto Mt. Union Road.

40.2 Bear left up the steep hill to remain on Mt. Union Road.

41.4 *Caution:* Steep descent and a stop sign at the bottom.

41.6 Turn right at the stop sign onto North Shore Drive.

46.0 End the ride at the bike concession area.

Challenge elevation profile

Beaver County Rides

Two exciting rides leave from Brady's Run Park in Beaver County. A short ramble slowly climbs the South Branch of Brady's Run amidst the region's picturesque farms, orchards, and woodlands. Gentle rollers along croplands and pastures are a prelude to a fantastic descent back down to the park. A longer cruise explores the western reaches of Beaver County and drops to Fredericktown, Ohio, where remnants remind us of its life long ago. Negley offers a chance to refuel as you cruise back into Pennsylvania and Darlington. A few tough hills will offer some challenge before a thrilling descent back to Brady's Run Park. Plan your tour in early April and enjoy a pancake breakfast, with syrup of course, during Brady's Run Park's Maple Syrup Festival.

Heading out for the shorter ramble, be sure you have your necessary supplies. There are no facilities of any kind once you leave Brady's Run Park. The longer cruise option has several stores and restaurants at the midpoint in Negley, Ohio, making it a perfect rest stop for your ride.

Both rides follow the same route for the first 7.3 miles. You'll be following the South Branch of Brady's Run upstream, gaining elevation for about 7 miles. Though there are several short, steep climbs, the route is mostly gradual, with woodlands and small farms surrounding this ideal biking road. At Mile 7.3 the ramble turns right onto Old Blackhawk Road and gently rolls for the next 7 miles. An exhilarating but manageable descent brings you back to the park. If you are looking for a flat ride, look elsewhere. The effort required for completing the ramble is not high, but it may not be suited for beginning cyclists.

The cruise branches off for more adventure in the far western portion of Beaver County, with a jaunt into Ohio. After an effortless 5 miles, you must use caution on the descent at Mile 12.1. There is a very tight turn and a one-lane bridge to negotiate at the bottom of this steep hill leading to Fredericktown. Just after the bridge, pull over to the left to view the remains of Culbertson's Gristmill, circa the 1840s. An old post office and general store adjacent to the mill make for a good photo op and pleasant rest stop.

A mile climb out of the creekbed greets you as you make your way north to Negley, Ohio. If planning a break in Negley, look to the left at the stop sign for Corral Steak House and Gorby's Grocery. Otherwise, turn right to follow the North Fork of Little Beaver Creek for an easy 6.5-mile spin to Darlington. There are a few convenience stores just past Darlington where you can refuel, which might be wise—the next few miles contain some nasty hills. At Mile 30.6 you'll hook back

up with the ramble route and enjoy an easy ride back to Brady's Run Park.

Beaver County's largest park, 2,000-acre Brady's Run Park offers plenty of other recreational activities to fill your day. In addition to a small trout-stocked lake, there are several miles of hiking trails encircling the park, plenty of picnic facilities, an ice arena that is open year round, a horse arena, tennis courts, and one of the largest horseshoe facilities in the state. If the weather is right, consider a visit to Brady's Run Park in early April when the Maple Syrup Festival is in full swing. You're guaranteed a sweet ending to a sweet bike ride.

LOCAL INFORMATION

♦ Beaver County Recreation and Tourism Development, 526 Brady's Run Road, Beaver Falls, PA 15010; (724) 891–7030.

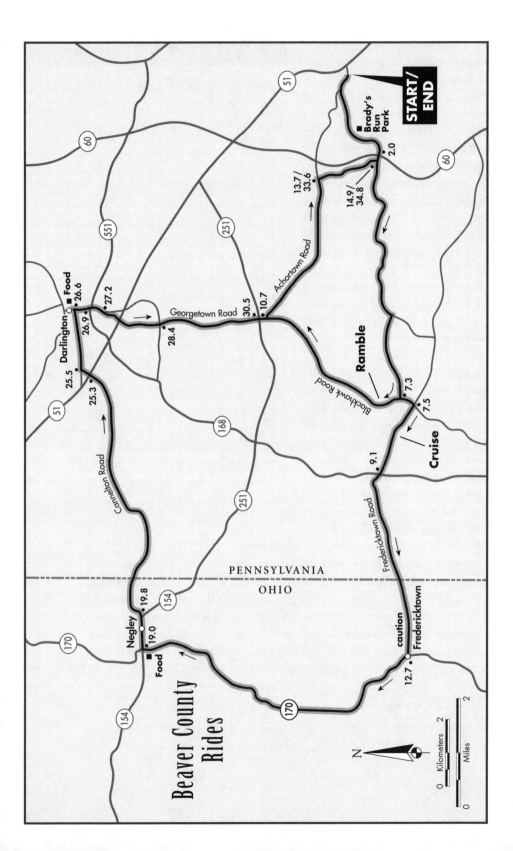

Beaver County Rides

START/END

Brady's Run Park

2.0

13.7/33.6

14.9/34.8

Achortown Road

251

Ramble

Georgetown Road

30.5
10.7

26.9

27.2

26.6 ■ Food

Darlington

25.5

25.3

Blackhawk Road

7.3

7.5

Cruise

28.4

168

9.1

251

Cannelton Road

Fredericktown Road

PENNSYLVANIA

OHIO

19.8

154

Negley

19.0

Food

caution

Fredericktown

12.7

170

N

0 Kilometers 2

0 Miles 2

0.0 Turn right out of the parking lot onto Brady's Run Road. Restrooms are scattered throughout the park for the next 2 miles.

1.7 Pass a popular picnic area in the park.

2.0 Turn right at the stop sign onto Park Road. In 0.2 mile bear left onto State Route 4012/Brady's Run Road, which eventually becomes Groscost Road.

7.3 Turn right at the stop sign onto State Route 4029/Old Blackhawk Road. (*Note:* The longer cruise route turns left here.)

10.7 Turn right onto State Route 4010/Achortown Road.

13.7 Turn right at the stop sign onto State Route 4019/Park Road.

14.9 Bear left to stay on Park Road.

15.1 Turn left onto Brady's Run Road and enter Brady's Run Park.

17.1 End the ride at the parking lot.

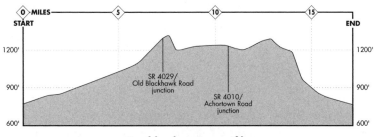

Ramble elevation profile

0.0 Turn right out of the parking lot onto Brady's Run Road. Restrooms are scattered throughout the park for the next 2 miles.

1.7 Pass a popular picnic area in the park.

2.0 Turn right at the stop sign onto Park Road. In 0.2 mile bear left onto State Route 4012/Brady's Run Road, which eventually becomes Groscost Road.

7.3 Turn left at the stop sign onto State Route 4029/Old Blackhawk Road. (*Note:* The shorter ramble route turns right here.)

7.5 Turn right at the stop sign onto State Route 4022/Lisbon Road.

9.1 Continue straight at the stop sign on SR 4022. Cross Pennsylvania Highway 168 and go 0.1 mile; turn left onto State Route 4024/Fredericktown Road.

11.2 Enter Ohio.

(continued)

12.1 Use caution on the upcoming descent. There is a tight turn and a one-lane bridge at the bottom of the hill.

12.6 After crossing the bridge, the remains of Culbertson's Gristmill will be on your left, as well as an old post office and general store.

12.7 Turn right at the stop sign onto OH 170 at the circa 1885 Methodist Episcopal Church.

19.0 Turn right at the stop sign onto Ohio Highway 154 in Negley. To the left at this intersection is the Corral Steak House restaurant and Gorby's Grocery.

19.7 Gorby's East End Market is on the left.

19.8 Turn left onto Darlington Road, which becomes State Route 4004/Cannelton Road.

25.3 Continue straight at the stop sign, crossing PA 51.

25.5 Turn right at the stop sign onto Darlington Road.

26.6 Turn right at the stop sign onto Pennsylvania Highway 551 South in Darlington. The Classic Express Shop is on the right at this intersection.

26.9 Continue straight at the stop sign on PA 551 South. (PA 168 goes off to the right at this intersection.) Go to the next intersection and continue straight on Old Darlington Road. (PA 551 South goes off to the left.) There is a convenience store on the left after the intersection.

27.2 Turn right onto Georgetown Road.

28.4 At the stop sign, jog left, then right, to stay on Georgetown Road.

30.5 Continue straight at the stop sign on SR 4029. Cross Pennsylvania Highway 251. In 0.1 mile turn left onto State Route 4010/Achortown Road. You just rejoined the ramble route.

33.6 Turn right at the stop sign onto State Route 4019/Park Road.

34.8 Bear left to stay on Park Road.

35.0 Turn left onto Brady's Run Road and enter Brady's Run Park.

37.0 End the ride at the parking lot.

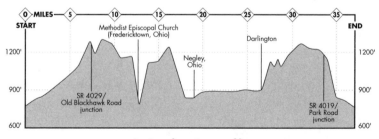

Cruise elevation profile

LOCAL EVENTS/ATTRACTIONS

♦ Maple Syrup Festival. Annual event usually held in early April in Brady's Run Park celebrates the arrival of maple syrup from the park's trees. Tours of the syrup-making process, pancake breakfasts, crafts, and entertainment. Call the Beaver County Conservation Department at (724) 774–7090.

RESTAURANTS

♦ Corral, 50597 Richardson Avenue, Negley, OH 44441; (330) 426–2910. Steakhouse located on the route at the midpoint of the cruise.
♦ Jerry's Curb Service, 1521 Riverside Drive, Beaver, PA 15009; (724) 774–4727. Popular '50s-theme carhop that has been serving for more than fifty-five years. About 2.5 miles from the ride's start.

Following riverbeds and streambeds is often a good way to avoid Pennsylvania's hills.

ACCOMMODATIONS

♦ The McKinley Place B&B, 132 McKinley Road, Beaver Falls, PA 15010; (724) 891–0300 or (866) 891–7502. Charming colonial inn close to the route in Darlington. Moderate. Also offers massage services.

BIKE SHOP

♦ Snitger's Bicycle Store, 399 Third Street, Beaver, PA 15009; (724) 774–5905.

RESTROOMS

On the ramble route:
♦ Mile 0.0: at the start and at various locations within Brady's Run Park
On the cruise route:
♦ Mile 0.0: at the start and at various locations within Brady's Run Park
♦ Mile 19.0: several location in Negley, Ohio
♦ Mile 26.6: Classic Express Shop
♦ Mile 26.9: convenience store on the left

MAP

♦ *DeLorme Pennsylvania Atlas & Gazetteer,* map 56

Saxonburg Cruise

The Saxonburg Cruise takes cyclists through the green, rolling countryside of southern Butler County. An easy day ride for the intermediate cyclist, the cruise does offer frequent rollers to keep the cycling interesting and provide great sweeping views. Enjoy quiet country roads lined with meticulously kept farms full of typical and several not-so-typical creatures. Plan to spend time after the ride in Saxonburg and enjoy lunch at the historic and renowned Hotel Saxonburg. Or relax in Roebling Park and visit the Saxonburg Museum, where exhibits on the community's founding and development are proudly displayed. Consider a tour in early September and enjoy the popular Saxonburg Festival of the Arts.

Starting at Roebling Park, you'll have several opportunities to pick up supplies in Saxonburg as you cycle through this quaint little town. You'll follow Saxonburg Boulevard south for the first few miles. Though the scenery isn't spectacular along this faster road, it offers a pleasant warm-up as you gradually lose elevation all the way to Cherry Valley Road. The cruise then turns much more rural and starts requiring more effort.

Once you regain the elevation, the cruise winds its way north over some of Butler County's best cycling roads. The route remains very rural, with numerous small farms and pastures dotting the landscape. Expect many breeds of cows, sheep, horses, even llama and elk. At Mile 10.9 consider a short detour to the right on Deer Creek Road for a good photo op of the elk.

If you're looking for a little shorter cruise, take a shortcut back to Saxonburg at Mile 17.8. After you cross the one-lane bridge, stay to the right on Saxonburg Boulevard and follow it for 2.1 miles to Main Street in Saxonburg. Turn left and ride through town until you reach the T intersection and Rebecca Street. You'll shave off about 8 miles. If you continue on, the small loop to the north of Saxonburg offers similar topography and scenery. Though there are no major climbs, a few short stubborn hills will force many to their granny gear.

After your cruise, consider spending a little time in small, historic Saxonburg. The town was founded in the early 1830s by Charles and John Roebling, who led a group of Germans looking for opportunities not found in their native country. John A. Roebling, an engineer, set up a factory near the town that manufactured wire rope. Roebling developed and patented his wire rope technology, leading to its use in river ferries, canal bridges, and eventually suspension bridges. The Saxonburg Museum, located next to Roebling Park, depicts the growth and development of Saxonburg as well as the engineering career of Roebling. You'll leave the museum knowing everything you wanted to know about wire rope but were afraid to ask.

Walk from the museum back up to the Memorial Church at the end of Main Street. Take a stroll through the heart of town and past its many interesting shops and boutiques. Look for the Main Stay B&B on the right and, just past it, Hotel Saxonburg, circa 1832. The several restaurants in town offer a variety, and cyclists won't have a problem finding something suitable for their attire or hunger pains. Early September, when the Saxonburg Festival for the Arts is in swing, is a wonderful time to visit. Look out for the crowds and traffic, however, during the Penn's Colony Festival, held nearby during the last two weekends in September.

THE BASICS

Start: From the parking lot at Roebling Park/Saxonburg Museum in Saxonburg.

Length: 28 miles.

Terrain: Moderate. Quite a few short, steep climbs mixed in with plenty of gentle cycling.

Traffic and hazards: The route is mostly rural. Use caution on Saxonburg Boulevard; traffic is fast, and the shoulder is not always present. Entire route is paved and in good shape. Use caution at Miles 13.3 and 19.4, as stop signs are located at the bottom of hills.

Getting there: From Pittsburgh take Pennsylvania Highway 8 North and turn right on Pennsylvania Highway 228 East. Follow PA 228 for 5.5 miles and bear left onto Saxonburg Boulevard. Follow 2 miles to Main Street in Saxonburg. Turn right and follow Main Street for 0.2 mile, then turn left onto Rebecca Street. Go 0.1 mile to Roebling Park/Saxonburg Museum on the right.

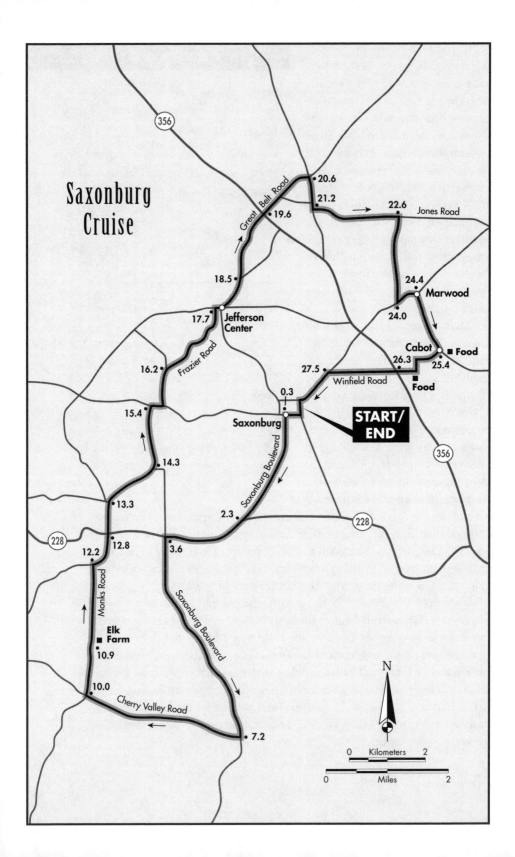

Saxonburg Cruise

356

Great Belt Road

20.6
21.2
19.6
22.6   Jones Road

18.5

17.7   Jefferson
Center

Frazier Road

24.4   Marwood

24.0

16.2

Cabot   ■ Food
26.3   25.4

27.5   Winfield Road

■ Food

0.3

Saxonburg

START/
END

356

15.4

Saxonburg Boulevard

14.3

13.3

228

2.3

228

12.8

12.2

3.6

Monks Road

Saxonburg Boulevard

Elk
Farm
10.9

10.0

Cherry Valley Road

7.2

N

0   Kilometers   2

0   Miles   2

0.0 Turn left out of the Roebling Park parking lot onto Rebecca Street, and in 0.1 mile turn right at the stop sign onto Main Street.

0.3 Turn left onto State Route 2005/Pittsburgh Street, which becomes SR 2005/Saxonburg Boulevard.

2.3 Continue straight as the road becomes PA 228 West.

2.9 There is a gas station and convenience store on the right.

3.6 Turn left onto State Route 2007/Saxonburg Boulevard.

7.2 Turn right onto Cherry Valley Road.

10.0 Turn right at the stop sign onto Deer Creek Road.

10.9 Continue straight at the stop sign on Monks Road. An elk farm will be on the right.

12.2 Turn right at the stop sign onto Sandy Hill Road.

12.8 Turn right at the stop sign onto PA 228, then make the immediate left on Spring Valley Road.

13.3 Bear right to remain on Spring Valley Road.

14.3 Bear left at the stop sign onto Victory Road.

15.1 Ride with caution; tight turn on the descent and a stop sign at the bottom.

15.4 Turn right at the stop sign onto State Route 2012/Dinnerbell Road.

15.6 Turn left onto Frazier Road.

16.2 Bear right at the Y intersection to remain on Frazier Road.

17.7 Turn right at the stop sign onto State Route 2010. In 0.1 mile, just after the one-lane bridge, turn left, then immediately bear left again onto Great Belt Road. (*Note:* If you want a shortcut back to Saxonburg, stay to the right on SR 2010 after the one-lane bridge and follow for 2.1 miles to Main Street. Turn left onto Main Street and follow it to Rebecca Street.)

18.5 Bear to the left to remain on Great Belt Road.

19.4 *Caution:* Control your speed on the upcoming descent; there is a stop sign at the bottom.

(continued)

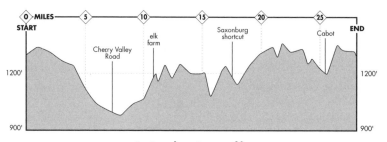

Cruise elevation profile

19.6 Continue straight at the stop sign on Great Belt Road. Cross Pennsylvania Highway 356.

20.6 Turn right at the stop sign onto Bonnie Brook Road.

21.2 Turn left onto Jones Road.

22.6 Turn right at the stop sign onto Keasey Road.

24.0 Turn left at the stop sign onto Marwood Road.

24.4 Turn right onto Helmbold Avenue. If you desire, you can hop on the rail-trail just before Helmbold Avenue for this 1-mile segment.

25.4 Turn right at the stop sign onto SR 2010/Winfield Road. The Cabot Country Inn is on the right.

26.3 Continue straight at the stoplight to remain on SR 2010/Winfield Road. The Planet Mart convenience store is on the left.

27.5 Turn left at the stop sign onto Neupert Road.

28.1 Turn left onto Rebecca Street, then turn left into Roebling Park/Saxonburg Museum parking lot to end the ride.

LOCAL INFORMATION

♦ Butler County Chamber of Commerce, 112 Woody Drive, Butler, PA 16003; (724) 283–2222.

LOCAL EVENTS/ATTRACTIONS

♦ Saxonburg Festival of the Arts. Held annually in early September on Main Street and Roebling Park in Saxonburg; (724) 352–3043. Art and photography exhibits, quilt show, trolley rides, crafts, car show, and food, including Bavarian almonds.

♦ Penn's Colony Festival, Saxonburg. Last two weekends in September; (412) 487–6922. Very large festival celebrating eighteenth-century America. Battle reenactments; festival foods; fine crafts; colonial entertainment, music, theater, and dance. $6.00 adult; $3.50 child.

RESTAURANTS

♦ Hotel Saxonburg, 220 Main Street, Saxonburg, PA 16056; (724) 352–4200. Cozy atmosphere and delicious food in historic building. Located on the route in Saxonburg. Closed Monday.

ACCOMMODATIONS

♦ The Main Stay B&B, 214 Main Street, Saxonburg, PA 16056; (724) 352–9363. Hundred-and-fifty-year old English Country–style home located on the route in Saxonburg. Moderate.

BIKE SHOP

♦ Gatto Cycle Shop, 117 East Seventh Avenue, Tarentum, PA 15084; (724) 224–9256.

RESTROOMS

♦ Mile 0.0: various locations in Saxonburg
♦ Mile 25.4: Cabot Country Inn

MAP

♦ *DeLorme Pennsylvania Atlas & Gazetteer,* map 57

You'll meet all kinds of interesting creatures on the Saxonburg Cruise.

Punxsutawney Challenge

T he Punxsutawney Challenge is a physically demanding ride through the undulating woodlands and farmlands of Jefferson, Armstrong, and Indiana Counties. Stop in the Amish towns of Dayton and Smicksburg to browse the quaint specialty shops. Share the quiet country roads with horse-drawn buggies, and watch Amish farmers working their fields with teams of horses. Be challenged by the constant rolling terrain but charmed by one-room schoolhouses and simple lifestyles. After the ride, enjoy the friendly town of Punxsutawney and meet its most popular resident, Punxsutawney Phil.

If Candlemas day be sunny and bright, winter again will show its might;
If Candlemas day be cloudy and grey, winter soon will pass away.
—Seventeenth-century proverb

There are many connections with Groundhog Day to centuries-old European traditions, but basically it means that if the groundhog sees his shadow on February 2, there will be six more weeks of winter. Punxsutawney Phil, the local weather-forecasting groundhog, makes his way out of his burrow each year in front of 30,000 or more faithful followers to predict the weather for the rest of the winter. Through the years, Phil has proven to be more accurate than our local meteorologists—and more entertaining.

It's unlikely that you'll be cycling the Punxsutawney Challenge on February 2. But do consider Fourth of July week when the Punxsutawney Groundhog Festival is in full swing. Besides the typical festival stuff, you'll enjoy an awesome vintage car cruise and lots of entertaining shows. But most of all, you'll get a chance to meet Phil.

Within 1 mile the challenge takes you out of town toward the west amid the farms and rolling countryside of southern Jefferson County. You'll breeze through easier terrain for the first 7 miles, but then the going gets a little tough. The ascents start getting longer and steeper, and no services are available until the town of Dayton, in eastern Armstrong County. Several restaurants and stores in Dayton should make a welcome rest stop.

Heading east again, you'll enter the northern reaches of Indiana County and the heart of the region's Amish country. About 300 Amish families live near Smicksburg, and the town is full of shops peddling Amish wares. Thee Village Eatinghouse Restaurant and Bakery is along the route and a good spot for lunch. Though several hills remain after Smicksburg, the gradients ease a bit. When you leave US 119, you've got it licked.

Make sure you are prepared to complete the route as designed. Though other roads on your own map may appear to be suitable shortcuts, almost all are unpaved. I've explored many so that I might offer a shorter cruise option but always ended up on surfaces unsuited for road bikes. Even the Smicksburg/Dayton Amish Country scenic driving road map includes several unpaved roads. If you plan on venturing off the route, take a mountain bike.

Back in Punxsutawney, head to Barclay Square, a beautifully preserved town square named for the town's founding father, Reverend David Barclay. Adjacent to the square is the small Groundhog Zoo, home to Punxsutawney Phil and family. Also bordering the square is the Pantall Hotel, a historic 1888 hotel boasting the beautiful Coach Light Bar, a restored curly maple stained cherry bar with ornate columns and arches. If you're interested in 3 more miles of cycling and another grueling climb, just follow Punxsutawney Phil's footprints from town up to Gobbler's Knob. This is the site of Phil's annual forecast that draws fans and reporters from around the world. Stand on Phil's platform, look for your shadow, and make your own predictions.

THE BASICS

Start: From the Punxy Plaza parking lot on West Mahoning Street in Punxsutawney.

Length: 39 miles.

Terrain: Very hilly; not suitable for beginners. Expect an intense workout.

Traffic and hazards: Some tight turns on descents, particularly at Miles 9.1 and 10.1. Maintain safe speed. Most of the route is rural and carries light but fast traffic. U.S. Highway 119 near the end of the route has more traffic, but a wide shoulder is present. Be prepared for many horse-drawn buggies along the route and the road obstacles they leave behind.

Getting there: Follow US 119 North to the main intersection in downtown Punxsutawney. Turn left at this stoplight onto West Mahoning, also Pennsylvania Highway 36 North. Go approximately 0.5 mile to the Punxy Plaza shopping area on the left. Lots of free parking available.

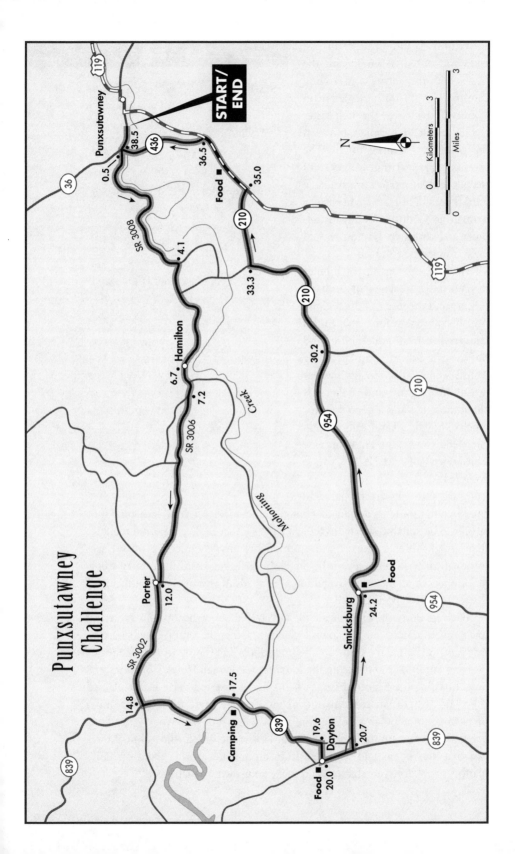

Punxsutawney Challenge

START/END

Punxsutawney

119

436

38.5

36.5

Food

35.0

210

33.3

4.1

SR 3008

0.5

36

210

Hamilton

6.7

7.2

SR 3006

30.2

954

210

Mahoning

Creek

Porter

12.0

SR 3002

Smicksburg

24.2

Food

954

17.5

14.8

Camping

839

19.6

Dayton

20.7

Food

20.0

839

N

Kilometers

Miles

0   3

0   3

0.0 Turn left out of the shopping plaza onto PA 36 North/West Mahoning Street.

0.5 Turn left onto State Route 3008/Perry Street (not the sharp left onto Pennsylvania Highway 436 South).

4.1 Turn right to stay on SR 3008.

6.7 In the village of Hamilton, jog right, then left onto State Route 3009.

7.2 Continue straight on State Route 3006.

12.0 Turn left at the stop sign onto State Route 3002 in Porter.

14.8 Turn left at the stop sign onto Pennsylvania Highway 839 South.

17.5 The Milton Loop Recreation Area (Mahoning Reservoir) and campground is on the right.

19.6 Turn right at the stop sign to remain on PA 839 South/Main Street.

20.0 Turn left in the center of Dayton onto PA 839 South/State Street. There are several restaurants and stores around this intersection.

20.7 Turn left onto State Route 1022, which becomes State Route 4022 in Indiana County.

24.2 Turn left at the stop sign onto Pennsylvania Highway 954 North/West Kittanning Street in Smicksburg. Several Amish stores and restaurants are in town.

24.4 Thee Village Eatinghouse Restaurant and Bakery is on the right.

30.2 Continue straight on Pennsylvania Highway 210 North.

33.3 Turn right at the stop sign onto PA 210 North.

35.0 Turn left at the stop sign onto US 119 North.

35.5 There is a Gulf station convenience store on the left.

35.8 A Dairy Queen is on the left.

36.0 The Plantation B&B is on the right.

36.5 Turn left onto PA 436 North.

38.5 Turn right at the stop sign onto PA 36 South.

39.0 End the ride back at Punxy Plaza.

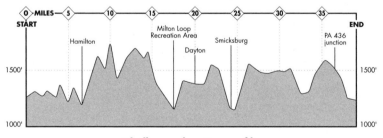

Challenge elevation profile

LOCAL INFORMATION

♦ Punxsutawney Area Chamber of Commerce, 124 West Mahoning Street, Punxsutawney, PA 15767; (814) 938–7700 or (800) 752–PHIL.

LOCAL EVENTS/ATTRACTIONS

♦ Groundhog Festival. Held annually in downtown Punxsutawney during Fourth of July week. Nightly shows and free entertainment, Food Alley, crafts, classic car cruise. Call the chamber of commerce for info at (800) 752–PHIL.

♦ Groundhog's Day Festival. February 2 and a few days leading up to it. Though it's not likely you would be cycling then, the town throws an exciting festival culminating in the trek up to Gobbler's Knob. Call the chamber for info.

RESTAURANTS

♦ Thee Village Eatinghouse Restaurant and Bakery, Route 954, Smicksburg, PA 16256; (814) 257–8035. Great lunch spot along the route in Amish town of Smicksburg.

Gobbler's Knob, where Punxsutawney Phil makes his yearly weather predictions.

♦ Punxy Phil's Family Restaurant, 116 Indiana Street, Punxsutawney, PA 15767; (814) 938–1221. Good local spot to start off your day.

ACCOMMODATIONS

♦ Pantall Hotel, 135 East Mahoning Street, Punxsutawney, PA 15767; (814) 938–6600 or (800) 872–6825. Historic hotel in center of town with great authentic Victorian bar. This is where Bill Murray stayed when he filmed *Groundhog Day*.

♦ Plantation Bed & Breakfast, RR 1, Box 112, Punxsutawney, PA 15767; (814) 939–7371. Old-world charm at reasonable rates. Along the route.

BIKE SHOP

♦ Biker's High, 515 Liberty Boulevard, DuBois, PA 15801; (814) 371–6210.

RESTROOMS

♦ Mile 0.0: various stores and restaurants in Punxy Plaza
♦ Mile 20.0: various locations in Dayton
♦ Mile 24.2: various locations in Smicksburg
♦ Mile 35.5: Gulf station/store

MAP

♦ *DeLorme Pennsylvania Atlas & Gazetteer*, map 59

16

Indiana County Classics

Known as the Christmas Tree Capital of the World and home-town of legendary actor Jimmy Stewart, Indiana is the base for two fantastic century rides. Whether your goal is a metric or an English century, you're sure to be challenged and even awed by the green, rolling pastures and farms that blanket Indiana County. Cycle through the largest Amish settlement in Western Pennsylvania, and share the roads with horse-drawn buggies. Cycle through fields bursting with conifers, and photograph two of the county's picturesque covered bridges. Be challenged by Indiana's often-rugged landscape, and painfully realize that this will not be your easiest century. After the ride, enjoy the friendly town of Indiana, and discover that its pace of life hasn't changed much since Jimmy Stewart walked the same streets decades ago.

Whichever route you are planning to do, make sure to stock up on energy foods. There are very few stores along the route and a lot of hills to climb. There are a number of stores along PA 286, especially toward Indiana, that should meet all your needs.

Both century rides start from the small Getty Heights Park on Rustic Lodge Road. Restrooms and water are available here, as well as picnic sites. You only have several miles to ride before you must decide on which route you intend to ride. At Mile 7.9 the English century route dips south onto Pennsylvania Highway 217 and runs to Blairsville. Though the town does have a few historic sites, you'll probably just take in Sheetz, the convenience store that is a popular stop with local cyclists.

The route leaves Blairsville to run north through a peaceful and scenic region of rolling hills, streams, and farms. But it's not until you cross US 422 and head north do you really notice the tree farms. Concentrated in the northern areas of the county, the numerous Christmas tree farms justify Indiana's long-lived claim to be Christmas Tree Capital of the World. Guys, you may not be able to find many restrooms along the route, but you won't have a hard time finding a tree.

Toward the northernmost segment of the routes, the English century option branches off from the metric route and does another loop farther to the north. This is one loop you don't want to miss. The largest Amish settlement in Western Pennsylvania lies in these parts, and cycling through it is certainly special. The past and the present coexist peacefully here, with equal numbers of automobiles and horse-drawn buggies sharing the roads. And be prepared to wave—everyone else does.

Both routes merge and share the

THE BASICS

Start: From Getty Heights Park in Indiana.

Length: 65 miles for the metric century and 101 miles for the English century.

Terrain: Though the real mountains lie just to the east of Indiana, both century routes have their share of hills. The amount of climbing limits these rides to experienced, fit cyclists.

Traffic and hazards: The routes outside Indiana are mostly rural, but they include some cycling on higher-speed-limit roads. Experienced cyclists should not have a problem with any of them. Do use caution at Mile 19.2/41.6 for the short segment on U.S. Highway 422. Stay on the shoulder. Be aware of horse-drawn buggies on the northernmost segment of the routes. Riding in the town of Indiana is relatively easy.

Getting there: From US 422, Pennsylvania Highway Route 286 North toward Indiana. After 1.3 miles turn right onto Rustic Lodge Road. Go 0.1 mile to Getty Heights Park on the left. Free parking.

same roads back to Indiana. It's during these last 25 miles or so that you'll encounter some of the toughest and longest hills. If you're the kind who likes to get the hills out of the way early, consider doing the route in reverse. Once you circle around the airport near the ride's end, it's easy going the rest of the way.

Before or after your ride, plan on spending some time in the delightful town of Indiana. Home to the Indiana University of Pennsylvania and its 13,000 students, the town may be best known as the home of one of America's most beloved film stars, Jimmy Stewart. Fans will enjoy the Jimmy Stewart Museum, which highlights Stewart's accomplishments in film and TV as well as his roles as family man, military hero, and world citizen. A pleasant stroll around Indiana will take in his birthplace, boyhood home, and a bronze statue dedicated to Stewart on his seventy-fifth birthday. You might feel that you somehow stepped back in time and that the streets you are now walking are those of Bedford Falls.

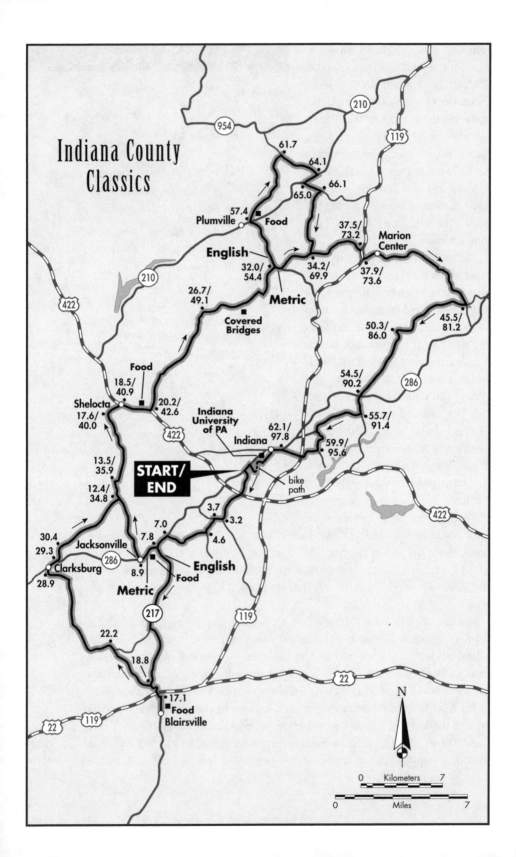

Indiana County Classics

210
954
119
61.7
64.1
66.1
65.0
37.5/
73.2
Marion
Center
57.4
Plumville
Food
English
32.0/
54.4
34.2/
69.9
37.9/
73.6
Metric
45.5/
81.2
26.7/
49.1
50.3/
86.0
Covered
Bridges
54.5/
90.2
210
286
Food
18.5/
40.9
20.2/
42.6
55.7/
91.4
422
Shelocta
17.6/
40.0
Indiana
University
of PA
62.1/
97.8
59.9/
95.6
422
Indiana
13.5/
35.9
START/
END
bike
path
12.4/
34.8
3.7
422
3.2
7.0
30.4
7.8
4.6
29.3
Jacksonville
286
Clarksburg
8.9
English
28.9
Food
Metric
217
22.2
119
18.8
17.1
22
Food
Blairsville
22
119

N

Kilometers

0   7

0   Miles   7

METRIC CENTURY CLASSIC
MILES AND DIRECTIONS

0.0 Turn left out of Getty Heights Park onto Rustic Lodge Road.

0.5 Continue straight on State Route 3033/Rustic Lodge Road.

3.2 Turn right at the stop sign onto Old Pennsylvania Highway 56.

3.7 Turn left onto Hilltop Road.

4.6 Turn right onto Bethel Church Road.

7.0 Turn left at the stop sign onto PA 286 West.

7.8 Continue straight on PA 286 West. (*Note:* The English century route goes left here on Pennsylvania Highway 217 South.)

8.6 Frank's Inn is on the left, and in 0.2 mile, Pap's Grocery is on the right.

8.9 Turn right onto State Route 3031/McIntyre Road.

12.4 Continue straight on SR 3031. (*Note:* The English century route joins the metric route here from the left.)

12.7 Turn right to remain on SR 3031.

13.5 Turn right at the stop sign onto State Route 3056.

13.7 Turn left onto State Route 3037/Craig Road.

15.0 Continue straight at the stop sign on SR 3037/Sportsman Club Road.

17.6 Turn right at the stop sign onto Pennsylvania Highway 156.

18.5 Turn right after the bridge onto Main Street, which becomes Shelocta Road.

19.2 Turn right at the stop sign onto US 422 East. Ride with caution.

19.8 There is a BP service station and market on the left.

20.2 Turn left onto State Route 4001/Five Points Road.

26.1 Bear right onto State Route 4009/Five Points Road.

26.7 At the stop sign, bear right onto Pennsylvania Highway 954 South.

27.4 Bear left at the stop sign onto State Route 4006/Five Points Road. In this stretch you'll see two of Indiana County's four covered bridges. The first, Trusal Covered Bridge, was built in 1870 and is the shortest and oldest in the area. The second bridge, Harmon Covered Bridge, was built in 1910. It's the youngest of the area's bridges and cost a whopping $525 to build.

30.3 Bear left to remain on SR 4006/Five Points Road.

(continued)

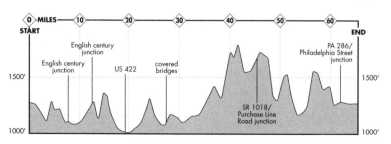

Metric century classic elevation profile

32.0 Turn right onto Pennsylvania Highway 85 at the stop sign. (*Note:* This is where the English century goes to the left.)

32.2 Turn left onto SR 4006/Ambrose Road.

34.2 Continue straight at the stop sign on Pennsylvania Highway 406/Brady Road. (*Note:* This is where the English century rejoins the metric route.)

37.5 Turn right onto U.S. Highway 119 South. Caution, faster traffic.

37.9 Turn left onto Pennsylvania Highway 403 South.

38.3 Continue straight on Main Street, as PA 403 goes to the right.

38.6 Bear right onto Decker Point Road.

42.6 Turn right at the stop sign onto State Route 1035/Pickering Run Road, and in 0.1 mile turn left onto Pine Vale Road.

43.0 Turn right onto State Route 1020.

44.0 Turn right onto Smith Street.

45.5 Turn right at the stop sign onto State Route 1018/Purchase Line Road.

49.2 Continue straight. Road becomes State Route 1012.

49.5 Continue straight at the stop sign on SR 1012/Barr Slope Road. There is a BP service station and market on the left at this intersection.

50.3 Turn left onto Kirkland Road at the top of the hill.

53.4 Bear left at the stop sign onto Tanoma Road. Do not take the earlier left onto Braughler Road.

54.5 Turn left at the stop sign onto PA 286, then make the immediate right on State Route 1005/Allen Bridge Road.

55.7 Turn right onto State Route 1008/Hood School Road.

58.6 Turn left at the stop sign onto State Route 1006/Airport Road.

58.8 Turn right onto State Route 1001/Geesy Road.

59.9 Turn right onto SR 1001/Stormer Road.

60.9 Turn right at the stop sign onto State Route 1002.

62.1 Turn left at the stoplight onto PA 286/Philadelphia Street.

62.5 There is a Sheetz convenience store on the left with restrooms.

62.8 Turn left onto PA 954 South/South Sixth Street at the stoplight in the center of town.

62.9 Make a soft right onto Wayne Avenue just after the stoplight at School Street.

63.5 Turn right at the stoplight onto Maple Street.

63.9 Turn left onto an unmarked access road between the tennis courts. Hop onto the bike lane for 0.3 mile.

64.2 Leave the bike lane and turn left onto South Thirteenth Street.

64.4 Turn right at the stop sign onto Rose Street.

(continued)

64.9 Turn left onto Saltsburg Avenue.

65.4 Turn left at the stop sign onto Rustic Lodge Road.

65.5 Turn left into Getty Heights Park and end of ride.

ENGLISH CENTURY CLASSIC
MILES AND DIRECTIONS

0.0 Turn left out of Getty Heights Park onto Rustic Lodge Road.

0.5 Continue straight on State Route 3033/Rustic Lodge Road.

3.2 Turn right at the stop sign onto Old Pennsylvania Highway 56.

3.7 Turn left onto Hilltop Road.

4.6 Turn right onto Bethel Church Road.

7.0 Turn left at the stop sign onto PA 286 West.

7.8 Turn left onto PA 217 South. (*Note:* The metric century route goes straight here on PA 286 West.)

17.1 Turn right at the stop sign onto PA 217 South/South Walnut Street.

17.5 Turn left into Sheetz convenience store. After your stop, turn right out of Sheetz and head back on PA 217 North.

17.9 Turn left on PA 217 North.

18.8 Turn left onto State Route 3009.

22.2 Turn left onto State Route 3007.

28.9 Turn right at the stop sign onto PA 286.

29.3 Bear left onto State Route 3025 just past Clarksburg Valley Inn.

30.4 Bear right to remain on SR 3025/Park Drive.

33.4 Young Township Park is on the left; restrooms and picnic area.

34.8 Turn left onto State Route 3031/McIntyre Road. (*Note:* The metric route rejoins the English century route here.)

(continued)

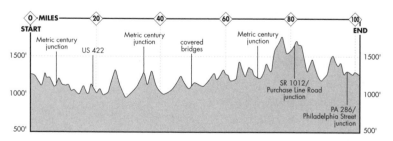

English century classic elevation profile

35.1 Turn right to remain on SR 3031.

35.9 Turn right at the stop sign onto State Route 3056.

36.1 Turn left onto State Route 3037/Craig Road.

37.4 Continue straight at the stop sign onto SR 3037/Sportsman Club Road.

40.0 Turn right at the stop sign onto Pennsylvania Highway 156.

40.9 Turn right after the bridge onto Main Street, which becomes Shelocta Road.

41.6 Turn right at the stop sign onto US 422 East. Ride with caution.

42.2 There is a BP service station and market on the left.

42.6 Turn left onto State Route 4001/Five Points Road.

48.5 Bear right onto State Route 4009/Five Points Road.

49.1 At the stop sign, bear right onto Pennsylvania Highway 954 South.

49.8 Bear left at the stop sign onto State Route 4006/Five Points Road. In this stretch you'll see two of Indiana County's four covered bridges. The first, Trusal Covered Bridge, was built in 1870 and is the shortest and oldest in the area. The second bridge, Harmon Covered Bridge, was built in 1910. It's the youngest of the area's bridges and cost a whopping $525 to build.

52.7 Bear left to remain onto SR 4006/Five Points Road.

54.4 Turn left at the stop sign onto Pennsylvania Highway 85. (*Note:* This is where the metric option goes to the right.)

56.9 Continue straight on Pennsylvania Highways 85 and 210.

57.1 The Beresnyak Market is on the right.

57.4 Turn right onto Rossmoyne Road.

59.9 Turn left onto Pearce Road.

61.1 Turn right at the stop sign on Griffith Road.

61.7 Turn right onto State Route 4018.

64.1 Turn right at the stop sign onto PA 210 South.

65.0 Turn left onto State Route 4015. The turn is on a downhill.

66.1 Turn right at the stop sign onto SR 4015/Georgeville Road.

69.9 Turn left onto SR 4006/Brady Road at the bottom of the hill. (*Note:* This is where the metric route rejoins the English century route for the last time.)

73.2 Turn right onto U.S. Highway 119 South. *Caution:* faster traffic.

73.6 Turn left onto Pennsylvania Highway 403 South.

74.0 Continue straight on Main Street as PA 403 goes to the right.

74.3 Bear right onto Decker Point Road.

78.3 Turn right at the stop sign onto State Route 1035/Pickering Run Road, and in 0.1 mile, turn left onto Pine Vale Road.

78.7 Turn right onto State Route 1020.

79.7 Turn right onto Smith Street.

(continued)

81.2 Turn right at the stop sign onto State Route 1018/Purchase Line Road.

84.9 Continue straight. Road becomes State Route 1012.

85.2 Continue straight at the stop sign on SR 1012/Barr Slope Road. There is a BP service station and market on the left at this intersection.

86.0 Turn left onto Kirkland Road at the top of the hill.

89.1 Bear left at the stop sign onto Tanoma Road. Do not take the earlier left onto Braughler Road.

90.2 Turn left at the stop sign onto PA 286, then make the immediate right onto State Route 1005/Allen Bridge Road.

91.4 Turn right onto State Route 1008/Hood School Road.

94.3 Turn left at the stop sign onto State Route 1006/Airport Road.

94.5 Turn right onto State Route 1001/Geesy Road.

95.6 Turn right onto SR 1001/Stormer Road.

96.6 Turn right at the stop sign onto State Route 1002.

97.8 Turn left at the stoplight onto PA 286/Philadelphia Street.

98.2 There is a Sheetz convenience store on the left with restrooms.

98.5 Turn left onto PA 954 South/South Sixth Street at the stoplight in the center of town.

98.6 Make a soft right onto Wayne Avenue just after the stoplight at School Street.

99.2 Turn right at the stoplight onto Maple Street.

99.6 Turn left onto an unmarked access road between the tennis courts. Hop onto the bike lane for 0.3 mile.

99.9 Leave the bike lane and turn left onto South Thirteenth Street.

100.1 Turn right at the stop sign onto Rose Street.

100.6 Turn left onto Saltsburg Avenue.

101.1 Turn left at the stop sign onto Rustic Lodge Road.

101.2 Turn left into Getty Heights Park and end of ride.

LOCAL INFORMATION

♦ Indiana County Tourist Bureau, Indiana Mall, 2334 Oakland Avenue, Suite 7, Indiana, PA 15701; (724) 463–7505.

LOCAL EVENTS/ATTRACTIONS

♦ Jimmy Stewart Museum, Indiana Library Building, 845 Philadelphia Street, Indiana, PA 15701; (724) 349–6112 or (800) 83–JIMMY. Interesting exhibits, displays, gallery talks, and film presentations highlight the actor's life and work. $5.00 adults, $3.00 child.

♦ Indiana Five Points Classic Bike Race. Held late May/early June. Includes several categories of road races and one recreational ride. Prize money. For info, call (724) 349–7688.

RESTAURANTS

♦ Rouki's Restaurant, 665 Philadelphia Street, Indiana, PA 15701; (724) 465–7200. Located in the center of town, with a Jimmy Stewart/*It's a Wonderful Life* theme.
♦ The Coney, 642 Philadelphia Street, Indiana, PA 15701; (724) 465–8092. Long-standing, casual hangout for wings, beer, and fun.

ACCOMMODATIONS

♦ Four Sisters B&B, 1500 Philadelphia Street, Indiana, PA 15701; (724) 349–3623. Moderate; in-town location.
♦ Holiday Inn, 1395 Wayne Avenue, Indiana, PA 15701; (724) 463–3561 or (800) 477–3561. Moderate; located 2 miles south of town.

The Amish region of northern Indiana County.

BIKE SHOP

♦ Indiana Schwinn, 36 South Fifth Street, Indiana, PA 15701; (724) 349–6550.

RESTROOMS

On the metric century route:
♦ Mile 0.0: Getty Heights Park
♦ Mile 19.8: BP service station
♦ Mile 49.5: BP service station
♦ Mile 62.5: Sheetz and other locations in Indiana

On the English century route:
♦ Mile 0.0: Getty Heights Park
♦ Mile 17.5: Sheetz
♦ Mile 33.4: Young Township Park
♦ Mile 42.2: BP service station
♦ Mile 85.2: BP service station
♦ Mile 98.2: Sheetz and other locations in Indiana

MAPS

♦ *DeLorme Pennsylvania Atlas & Gazetteer*, maps 58, 59, 72, and 73

One of America's all-time favorite actors, Jimmy Stewart.

Prince Gallitzin Ramble

The Prince Gallitzin ramble offers the cyclist a gently rolling and scenic ride through northern Cambria County's Allegheny Plateau region. Stop at the many overlooks for outstanding vistas of 1,600-acre Lake Glendale and the rolling woodlands of Prince Gallitzin State Park. Plan a picnic at one of many lakeside sites, or stay overnight in the park's modern campground and cabins. After a morning of cycling, seek out the park's hiking and mountain biking trails, or simply spend the afternoon relaxing at Lake Glendale's safe and sandy beach. For more adventure, head to nearby Patton for an unforgettable trip underground in the Seldom Seen Valley Tourist Coal Mine.

Situated in the Allegheny Plateau region of northern Cambria County, Prince Gallitzin State Park's 6,000 acres are easy and exciting to explore. The Prince Gallitzin Ramble is a delightful and relatively easy spin around the park's main attraction, 1,600-acre Lake Glendale. A number of small bluffs around the lake provide some challenge but also great photo ops of the scenic lake.

Prince Gallitzin was named for a Russian Prince, Demetrius Gallitzin, who gave up a life of ease to establish a frontier mission in 1799. Father Gallitzin established Saint Michael's in the town of Loretto, a Catholic colony just about a dozen miles south of the present-day park. Refusing bishophood in other areas, Father Gallitzin remained at his parish in the Alleghenies and is now remembered as the "Apostle of Western Pennsylvania."

Just 2 miles into the ride, stop at the park office to pick up information about the park and of the surrounding region. The state park offers more than 12 miles of hiking trails, several mountain bike loops, recreational boating, warm-water fishing, great swimming beaches, and a campground with more than 400 sites and several modern cabins. The campground is located at Mile 4.7. Consider spending the night at the campground and starting the ramble from there.

Pack your camera for this trip. Plenty of lookouts are scattered along the ramble route and provide incredible views of Glendale Lake. In addition, several picnic areas can be found along the north shore at the ride's midpoint. If you didn't pack food and need some, Sir Barney's at Mile 12.1 is open daily and should be suitable. Noel's Family Drive-In at Mile 17.5 is another option.

Remember to pack your swimwear. The safe and sandy beach offers a relaxing end to your bike ride. Food concessions are available in season, as well as modern bathhouses and hundreds of picnic tables. Autumn is another great time to visit Prince Gallitzin. Consider coming in early October for the Apple Cider Festival and Crafts Show. This annual tradition offers apple cider pressing and apple butter boiling demonstrations in addition to the usual festival wares.

THE BASICS

Start: From Main Beach Parking Area 2 at Prince Gallitzin State Park.

Length: 20 miles.

Terrain: Moderate. A few flat segments with quite a few rollers. No difficult climbs.

Traffic and hazards: Moderate traffic. All roads are paved and in good condition with small to average shoulders. Ride with caution on Pennsylvania Highway 53, where there is more traffic.

Getting there: From U.S. Highway 22, follow PA 53 North for approximately 17.5 miles. Turn left on Marina Road (follow signs to Prince Gallitzin State Park). In 2.5 miles turn right into Main Beach Area. Follow the park road for 1.1 miles to Main Beach 2. Turn left and proceed 0.25 mile to the parking lot. Free and plentiful parking. Restrooms available.

LOCAL INFORMATION

♦ Prince Gallitzin State Park, 966 Marina Road, Patton, PA 16668; (814) 674–1000.

LOCAL EVENTS/ATTRACTIONS

♦ Apple Cider Festival and Crafts Show. Held at Prince Gallitzin State Park in early October; (814) 674–1000. Demonstrations, food, entertainment, crafts, pony rides, and hayrides.

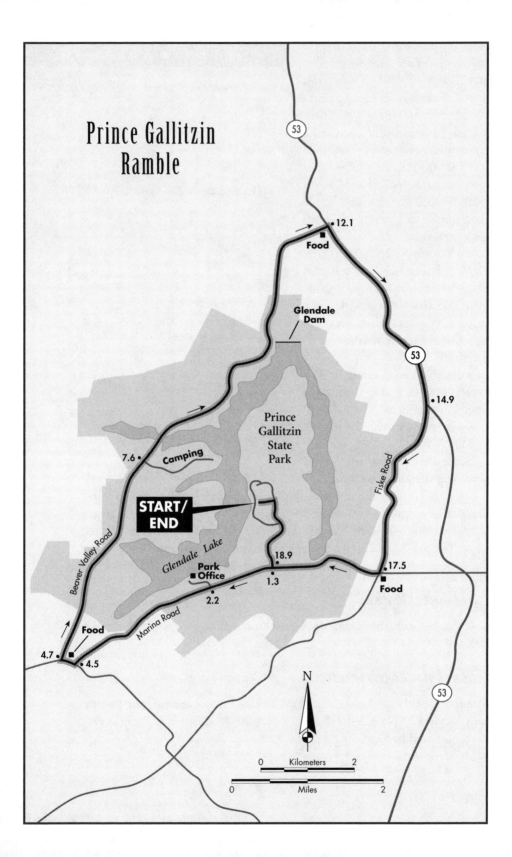

Prince Gallitzin
Ramble

53

• 12.1
Food

**Glendale
Dam**

53

• 14.9

Prince
Gallitzin
State
Park

7.6 •
Camping

Fiske Road

**START/
END**

18.9 •

• 17.5

Beaver Valley Road

Glendale Lake

**Park
Office**

1.3 •

Food

2.2 •

Food

Marina Road

4.7 •
• 4.5

53

N

0   Kilometers   2

0   Miles   2

0.0 Leave the parking lot the way you came in. In 0.25 mile, turn right onto the park road to exit the beach access area.

1.3 Turn right at the stop sign onto State Route 1026/Marina Road.

2.2 The Prince Gallitzin Park Office is on the right.

4.5 Turn right at the stop sign onto State Route 1025/Glendale Lake Road.

4.7 Turn right onto State Route 1021/Beaver Valley Road.

7.6 Crooked Run Campground (part of the state park) is on the right.

11.0 The Sleepy Valley Motel is on the left.

12.1 Turn right at the stop sign onto PA 53 South/Glendale Valley Boulevard. Just before the turn, Sir Barney's Restaurant is on the left. A convenience store is on the right. Ride with caution on PA 53.

14.9 Turn right onto State Route 1023/Fiske Road.

17.5 Turn right at the stop sign onto SR 1026/Marina Road. Noel's Family Drive-In is at this intersection.

18.9 Turn right into the Main Beach Area park road.

20.0 Turn left into Beach Area 2.

20.2 End the ride back at the beach parking lot.

♦ Seldom Seen Valley Tourist Coal Mine, P.O. Box 83, Patton, PA 16668; (814) 247–6305. An exciting trip underground explains the process of mining and shipping coal. Call for tour dates and schedules. $6.00 adult; $3.50 child.

RESTAURANTS

♦ Sir Barney's Restaurant, RR 1, Flinton, PA 16640; (814) 687–9235. Located on the route at Mile 12.1. Offers steaks, burgers, and pizza, eat-in or take-out.

ACCOMMODATIONS

♦ Prince Gallitzin State Park, 966 Marina Road, Patton, PA 16668. Campground and cabins. Very reasonable. Reserve by calling (888) PA–PARKS (888–727–2757).

♦ Miner's Rest, 807 Fourth Avenue, Patton, PA 16668; (814) 674–5532 or (888) 297–0332. Century-old Victorian hotel in downtown Patton, a few miles west of the state park. Moderate.

BIKE SHOP

♦ None in the area.

Curious creatures of our beautiful forests. Photo courtesy of the Allegheny National Forest Vacation Bureau

RESTROOMS

- Mile 0.0: beach bathhouse
- Mile 12.1: Sir Barney's Restaurant or at the convenience store

MAP

- *DeLorme Pennsylvania Atlas & Gazetteer,* map 60

State College Rides

Two fabulous but very different rides start from the Centre County Convention and Visitors Bureau on the Penn State University campus. A short ramble explores the "happy valley" on delightful country roads that constantly roll but never become difficult. The longer challenge climbs Bald Eagle Mountain as a warm-up to an even more difficult assault of the Allegheny Front. A continuous climb of more than 8 miles is required to reach the Allegheny Plateau and the Moshannon State Forest. A welcome rest stop at Black Moshannon State Park offers a chance to "cool off" before traversing Bald Eagle Mountain a second time on the return to State College. After the ride, seek out the Creamery, serving locally made ice cream to Penn State fans and friends for more than a hundred years.

Make sure you stop in the visitor center before your ride. The parking area you are in is restricted, but you can get a free parking pass to place on your windshield if you are just out for a bike ride. The staff is extremely helpful and can provide you with other cycling maps for rides starting from the visitor center.

Two rides are offered out of Penn State, and they couldn't be more different. The Happy Valley Ramble is an easy ride that takes in the pleasant country roads northwest of the sprawling Penn State campus. Though there are some rollers, the ride can be completed by beginners within several hours. A particularly pleasant segment is along Pennsylvania Highway 550, where you'll be following Buffalo Run. It's hard to imagine that you're only several miles away from the hustle and bustle of State College and Penn State's 41,000 students.

Former Pennsylvania Governor Tom Ridge leads cyclists in Pennsylvania's Keystone Ride. Photo courtesy of the Pennsylvania State Archives

The second ride, the Black Moshannon Challenge, is a far cry from the gently rolling valley ramble. The ride starts and finishes the same, but when you reach PA 550 early on, the challenge continues straight for an ascent of Bald Eagle Mountain. You'll be climbing for nearly 2 miles but will be rewarded with spectacular views and a thrilling descent. Now comes the hard part.

After breezing through Unionville, you'll start the climb up the Allegheny Plateau, one that will last for roughly 8 miles. Climbing the Allegheny Front is made bearable by the many opportunities to hop off the bike and enjoy the stunning views of the valley below. Despite its difficulty, this is one of the premier bike routes in Western Pennsylvania. A nice descent brings you to the midpoint of the ride—and a chance to cool off at Black Moshannon State Park.

Black Moshannon is the perfect place for your cooldown. Not only is the park at a high elevation but it also sits in a slight basin that traps the heavier cooler air, making cool summer days possible. If that's not enough, the cold 250-acre lake has an appealing sandy beach that is open from mid-May to early September. There are plenty of picnic facilities surrounding the lake if you brought your own lunch along. If you didn't, the park store and concession stand might come in handy. The park has an eighty-site campground as well as rustic and modern cabins. If the overall climbing effort of the challenge is too great, then consider breaking the route up into two days worth of riding and treating yourself to a cool, refreshing overnight at Black Moshannon.

Two good climbs are left once you leave the state park, and the second will take you back over Bald Eagle Mountain a second time. Reaching PA 550, you'll share the same roads with the ramble route as you head back to Penn State. Avoid some busy roads by hopping on the bike path that delivers you to Park Avenue. Enjoy the easy spin along the Penn State campus's northern border, or, if you know the campus layout, take a short detour to the Creamery. This much-beloved landmark with more than one hundred years of tradition serves up delicious flavors of locally made ice cream for the Nittany faithful. Try the Peachy Paterno. Anything named after JoePa has to be a winner.

LOCAL INFORMATION

♦ Centre County Convention and Visitors Bureau, 800 East Park Avenue, State College, PA 16803; (800) 358–5466.

LOCAL EVENTS/ATTRACTIONS

♦ Central Pennsylvania Festival of the Arts. Presented by State College and Penn State University during the second week of July; (814) 237–3682. One of the top art festivals in America, the show boasts the works of more than 1,000 visual and performing artists in addition to a sidewalk sale and exhibition with more than 350 booths.
♦ Penn State Football! If you've never attended a Penn State football game at Beaver Stadium, you must give it a try. With more than 100,000 supportive fans flocking to the game, the thrill begins well before kickoff and lasts long into the College Avenue night.

RESTAURANTS

♦ The Corner Room, 100 West College Avenue, State College, PA 16801; (814) 237–3051. When the locals say "Meet me at the corner," this is where they mean. Serving breakfast, lunch, and dinner daily since 1926.
♦ Ye Olde College Diner, 126 West College Avenue, State College, PA 16801; (814) 238–5590. Another Penn State tradition in the heart of downtown State College; popular for its grilled stickies.

THE BASICS

Start: From the Centre County Convention and Visitors Bureau.

Length: 20 miles for the ramble; 45 miles for the challenge.

Terrain: The ramble includes some rollers but nothing that is too difficult. The challenge has a number of difficult climbs and is suitable only for experienced, fit cyclists.

Traffic and hazards: The challenge route includes several descents where you need to maintain speed and control. Neither of the routes carries heavy traffic. Use caution when crossing U.S. Highways 322 and 220 at Mile 10.0 of the ramble and Mile 35.2 of the challenge.

Getting there: From the west or east, take US 322 (not US 322 Business) to the Penn State University exit. Follow Park Avenue for 0.8 mile and turn left onto Porter Road (adjacent to Beaver Stadium). Make the immediate left into the Centre County Convention and Visitors Bureau.

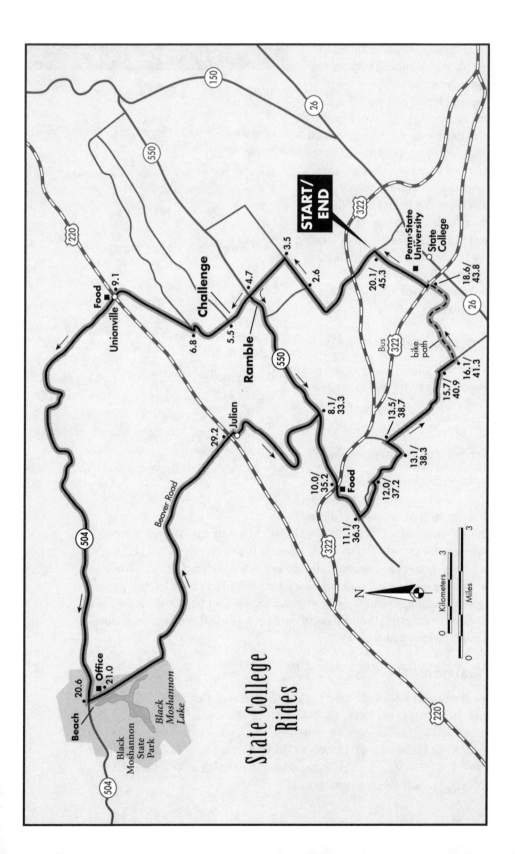

State College Rides

START/END

322

Penn State University

State College

150

26

550

322

220

Food
9.1

Unionville

Challenge

4.7

3.5

2.6

20.1/
45.3

18.6/
43.8

26

6.8

5.5

Ramble

550

Bus 322

bike
path

15.7/
40.9

16.1/
41.3

8.1/
33.3

13.5/
38.7

Julian

29.2

Beaver Road

10.0/
35.2

Food

12.0/
37.2

13.1/
38.3

504

11.1/
36.3

322

20.6

Office
21.0

Beach

Black Moshannon
State Park

Black
Moshannon
Lake

504

220

N

Kilometers   3

0

Miles   3

0

0.0 Turn right out of the visitor center onto Porter Road and continue to the stoplight. Go straight at the light onto State Route 3005/Fox Hollow Road.

2.6 Bear right onto SR 3005/Fox Hill Road.

3.5 Turn left onto South Fillmore Road.

4.7 Turn left at the stop sign onto PA 550 South.

5.1 Fillmore General Store is on the right.

8.1 Continue straight. *Note:* The challenge route joins here from the right.

10.0 Continue straight at the flashing light on PA 550 South. Use caution crossing PA 322 and PA 220. There is a Uni-Mart on the left at this intersection.

11.1 Turn left onto Meeks Lane.

12.0 Bear to the right onto Skytop Lane.

12.9 Continue straight at the stop sign onto Meeks Lane.

13.1 At the stop sign, turn left onto Scotia Road.

13.5 Turn right onto Circleville Road.

15.6 Turn left onto Bachman Lane.

15.7 Turn right at the stop sign onto Valley Vista Drive.

16.1 Continue straight at the stop sign on Science Park Road; in 0.1 mile turn left onto the bike path.

17.4 Cross Corl Street and continue on bike path.

18.6 When you reach the stoplight at North Atherton Street, leave the bike lane and go straight on East Park Avenue (cross North Atherton Street).

20.1 Turn right at the stoplight onto Porter Road, then make the immediate left into the visitor center.

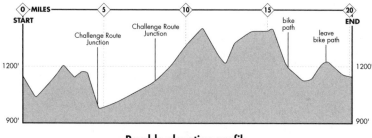

Ramble elevation profile

ACCOMMODATIONS

♦ Penn State's Nittany Lion Inn, 200 West Park Avenue, State College, PA 16803; (814) 865–8500. Upscale inn located on the Penn State Campus.

♦ Black Moshannon State Park, 4216 Beaver Road, Philipsburg, PA 16866. Campground and modern and rustic cabins. Reserve by calling (888) PA–PARKS (888–727–2757).

0.0 Turn right out of the visitor center onto Porter Road and continue to the stoplight. Go straight at the light on State Route 3005/Fox Hollow Road.

2.6 Bear right onto SR 3005/Fox Hill Road.

3.5 Turn left onto South Fillmore Road.

4.7 Continue straight at the stop sign onto State Route 3008.

5.5 Continue straight at the stop sign (SR 3008 goes to the right).

6.8 Continue straight at the stop sign at the top of the mountain on Unionville Pike Road.

9.1 Turn left onto US 220/Union Street in Unionville, then immediately bear right onto Pennsylvania Highway 504. Buckie's Pizza & Subs is on the left at this intersection.

20.6 Turn left onto State Route 3032/Julian Pike at Black Moshannon State Park. The beach and bathhouse/restrooms are to the right before the turn. Plenty of picnic facilities are scattered around the lake.

21.0 The park office is on the left.

29.2 Go straight at the stop sign on SR 3032 at the intersection with US 220 in Julian. In 0.1 mile bear right after the railroad tracks, then immediately bear left to remain on SR 3032, which becomes Julian Pike Road.

33.3 Turn right at the stop sign onto PA 550 South.

35.2 Continue straight at the flashing light on PA 550 South. Use caution crossing US 322/220. There is a Uni-Mart on the left at this intersection.

36.3 Turn left onto Meeks Lane.

37.2 Bear to the right onto Skytop Lane.

38.1 Continue straight at the stop sign onto Meeks Lane.

38.3 At the stop sign, turn left onto Scotia Road.

38.7 Turn right onto Circleville Road.

40.8 Turn left onto Bachman Lane.

40.9 Turn right at the stop sign onto Valley Vista Drive.

41.3 Continue straight at the stop sign onto Science Park Road; in 0.1 mile turn left onto the bike path.

42.6 Cross Corl Street and continue on bike path.

43.8 When you reach the stoplight at North Atherton Street, leave the bike lane and go straight on East Park Avenue (cross North Atherton Street).

45.3 Turn right at the stoplight onto Porter Road, then make the immediate left into the visitor center.

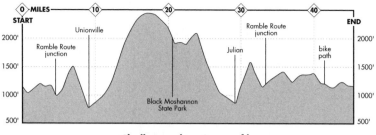

Challenge elevation profile

BIKE SHOP

♦ Bicycle Shop, 441 West College Avenue, State College, PA 16801; (814) 238–9422.

RESTROOMS

On the ramble route:
♦ Mile 0.0: visitor center
♦ Mile 10.0: Uni-Mart

On the challenge route:
♦ Mile 0.0: visitor center
♦ Mile 20.6: Black Moshannon State Park
♦ Mile 35.2: Uni-Mart

MAPS

♦ *DeLorme Pennsylvania Atlas & Gazetteer,* maps 61 and 62

Altoona Challenge

*C*rossing the Allegheny Mountains has always presented a problem. In the 1800s the Horseshoe Curve was built so that locomotives could circumvent the steep slopes. Today cyclists must rely on their own sheer muscle power. But once up and over the mountains, cyclists are rewarded with premier cycling roads and incredible views. The Altoona Challenge offers a stop at Horseshoe Curve National Historic Site to learn more of this engineering marvel and to get up close and personal with the roaring diesels. Cycle through sleepy Cambria County towns such as Loretto, whose Catholic roots are very evident. After a long, gradual descent, be challenged again by climbing the Alleghenies once more. After a thrilling descent back to Altoona, take the opportunity to explore the city's railroading heritage.

You might want to stop in Altoona to pick up some fuel for this ride. There's nothing available at the start and there are limited choices along the route. In fact, with 7 miles of climbing to start your morning, you had better be prepared. Before the going gets too tough, you can take a breather at the Horseshoe Curve National Historic Landmark.

Designed by Pennsylvania railroad Chief Engineer J. Edgar Thompson, the horseshoe curve circumvented the problem of the steep Allegheny Mountains. This engineering marvel was completed in 1854 and cleared the way for western expansion of the railroad. The Horseshoe Curve remains a very busy railroad line and hasn't been altered since its beginnings. You can climb the 194 steps to reach the tracks or pay a small charge for the inclined-plane funicular.

Whichever way you take to the tracks, you're sure to be thrilled by the power of the passing trains. Railroad buffs should also plan to stop at the Railroaders Memorial Museum in Altoona after the ride. The museum tells the historical, cultural, and social story of the railroad workers who once made Altoona the greatest railroad town in the world.

Speaking of diesel power—you'll need some of your own to finish the climb up the Alleghenies. Another 4 grueling miles and you'll reach the top of the ridge and enjoy some gentler riding. You'll breeze through the villages of Gallitzin and Sankertown before pulling into Loretto. Home to Saint Francis College, Loretto was founded by Demetrius Gallitzin, a Russian Prince who established a frontier mission in the late 1700s. A picnic area adjacent to the Our Lady of the Alleghenies Shrine makes a nice rest stop, and the Basilica of St. Michael the Archangel makes a great photo op. If you're not feeling religious today, head on up the street a short way to the Loretto Pub & Grill or Spanky's Tavern. Just past these hangouts is Smith Myer's Superette. Fuel up now—this is your last opportunity.

Some of the challenge route's best views occur in the next 10 miles. The scenery is fantastic and the cycling fairly easy as you slowly lose elevation on your way to Dysart. Your last difficult climb starts immediately after you cross Pennsylvania Highway 53 and extends for 4 miles, setting you up for a fantastic finish down PA 36. The route branches off to skirt the western edge of Altoona, avoiding city traffic. After your turn onto Fortieth Street near the ride's end, notice Allegro Restaurant on the right. You won't have any trouble replenishing carbs here.

THE BASICS

Start: From Leopold Park, just a few miles west of Altoona.

Length: 42 miles.

Terrain: Difficult. Two major climbs limit this ride to experienced, fit cyclists.

Traffic and hazards: Traffic is light throughout the ride. Traffic is fast and a little heavier on Pennsylvania Highway 36 near the end of the ride, but a nice shoulder is present. Watch for tight turns on the descent into Dysart beginning at Mile 28.0.

Getting there: From U.S. Highway 22 just west on Interstate 99, take the exit for Pennsylvania Highway 764 North toward Altoona. In approximately 2 miles turn left onto Fifty-eighth Street. Follow for 1.2 miles and turn left onto State Route 4008. Go 0.3 mile and turn left into Leopold Park. Free parking and restrooms are available.

LOCAL INFORMATION

◆ Allegheny Mountains Convention & Visitors Bureau, One Convention Center Drive, Altoona, PA 16602; (814) 943–4183 or (800) 842–5866.

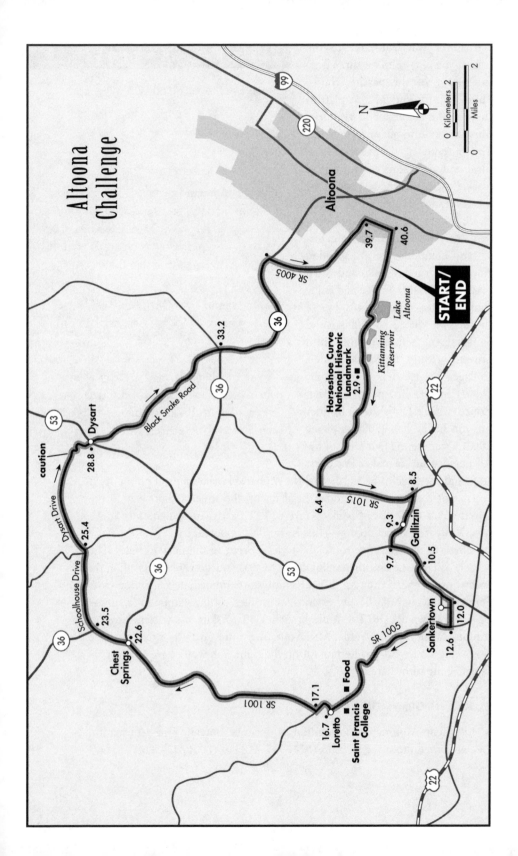

0.0 Leave the Leopold Park parking lot and return to SR 4008. Turn left at the stop sign.

2.9 The Horseshoe Curve National Historic Landmark is on the right. SR 4008 becomes State Route 1034 in Cambria County.

6.4 Turn left at the stop sign onto State Route 1015.

8.5 Turn right onto SR 1015/Forest Street.

9.3 Turn right at the stop sign to stay on SR 1015.

9.7 Turn left at the stop sign onto PA 53 South.

10.5 Turn right then make the immediate left onto Shaft Road.

11.7 *Caution:* rough railroad crossing. (*Note:* Shaft Road becomes Webster Street.)

12.0 Turn right at the stop sign onto Pennsylvania Avenue.

12.6 Turn right at the stop sign onto State Route 1005.

16.0 On the right you will pass the Our Lady of the Allegheny Shrine and the Basilica of St. Michael the Archangel.

16.4 Loretto Pub & Grill is on the left; Spanky's Tavern is on the right. Just ahead on the right is Smith Myer's Superette.

16.7 Turn right onto State Route 1001 at the Village Cross monument.

17.1 Turn right at the stop sign to stay on SR 1001.

22.6 Bear left onto PA 36 North.

23.5 Turn right onto State Route 1012/Schoolhouse Drive.

25.4 Turn left to stay on SR 1012 (just past the State Route 1019 turnoff, also to the left).

28.0 *Caution:* some tight turns coming up on your descent.

28.8 Go straight at the stop sign on State Route 1014/Black Snake Road. Cross PA 53.

33.2 Turn right at the stop sign onto State Route 4012, then make the immediate left onto PA 36 South.

(continued)

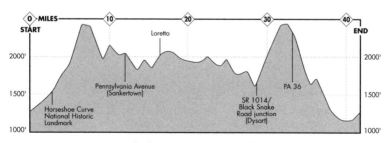

Challenge elevation profile

The Basilica of St. Michael the Archangel in Loretto.

CHALLENGE MILES AND DIRECTIONS (continued)

36.7 Turn right onto State Route 4005.

39.7 Turn right at the stoplight onto Broad Avenue. After turn, stay to the right to remain on Broad Avenue.

40.6 Turn right at the stop sign onto SR 4008/Fortieth Street. Allegro Restaurant is on the right.

41.5 Turn left into Leopold Park.

41.7 End of ride.

LOCAL EVENTS/ATTRACTIONS

♦ Altoona Railroaders Memorial Museum, 1300 Ninth Avenue, Altoona, PA 16602; (814) 946–0834. Interesting exhibits on Altoona's railroading heritage.

♦ Allegheny Portage Railroad National Historic Site, 110 Federal Park Road, Gallitzin, PA 16641; (814) 886–6150. Before the Horseshoe Curve, moving people and cargo over the Alleghenies was done in another peculiar way, memorialized at this site.

RESTAURANTS

♦ Allegro Restaurant, 3926 Broad Avenue, Altoona, PA 16601; (814) 946–5216. Award-winning restaurant featuring Italian cuisine. On the route.
♦ Loretto Pub & Grill, 196 Saint Mary Street, Loretto, PA 15940; (814) 471–0222. Convenient and casual place along the route.

ACCOMMODATIONS

♦ Days Inn, 2915 Pleasant Valley Boulevard, Altoona, PA 16602; (814) 944–4581. Moderate.
♦ The Tunnel Inn, 702 Jackson Street, Gallitzin, PA 16641; (814) 884–2975. Small inn just off the route in Gallitzin.

BIKE SHOP

♦ Pedal Power, 2501 Union Avenue, Altoona, PA 16602; (814) 942–4537.

RESTROOMS

♦ Mile 0.0: Leopold Park
♦ Mile 2.9: Horseshoe Curve Historical Site
♦ Mile 16.4: various locations in Loretto

MAPS

♦ *DeLorme Pennsylvania Atlas & Gazetteer,* maps 60, 61, 74, and 75

Canoe Creek Ramble

*S*tarting in Hollidaysburg, the Canoe Creek Ramble is an enchanting tour of the "loop" area of central Blair County. Enjoy fabulous views of surrounding mountains without needing to climb any on this gently rolling tour. Stop at Canoe Creek State Park and tour the limestone kilns that reflect the region's industrial heritage. Roll down Scotch Valley back to Hollidaysburg and cycle past its countless historic buildings reflecting many architectural styles. Plan a visit in late July and take in America's largest bicycling stage race, the International Tour de Toona.

The Canoe Creek Ramble is a delightful tour of the "loop" area, a fertile rolling valley nestled between Loop, Lock, and Brush Mountains. Starting in historic Hollidaysburg, the route quickly leaves the town for some fantastic country cycling. Mountains always appear, but the route turns just in time to avoid any real climbing obstacles.

The ramble winds along several streams and passes numerous farms in the unspoiled region of Blair County. A little past the ride's midpoint, you have an opportunity to stop at Canoe Creek State Park. This popular park offers a nice swimming area in its 155-acre lake as well as concessions and picnic areas. You can pick up a map at the park office near the entrance and cycle the park road or bike path to the main beach and picnic area.

The state park has a few interesting features. First, the park has several old quarry operations. Limestone, abundant around the park, was extracted and commonly used in Pennsylvania's once-thriving iron and steel industry. The remnants of the Blair Limestone Company's limekilns are the focus of the displays and historical programs at the park. These six massive cement furnace arches offer mute testament to the industrial significance of this limestone-rich valley.

Another interesting characteristic of the park is its large population of little brown bats. Educational programs are offered at the park about the bat nursery colony, which happens to be the largest in Pennsylvania. Look for them on summer evenings around the old church sanctuary. Holy colonization, Batman!

The route back to Hollidaysburg is mainly on Scotch Valley Road, another one of Blair County's pleasant, gentle, and scenic country roads. Turn on Allegheny Street and ride through the heart of the Hollidaysburg Historic District. The district includes hundreds of historic properties, many dating to the 1830s. Equally impressive as the quality of its historic buildings is the vast number of them. Those with an interest in architecture will surely want to take the walking tour of the town after their ride.

LOCAL INFORMATION

◆ Allegheny Mountains Convention & Visitors Bureau, One Convention Center Drive, Altoona, PA 16602; (814) 943–4183 or (800) 842–5866.

LOCAL EVENTS/ATTRACTIONS

◆ International Tour de Toona. Late July–early August. Largest professional bicycling stage race in America; (814) 949–7223.

RESTAURANTS

◆ U.S. Hotel Restaurant & Tavern, 401 South Juniata Street, Hollidaysburg, PA 16648; (814) 695–9924. Fine dining in historic tavern established in 1835.

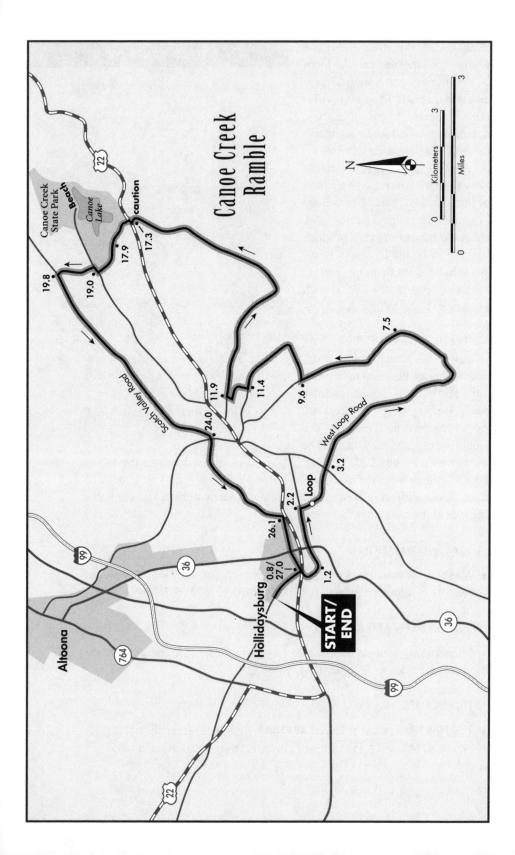

Canoe Creek Ramble

Canoe Creek State Park

Beach

Canoe Lake

caution

Scotch Valley Road

West Loop Road

Loop

Altoona

Hollidaysburg

START/END

N

Kilometers

Miles

22

99

36

764

22

99

36

36

19.8
19.0
17.9
17.3
11.9
11.4
9.6
7.5
24.0
3.2
2.2
26.1
1.2
0.8/27.0

0.0 Exit the park and turn right at the stop sign onto SR 1002/North Juniata Street.

0.8 Turn right at the stoplight onto Allegheny Street. Continue across US 22 and the railroad tracks, and turn left onto Bedford Street, keeping the BCO Mart and gas station on your left after the turn.

1.2 Turn left onto State Route 2014/Plank Road.

2.2 Stay to the right to remain on SR 2014.

3.2 Continue straight at the stop sign on West Loop Road.

7.5 Turn left at the stop sign onto State Route 2020/Lock Mountain Road.

9.6 Turn right onto East Loop Road.

11.4 Turn right onto White Bridge Road.

11.9 Turn right at the stop sign onto State Route 2022/Juniata Valley Road.

17.1 Use caution on the upcoming descent; stop sign at bottom of hill.

17.3 Turn right onto US 22 East, then make the immediate left onto State Route 1011/Turkey Valley Road.

17.9 Turn right into Canoe Creek State Park. In 0.3 mile arrive at the park office, where you can pick up information. Restrooms available. Option here to further explore the park. Otherwise, turn around and return to SR 1011.

18.5 Turn right onto SR 1011/Turkey Valley Road.

19.0 Bear right at the stop sign; in 0.1 mile bear left to remain on SR 1011.

19.8 Turn left at the stop sign onto Scotch Valley Road.

24.0 Continue straight at the flashing light on Scotch Valley Road.

26.1 Turn right onto US 22, then immediately bear right onto Allegheny Street.

27.0 Turn right at the stoplight onto North Juniata Street.

27.7 Turn left into the American Legion Memorial Park.

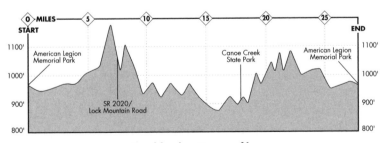

Ramble elevation profile

ACCOMMODATIONS

♦ Carriage House B&B, RR 2, Box 650, Hollidaysburg, PA 16648; (814) 696–4143. Two-hundred-year-old stone home.

♦ Canoe Creek State Park, RR2, Box 560, Hollidaysburg, PA 16648. Modern cabins available. Very reasonable. Reserve by calling (888) PA–PARKS (888–727–2757).

BIKE SHOP

♦ Spokes N Skis, 315 Logan Boulevard, Altoona, PA 16602; (814) 941–3888.

RESTROOMS

♦ Mile 0.0: American Legion Memorial Park
♦ Mile 18.2: Canoe Creek State Park office

MAP

♦ *DeLorme Pennsylvania Atlas & Gazetteer,* map 75

Cycle the Southern
Alleghenies Cruise

Starting in Martinsburg, the Cycle the Southern Alleghenies Cruise is a premier biking tour among the countless dairy farms of eastern Blair County. Nestled between two towering Allegheny ridges, the cruise rolls through the fertile valley and past picturesque farms of every variety. Stop in the small, friendly town of Williamsburg, or stay overnight in a B&B. Marvel at the many country churches, farmhouses, farm ponds and streams, and the horses and buggies of the area's Mennonites. Even though it lacks major tourist attractions and distractions, come see why this cruise has become one of my favorites in Pennsylvania.

Don't expect big-time attractions on this cruise. There are no wineries, museums, historic landmarks, or even state parks. That is probably the reason that, while living in Western Pennsylvania most of my life, I've never passed through this region. I've always stayed on the highways that just seem to bypass this part of the state. I never knew what I was missing.

I found out about the Martinsburg/Williamsburg area from Cycle the Southern Alleghenies (CSA), a coalition of tourism agencies for the seven county region of the Southern Alleghenies. They called their ride the Horse and Buggy Tour and placed their ride start in Williamsburg. Basically the same ride, the Cycle the Southern Alleghenies Cruise starts from Martinsburg simply because I prefer to start my rides from local and state-run parks. These types of

Start: From Morrison's Cove Memorial Park in Martinsburg.

Length: 35 miles.

Terrain: Moderate. No long mountain climbs, but several hills provide some challenge.

Traffic and hazards: Pennsylvania Highway 866 has fast traffic, but it is light. All other roads are very rural, and traffic is extremely light. Use caution on the steep descent into Williamsburg.

Getting there: Take Interstate 99 from Altoona or Bedford and exit at Pennsylvania Highway 36 for Roaring Spring. Follow to Roaring Spring; where the road splits take Pennsylvania Highway 164 approximately 5 miles to Martinsburg. At the stoplight at PA 866/Market Street in center of town, continue straight for 0.2 mile to Walnut Street. Turn right and go 1 block to Morrison's Cove Memorial Park on the left. Free parking.

parks tend to offer free parking and usually have restrooms, water, and picnic facilities available. I elected to change the title of the tour to Cycle the Southern Alleghenies Cruise, in honor of CSA's efforts in mapping out the many bike rides in the area and encouraging the use of the bicycle in touring this beautiful region.

The cruise may turn out to be one of your favorite bike rides in Western Pennsylvania, as it is now one of mine. The distance is just right, not too long or too short. There are no mountain passes, but there are several respectable climbs and enough of those gentle rollers that add up to a moderately demanding day in the saddle. You'll be cycling in a gentle and green rolling valley between two Allegheny ridges, Lock Mountain to the west and Tussey Mountain to the East. The looming mountain views are always evident and the valley scenery absolutely incredible, especially if you enjoy agricultural regions as I do. The number of farms is unbelievable, most meticulously kept and of the dairy variety.

About 20 miles into the cruise, you'll roll into Williamsburg after a nice descent. If you're looking for a place to stay, the Clubhouse B&B is right along the route at Mile 19.9 as you're heading into town. There are several casual restaurants in town, or you could head to Martin's General Store. You can pick up some snacks and drinks there as well as packaged sandwiches or salads. They offer several inside tables as well as restrooms. You won't find many diversions in Williamsburg, but it is still a small, friendly, likable town—sort of like Mayberry. Now run along, Opie. Rail-trail enthusiasts should look into some of the trails being developed in the vicinity.

Williamsburg sits at a lower elevation than Martinsburg, so you'll have a little more climbing after your break. Taking that into consideration, you might want to start your ride from Williamsburg if you're driving in from the north. You can get most of the climbing out of the way early, take a breather in Martinsburg, and have a steady decline while you cycle north back to

Farms make up most of eastern Blair County, near Martinsburg.

Williamsburg. Regardless, you're in for one sweet ride. Be sure to look into Cycle the Southern Alleghenies for other road and off-road rides in the region.

LOCAL INFORMATION

♦ Allegheny Mountains Convention and Visitors Bureau, One Convention Center Drive, Altoona, PA 16602; (800) 842–5866.

LOCAL EVENTS/ATTRACTIONS

♦ Williamsburg Community Farm Show. Mid to late August. Horse shows, contests, truck pulls, food, entertainment, and more. Call the visitor bureau for information at (800) 842–5866.

RESTAURANTS

♦ Pizza Star Restaurant, 104 East Allegheny Street, Martinsburg, PA 16662; (814) 793–4404. Pizza and other good stuff right in the middle of town.
♦ Martin's General Store, 300 High Street, Williamsburg, PA 16693; (814) 832–3534. Good stop for a quick bite during your ride.

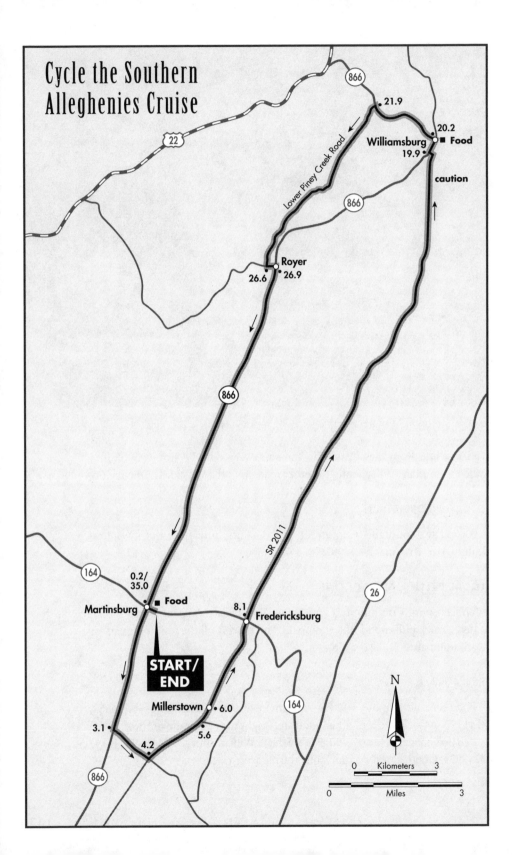

Cycle the Southern
Alleghenies Cruise

22

866

• 21.9

Lower Piney Creek Road

866

Williamsburg

20.2
■ Food
19.9

caution

Royer
26.6 • • 26.9

866

SR 2011

164

0.2/
35.0

Martinsburg ■ Food

8.1 ○ Fredericksburg

26

START/
END

Millerstown • 6.0

3.1 •

5.6

164

4.2

N

866

0   Kilometers   3

0   Miles   3

0.0 Turn right out of the parking lot onto Walnut Street and go back to PA 164/ East Allegheny Street. Turn left at the stop sign and continue 0.2 mile to the stoplight.

0.2 Turn left at the stoplight onto PA 866 South/Market Street.

3.1 Turn left onto State Route 2001/Henrietta Road.

4.2 Turn left onto Cross Roads Lane.

5.6 Bear left onto State Route 2005 at the stop sign and Mt. Pleasant United Church.

6.0 Continue straight on Millerstown Road.

8.1 Continue straight at the stop sign on State Route 2011/Clover Creek Road. Cross PA 164.

19.4 Use caution on the upcoming descent.

19.9 Bear left at the bottom of the hill and continue to the stop sign. Turn right onto PA 866 North/High Street. The Clubhouse B&B is on the right after the turn.

20.2 Turn left onto PA 866 North/First Street. On the right at this turn is Martin's General Store.

20.3 Bear right at the stop sign to remain on PA 866 North.

21.9 Turn left before the bridge onto Lower Piney Creek Road. After this turn, continue straight (up the hill), where the road splits.

26.6 Turn left at the stop sign onto State Route 2020/Lock Mountain Road.

26.9 Turn right at the stop sign onto PA 866 South/Piney Creek Road.

35.0 Turn left at the stoplight onto PA 164 East/East Allegheny Street in the center of Martinsburg. There are several casual restaurants in town.

35.2 Turn right onto Walnut Street and go 1 block to Memorial Park on the left.

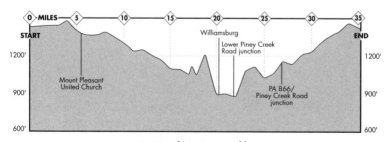

Cruise elevation profile

ACCOMMODATIONS

♦ Clubhouse B&B, 327 High Street, Williamsburg, PA 16693; (814) 832–9122. Reasonably-priced B&B located on the route in Williamsburg.

BIKE SHOP

♦ None in the area.

RESTROOMS

♦ Mile 0.0: Morrison's Cove Memorial Park
♦ Mile 20.2: Martin's General Store

MAP

♦ *DeLorme Pennsylvania Atlas & Gazetteer,* map 75

Pittsburgh City Cruise

*L*ocated at the confluence of the Monongahela, Allegheny, and Ohio Rivers, Pittsburgh is a modern, cosmopolitan city that still retains small-town friendliness and charm. The Pittsburgh City Cruise explores many of the distinct ethnic neighborhoods that characterize one of America's most livable cities. Cycle through the vibrant and colorful Strip District and pick up some fresh fruit to take on your ride. Challenge the hill in Highland Park while cycling past the renowned natural-habitat Pittsburgh Zoo. Enjoy a lunch and the trendy shops and boutiques in Squirrel Hill. Ride through the campus of the University of Pittsburgh and marvel at its Cathedral of Learning. Cycle up East Carson Street on Pittsburgh's South Side for a different flavor of this unique city. Finally, enjoy riding through the heart of Pittsburgh's downtown, where the city's passion for sports and the performing arts is proudly displayed.

In terms of traffic, this is by far the most difficult ride in this book, but it is also the most interesting and colorful. I've ridden Pittsburgh numerous times without any problems, but I always ride with caution and only on Saturday and Sunday mornings. If you're not familiar with Pittsburgh, this short city tour of 19 miles will pass many distinct neighborhoods and places of interest. I guarantee that you'll find something of interest that will bring you back for another visit.

Start: From the pay parking lot at the Boardwalk Entertainment Complex on Smallman Street. Fees range from $3.00 to $5.00 per vehicle.

Length: 19 miles.

Terrain: Several hills add some challenge to a mostly gentle ride.

Traffic and hazards: This is city riding! Although short in length, this ride is not suitable for children or beginners due to heavier city traffic, thus the cruise label. The cruise should only be attempted during Saturday and Sunday mornings, when traffic in the city is light. Pay particular attention to car doors opening ahead of you. Always use hand signals—and stay alert.

Getting there: From the Point State Park area, take Liberty Avenue away from the point. Turn left onto Tenth Street and go 1 block to Penn Avenue and turn right. Go 1 long block to Eleventh Street and turn left. Go 1 block and turn right onto Smallman Street. Go 0.3 mile to the Boardwalk Entertainment Complex on the left. This is a pay lot. If you are lucky, you may find free street parking in the vicinity, but don't count on it.

Located at the junction of three mighty rivers, Pittsburgh is a mix of sophisticated urban life and tree-lined streets that are reminiscent of an earlier time. In fact, when describing the city to outsiders, I always mention its unique ethnic neighborhoods that offer varieties of food, culture, and celebrations—that and the Pittsburgh Steelers.

No need to pack any extra fuel for this ride. There are multitudes of stores and eateries along the route. But remember that this *is* a city. Be sure to lock your bike, including your front wheel.

Turn left out of the parking lot onto Smallman Street. You are now in the heart of Pittsburgh's nightlife district. This area offers everything from industrial rock to jazz, disco to hip-hop, whatever that is. Continue a few blocks down Smallman Street until you come to Eighteenth Street. Primanti Brothers restaurant (on the right) may very well be the one dining establishment that best exemplifies the "burgh." It's at its best after midnight.

After Primanti's, note that the street running parallel to Smallman on the right is Penn Avenue. This is the heart of Pittsburgh's renowned "Strip District." For an authentic Pittsburgh experience, stroll Penn Avenue on a Saturday morning. Flower markets and produce stands add color to a bustling marketplace full of antiques, specialty, and ethnic food stores. The aroma of vendor foods and roasting coffee adds to a feast for the senses.

After a relatively mild cruise through the Lawrenceville section of Pittsburgh, you'll begin the toughest climb on the tour. The ascent to Highland Park will pass the Pittsburgh Zoo & Aquarium, one of America's finest natural-habitat zoos. Riding through beautiful Highland Park will offer a reprieve from busy city traffic.

After cycling through the neighborhoods of Highland Park, East Liberty, Shadyside, and Point Breeze, you'll pull into Squirrel Hill. You can easily spend an entire day here strolling the kosher delis, bakeries, bookstores, and specialty shops. A Starbucks Coffee at Mile 10.8 makes a good stop. Continue through Squirrel Hill and enter Schenley Park. Enjoy some great views of the city from here. If you have a park map, consider lengthening the cruise with a spin through this fine city park.

Before you leave Schenley Park, the Phipps Conservatory and Botanical Gardens will be on the left. The conservatory, housed in an 1893 Victorian glasshouse, offers 2.5 acres of plants, butterflies, and special exhibits throughout the year. The tropical palm court, the mainstay of the conservancy, is alone worth the admission. Passing Phipps, look to the right to view the scholarly buildings of Carnegie Mellon University, one of the finest academic institutions in the country.

After you pass the Carnegie Library on the right, you'll turn right onto Forbes Avenue and arrive at the Carnegie Museum of Natural History. Every young child in the region has visited here on one school field trip or another. It's best known for its dinosaur collection, one of the finest in the world. Swing around the block and hop onto Fifth Avenue. The tall building on the left is the Cathedral of Learning, located on the campus of the University of Pittsburgh.

Cyclists enjoying the wide-open streets on a Sunday morning in Pittsburgh.

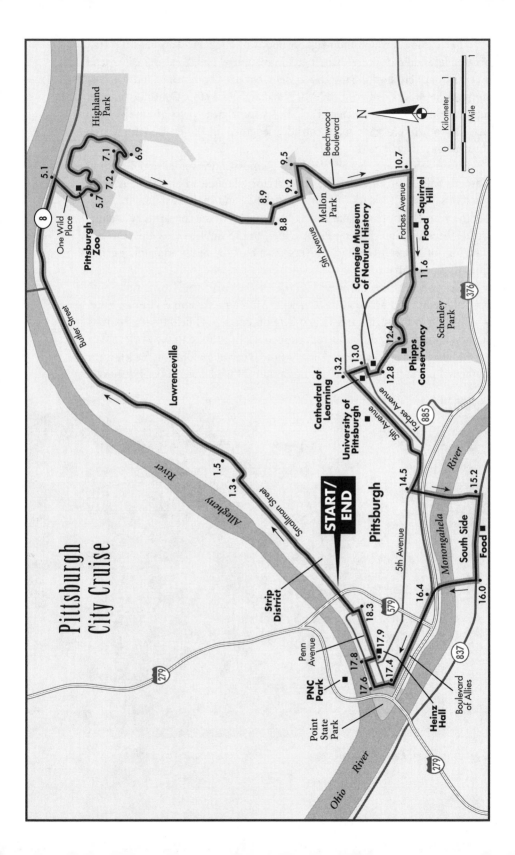

Pittsburgh City Cruise

0.0 Turn left out of the parking lot onto Smallman Street.

0.2 Primanti Brothers restaurant is on the right at Eighteenth Street. One block to the right (Penn Avenue) is Pittsburgh's Strip District.

1.3 Turn right onto Thirty-second Street and go 1 block. Turn left at the stoplight onto Penn Avenue.

1.5 Bear left at the stoplight and Y intersection onto Butler Street. Proceed through Lawrenceville.

5.1 Turn right at the stoplight onto One Wild Place. You'll have a long climb past the Pittsburgh Zoo.

5.7 Bear left at the stop sign onto Lake Drive.

6.8 Bear right onto Connecting Road.

6.9 Make a sharp right at the stop sign onto Farmhouse Drive.

7.1 At the top of the hill, bear left at the stop sign onto Reservoir Drive.

7.2 Turn left onto North Highland Drive and exit the park.

8.8 Turn left at the stoplight onto Alder Street.

8.9 Turn right at the stop sign onto Shady Avenue.

9.2 Turn left at the stoplight onto Fifth Avenue.

9.5 Turn right at the stoplight onto Beechwood Boulevard.

10.7 Turn right at the stoplight onto Forbes Avenue. In 0.1 mile Starbucks will be on the right.

11.6 Bear left at the stop sign onto Schenley Drive.

12.4 Bear right at the stop sign, keeping Phipps Conservancy on your left.

12.8 Bear right, keeping the Carnegie Library on your right.

12.9 Turn right at the stoplight onto Forbes Avenue.

13.0 Turn left at the stoplight onto South Bellefield Avenue. Before the turn, the Carnegie Museum of Natural History is on the right.

13.2 Turn left at the stoplight onto Fifth Avenue. The Cathedral of Learning will be on your left.

(continued)

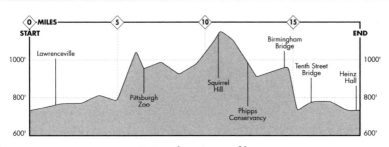

Cruise elevation profile

14.5 Turn left at the stoplight onto Birmingham Bridge. Cross the Monongahela River.

15.2 Turn right after the bridge and at stoplight onto East Carson Street. Cycle through the South Side District. In 0.3 mile Fat Heads South Shore Saloon will be on the right; 0.2 mile later a Starbucks will be on the left.

16.0 Turn right at the stoplight onto South Tenth Street. Cross the Mon again on the Tenth Street Bridge.

16.4 Turn left at the stoplight onto Second Avenue. The County Jail is on the left.

16.8 At the T intersection and with the Pittsburgh sports mural in front of you, bear right and then make the immediate right onto Court Place.

16.9 At the stoplight continue straight with caution onto Boulevard of the Allies.

17.2 Continue straight. For a detour to Market Square, turn right here and proceed several blocks.

17.4 Turn right at the stoplight onto Commonwealth Place. Stay on Commonwealth as it bends to the left toward the Hilton Hotel. Cross Liberty Avenue, keeping the hotel on your right and Point State Park on your left.

17.6 Turn right at the stop sign onto Ft. Duquesne Boulevard. PNC Park and Heinz Field are located to your left across the Allegheny River.

17.8 Turn right at the stoplight onto Sixth Street.

17.9 Turn left at the stoplight onto Penn Avenue. Heinz Hall is on the right.

18.3 Turn left at the stoplight onto Eleventh Street just past the Convention Center.

18.4 Turn right onto Smallman Street. In 0.1 mile the Senator John Heinz Regional History Center is on the right.

18.7 End the ride at the Boardwalk Complex parking lot.

Inside this impressive structure are the Nationality Rooms—twenty-six rooms that offer an enchanting insight into Pittsburgh's diverse ethnic heritage.

Cross the Birmingham Bridge and the Monongahela River (the Mon) and turn right onto East Carson Street for an interesting ride through Pittsburgh's eclectic South Side. Coffeehouses, bars, antiques dealers, ethnic restaurants, and more bars line Carson and add flavor to this distinctly Pittsburgh neighborhood. At Mile 15.5 my favorite casual restaurant, Fat Heads South Shore Saloon, offers humongous sandwiches, the very best wings, and every draft beer imaginable. Another Starbucks is located on the left after Fat Heads.

Cross the Tenth Street Bridge and the Mon again, and turn left onto Second Avenue. The funny-looking building on the left is the Allegheny County Jail, where residents enjoy HBO, air-conditioning, and stunning river views. How cozy. Continue onto the Boulevard of the Allies. At Market Street consider a short detour to the right to Market Square. You can view the beautiful courtyard of the PPG complex and stroll the shops and markets surrounding the city square.

After passing Point State Park, turn right onto Ft. Duquesne Boulevard. Look for beautiful PNC Park, home of the Pittsburgh Pirates, on the left across the Allegheny River. Just downriver from PNC Park is Heinz Field, home of the Pittsburgh Steelers. With plenty of professional and collegiate sports teams, Pittsburgh is a sports fan's paradise. With black spandex and a gold jersey, you'll fit right in.

Cycling down Penn Avenue, you'll enter Pittsburgh's cultural district. Heinz Hall for the Performing Arts offers outstanding acoustics and a truly elegant setting for the Pittsburgh Symphony Orchestra and other performers. The Benedum Center, a splendidly renovated theater from the golden years of vaudeville, boasts one of the largest stages in the country.

Just before the end of your cruise, the Senator John Heinz Pittsburgh Regional History Center will be located on the right. Housed in an 1898 ice company building, the Center's seven floors offer insight into 300 years of Pittsburgh's history and heritage. You can pick up other information on Pittsburgh at the Heinz History Center, just a short walk from the start and end of the cruise.

For a longer bike tour of Pittsburgh, consider the Great Ride, held on the last Sunday in July, or Pedal Pittsburgh, held in mid-May. These events offer a variety of rides for all ability levels and offer wonderful rest stops. The longer route options take in more of Pittsburgh's hills and will definitely challenge any cyclist. Enjoy unsurpassed views of one of America's most livable cities from atop Mount Washington. The only thing that beats the view is the thrilling ride back down to the Mon—that and the Pittsburgh Steelers.

LOCAL INFORMATION

♦ Greater Pittsburgh Convention & Visitors Bureau, Regional Enterprise Tower, 425 Sixth Avenue, Thirtieth Floor, Pittsburgh, PA 15219; (412) 281–7711.

♦ Information is also available at the Senator John Heinz Regional History Center, 1212 Smallman Street, Pittsburgh, PA 15222; (412) 454–6000.

LOCAL EVENTS/ATTRACTIONS

♦ The Great Ride. Last Sunday in July; (412) 255–2493. Mass bicycle ride through the heart of Pittsburgh, highlighting parks and the city's diverse ethnic neighborhoods.

♦ Three Rivers Arts Festival. Held at various locations in downtown Pittsburgh for seventeen days in early June. Popular annual festival for the visual and performing arts. Notorious for attracting rain. Call (412) 281–8723 for information.

RESTAURANTS

♦ Primanti Brothers, 46 Eighteenth Street, Pittsburgh, PA 15222; (412) 263–2142. Pittsburgh institution known for its unique sandwiches. On the route.

♦ Fat Heads South Shore Saloon, 1805 East Carson Street, Pittsburgh, PA 15203; (412) 431–7433. Oversized sandwiches, great wings, beer. It's what Pittsburgh is all about.

ACCOMMODATIONS

♦ The Priory—A City Inn, 614 Pressley Street, Pittsburgh, PA 15212; (412) 231–3338. A small, upscale European-style inn located on Pittsburgh's North Side, close to the cruise route.

♦ Sheraton Station Square Hotel, 7 Station Square, Pittsburgh, PA 15219; (412) 261–2000. Upscale chain with a great location on the Monongahela River. Lots of restaurants and entertainment nearby.

BIKE SHOP

♦ Pittsburgh Pro Bicycles, 2012 Murray Avenue, Pittsburgh, PA 15217; (412) 521–2453.

RESTROOMS

♦ This is a city ride. There are many locations along the route.

MAP

♦ *DeLorme Pennsylvania Atlas & Gazetteer,* map 71

Hickory Rides

The Hickory ramble and cruise offer an outstanding tour of Washington County's small villages and bucolic countryside. Starting in Cecil Park, both routes roll through Venice, Southview, and Hickory before a decision must be made regarding the ride's length. The cruise adds only 7 miles to the ramble route but includes several challenging hills. Both routes join and then offer some of the gentlest cycling in the county. One long but gradual hill sets cyclists up for an easy sprint to the finish. Consider a visit in early October, and take in Hickory's popular Apple Festival, offering America's favorite fruit in every imaginable form.

Less than 3 miles from the hustle and bustle of Allegheny County, these two country rides in the Hickory area are a refreshing change of pace. In this northwest region of Washington County, it's hard to find a store or restaurant, let alone traffic and sprawl. Both of these rides offer a pleasant and relatively easy morning of cycling for those looking for a quick and convenient getaway.

Both rides begin by passing through the small villages of Venice and Southview. A short segment on Baker Road might very well be the best country road cycling in the area. After a short climb you'll enjoy a long, gradual descent for several miles past rustic farmhouses and one not-so-rustic mansion. A very pleasant stretch along Cherry Valley Reservoir is followed by a short but grueling climb up to PA 50 in Hickory. Though both routes turn right, those doing the ramble may want to head left if they need a store. One is located at the intersection with Pennsylvania Highway 519 in less than 0.5 mile.

Start: From Cecil Park on Pennsylvania Highway 50 near Venice.

Length: 23 miles for the ramble; 30 miles for the cruise.

Terrain: The shorter ramble has several hills that will challenge beginners. The cruise includes the same hills as the ramble but adds two more fairly difficult climbs, making it a good intermediate ride.

Traffic and hazards: Use caution on PA 50; traffic is fast. The remaining roads are rural and lightly traveled.

Getting there: From Interstate 79, take the Bridgeville exit and head west on PA 50 toward Cecil. Continue for approximately 6.5 miles to Cecil Park on the left. Free parking.

The ramble turns left off PA 50 on McCarrell Road for an exhilarating descent followed by a segment of approximately 6 miles of very gentle cycling. The cruise stays on PA 50 for a few miles. At Mile 12.2 consider a stop at the popular local restaurant, the Cherry Hill Grill. Just after the grill, a small Amoco convenience store at Mile 12.8 is your last chance to refuel.

The cruise then ventures off PA 50 for an additional loop that includes two good climbs. Both climbs are well within the cruise category but will offer some challenge to intermediate cyclists. After the descent to Pennsylvania Highway 18, the route remains gentle for a good stretch and hooks back up with the ramble route at McCarrell Road. Both routes pass through the village of Westland before turning onto Hornhead Road for a fairly long, but mostly gradual ascent. Once you reach PA 50, it's easy going the rest of the way; just ride with caution on this stretch.

Rail-trail enthusiasts might want to look into the Montour Trail, which passes adjacent to Cecil Park. It's in varying stages of development but will tie in to the Allegheny Highlands Trail when completed. Someday soon you'll be able to hop on the Montour Trail and cycle on a continuous succession of trails and towpaths all the way to Washington, D.C. Though out-and-back rides on trails can be somewhat monotonous, with a good map and a little creativity, you can fashion interesting loops using just sections of trails and eliminate dangerous road segments in the process.

LOCAL INFORMATION

♦ Washington County Tourism Promotion Agency, 273 South Main Street, Washington, PA 15310; (724) 228–5520 or (800) 531–4114.

LOCAL EVENTS/ATTRACTIONS

♦ Apple Festival. Held in early October in Hickory; (724) 356–7824. Exceptional country festival with an apple theme. Live music, antique machines and autos, children's activities, hayrides, cornmeal grinding, pie eating, and lots of food, especially apples.

♦ Meadowcroft Museum of Rural Life, 401 Meadowcroft Road, Avella, PA 15312; (724) 587–3412. Two-hundred-acre outdoor museum recreating a nineteenth-century village. Also includes one of the oldest archaeological sites in North America. Open late May through September, Wednesday through Sunday.

RESTAURANTS

♦ Cherry Hill Grille, 186 Main Street, PA 50, Hickory, PA 15340; (724) 356–1001. Serves breakfast, lunch, and dinner. Closed Sunday. On the cruise route.

ACCOMMODATIONS

♦ Knights Inn, 111 Hickory Grade Road, Bridgeville, PA 15017; (412) 221–8110. Reasonably priced chain hotel not far from the ride's start.

BIKE SHOP

♦ TRM Cycles, 719 Washington Road, Pittsburgh, PA 15228; (412) 343–6885.

RESTROOMS

On the ramble route:
♦ Mile 0.0: Cecil Park
♦ Mile 11.8: Mt. Pleasant Township Park
On the cruise route:
♦ Mile 0.0: Cecil Park
♦ Mile 12.2: Cherry Hill Grille
♦ Mile 12.8: Amoco station

MAP

♦ *DeLorme Pennsylvania Atlas & Gazetteer,* map 70

RAMBLE MILES AND DIRECTIONS

0.0 Turn left out of Cecil Park onto PA 50 West. In 0.75 mile cross Pennsylvania Highway 980.

1.0 Turn right onto State Route 4039/Southview Road.

2.0 Bear left to remain on SR 4039/Southview Road.

(continued)

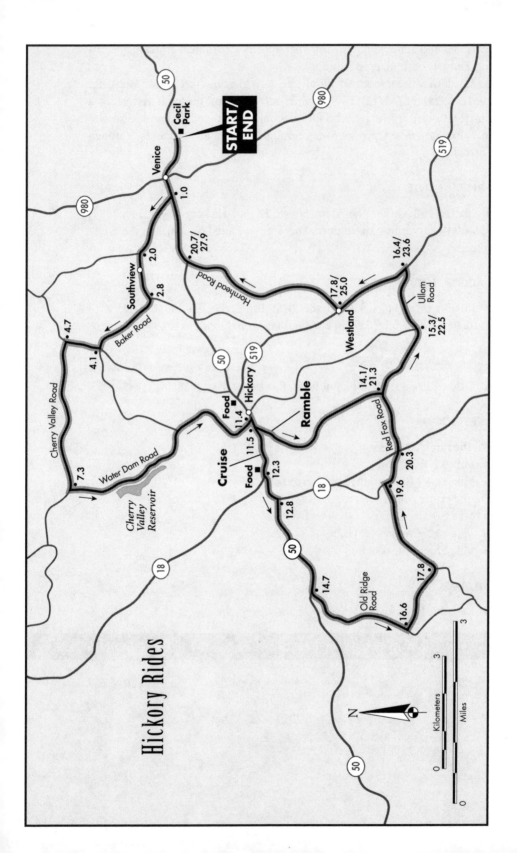

Hickory Rides

START/
END

Cecil
Park

Venice

50

980

519

980

1.0

20.7/
27.9

2.0

Southview

2.8

Baker Road

4.7

4.1

Hornhead Road

16.4/
23.6

17.8/
25.0

Westland

Ullom
Road

15.3/
22.5

Cherry Valley Road

7.3

Water Dam Road

Cherry Valley
Reservoir

50

519

Food

Hickory

11.4

Food

11.5

Cruise

12.3

Ramble

14.1/
21.3

Red Fox Road

20.3

19.6

18

12.8

50

14.7

Old Ridge
Road

17.8

16.6

18

50

N

Kilometers 3

Miles

0

3

0   3

2.8 Turn right onto Baker Road.

4.1 Turn right at the stop sign onto State Route 4037/Fort Cherry Road.

4.7 Turn left onto State Route 4016/Cherry Valley Road.

7.3 Turn left at the stop sign onto State Route 4015/Water Dam Road.

11.4 Turn right at the stop sign onto PA 50 West. (*Note:* If you go left instead, there is a store located within 0.5 mile.)

11.5 Turn left onto State Route 4047/McCarrell Road. (*Note:* The cruise route goes straight here.)

11.8 Mt. Pleasant Township Park is on the right. Picnic facilities and restrooms available. *Caution:* The turn into the park is on a downhill.

14.1 Bear left to remain on SR 4047/McCarrell Road. (*Note:* The cruise rejoins the ramble route here.)

15.3 Continue straight at the stop sign onto Ullom Road. (SR 4047 goes to the right.)

16.4 Turn left at the stop sign onto PA 519 North.

17.8 Turn right onto State Route 4041/Hornhead Road.

20.7 Bear right at the stop sign onto PA 50 East.

22.8 Turn right into Cecil Park.

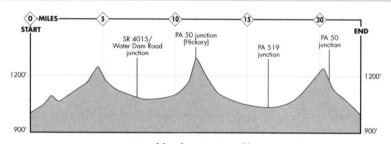

Ramble elevation profile

0.0 Turn left out of Cecil Park onto PA 50 West. In 0.75 mile, cross Pennsylvania Highway 980.

1.0 Turn right onto State Route 4039/Southview Road.

2.0 Bear left to remain on SR 4039/Southview Road.

2.8 Turn right onto Baker Road.

4.1 Turn right at the stop sign onto State Route 4037/Fort Cherry Road.

4.7 Turn left onto State Route 4016/Cherry Valley Road.

(continued)

7.3 Turn left at the stop sign onto State Route 4015/Water Dam Road.

11.4 Turn right at the stop sign onto PA 50 West. (*Note:* If you go left instead, there is a store located within 0.5 mile.)

11.5 Continue straight on PA 50 West. (*Note:* The ramble turns left here.)

12.2 The Cherry Hill Grille is on the right.

12.3 Keep to the left on PA 50 West at the junction with PA 18.

12.8 Bear right to remain on PA 50 West. There is a small Amoco convenience store on the left.

14.7 Turn left onto State Route 4035/Old Ridge Road.

16.6 Turn left to remain on SR 4035.

17.8 Turn left to remain on SR 4035/now Eberle Road.

19.6 Bear right, then continue straight to remain on SR 4035/Eberle Road.

20.3 Continue straight at the stop sign onto State Route 4045/Red Fox Road. Cross PA 18.

21.3 Turn right at the stop sign onto State Route 4047/McCarrell Road. (*Note:* The ramble rejoins the cruise route here.)

22.5 Continue straight at the stop sign onto Ullom Road. (SR 4047 goes to the right.)

23.6 Turn left at the stop sign onto PA 519 North.

25.0 Turn right onto State Route 4041/Hornhead Road.

27.9 Bear right at the stop sign onto PA 50 East.

30.0 Turn right into Cecil Park.

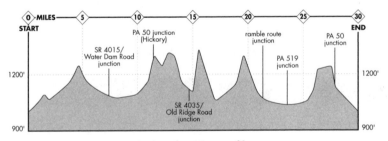

Cruise elevation profile

Mingo Creek Rides

Mingo Creek County Park in eastern Washington County is the base for two short but sweet country rides. After exploring the full length of the scenic and serene Mingo Creek County Park, the ramble offers a fine sample of rural Washington County in a relatively easy 14 miles. The 30-mile cruise adds more variety, more hills, more views, plus the opportunity to enjoy the refreshing wares of a working dairy farm. After your ride, be sure to spend some relaxing moments along Mingo's unspoiled trout stream or on one of the park's many hiking paths in search of its abundant wildflowers and wildlife.

Mingo Creek County Park comprises 2,600 gorgeous acres in eastern Washington County. Great for families, the park offers numerous picnic facilities, playgrounds, ball fields, a stocked trout stream, two picturesque covered bridges, a short bike path, and 17 miles of bridle paths for horse enthusiasts. Administered by the Washington County Department of Parks and Recreation, Mingo Park conducts a variety of programs, such as nature walks, workshops, arts and crafts, hayrides, and day camps. Stop at the park office for a map and a schedule of events.

Both the ramble and cruise follow Mingo Creek as it meanders through steep-sloped Mingo Creek Valley. You can't miss the Henry Covered Bridge at Mile 1.9. This bridge is the most photographed in the area, and rightfully so. Cycling just steps away from the cool stream, you'll find yourself appreciating the park's tranquility while keeping an eye out for that special spot to enjoy after the ride. There are plenty. Once you leave the park boundary, you'll

Start: From the Park Shelter 3/4/5 parking lot, just past the Ebenezer covered bridge.

Length: 14 miles for the ramble; 30 miles for the cruise.

Terrain: The ramble contains a few rollers plus one 0.75-mile climb that will challenge a beginner. The cruise offers several additional climbs that will provide a good workout.

Traffic and hazards: Traffic is light in Mingo Creek County Park, more so when you leave the park boundary on the ramble route. The cruise also uses lightly traveled country roads. Use caution on the short segment of Pennsylvania Highway 136.

Getting there: From Washington, follow PA 136 for approximately 6 miles to the intersection with Pennsylvania Highway 519. Continue east on PA 136 for 4.5 miles and turn left onto Sichi Hill Road. At the bottom of the hill, turn right at the T intersection on Sugar Run Road. Go 0.1 mile and turn right into Mingo Creek County Park. Continue 0.9 mile and turn right to the Shelter 3/4/5 access. Drive through the Ebenezer covered bridge and park in the free lot on the right. Restrooms, water, and picnic facilities are available here.

begin to gain some elevation on Little Mingo Creek Road. When you reach Munntown Road, you'll be reminded that you're still in Western Pennsylvania. You just can't escape the hills.

At Mile 8.6 the ramble and the cruise routes split. The ramble turns left onto Green Valley Road for an extremely easy ride all the way back to Mingo Park. The longer cruise option will drop down through Thomas to take in always-enjoyable Ross Road. Expect a very tough climb on Linnwood Road but great views and a thrilling descent to enjoy after. When you reach PA 136, turn right to go to the Spring House for an enjoyable and delicious break from your bike.

The Spring House is actually a working dairy farm that offers the farm's milk and dairy products as well as appetizing baked goods and fresh produce. The restaurant specializes in country-style cooking and is popular at breakfast and lunch. Several benches outside serve tired cyclists well. Open daily year-round, the Spring House is a welcome break from the road. Fuel up—more of Washington County's hills await you.

The hills on the cruise route are not extremely difficult. A 0.5-mile climb on Mitchell Road is steep, as is one on Church Road. In between you'll find lots of relaxing rollers amid some of Washington County's best farmlands. Though horses and cattle dominate, expect to see chickens, sheep, pigs, llamas, and an ostrich or two, in addition to the usual furry friends of our woodlands. Though the area lacks notable or exciting attractions, Washington County remains a popular and exceptional region to cycle. The lack of attractions can also be looked at as a lack of distractions. Hop on your bike and pedal great country roads—simple as that.

You'll drop back down to Mingo Creek Valley on Sundust Road and rejoin the ramble route on Sugar Run Road. The last few miles of both routes are a breeze. After you enter Mingo Creek Park, you can hop on the bike path at Mile 13.4/29.1, which takes you right back to the parking lot. Plan your visit in late September and enjoy the Covered Bridge Festival. Held at these and various other bridges in Washington and Greene Counties, the festival offers a variety of foods, crafts, exhibits, and entertainment.

RAMBLE MILES AND DIRECTIONS

0.0 Leave the parking lot the way you came in (through the covered bridge) and turn right onto Mingo Creek Road.

0.2 The Mingo Creek Park Office, on the left, is the best place for information.

0.9 Bear right at the stop sign to remain on Mingo Creek Road.

1.9 At the stop sign continue straight on Mingo Creek Road. The Henry Covered Bridge is on the right.

3.0 Turn left at the stop sign onto State Route 1016/Little Mingo Creek Road.

5.1 At the stop sign continue straight onto Barr Road.

6.0 Bear left at the stop sign onto Munntown Road.

7.5 Continue straight at the stop sign to remain on Munntown Road.

8.6 Turn left onto Green Valley Road. (*Note:* This is where the longer cruise option turns right.)

9.7 Turn left onto Sundust Road.

11.4 Turn left at the stop sign onto State Route 1059/Sugar Run Road.

13.2 Turn right onto Mingo Creek Road and enter park.

13.4 You have an option here to hop on the bike path, which will take you directly to the ride's end at the parking lot. Otherwise, continue straight.

14.2 Turn right to cycle through the Ebenezer Covered Bridge and to the ride's end-point.

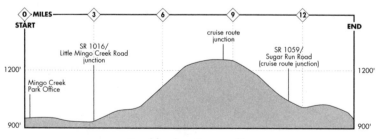

Ramble elevation profile

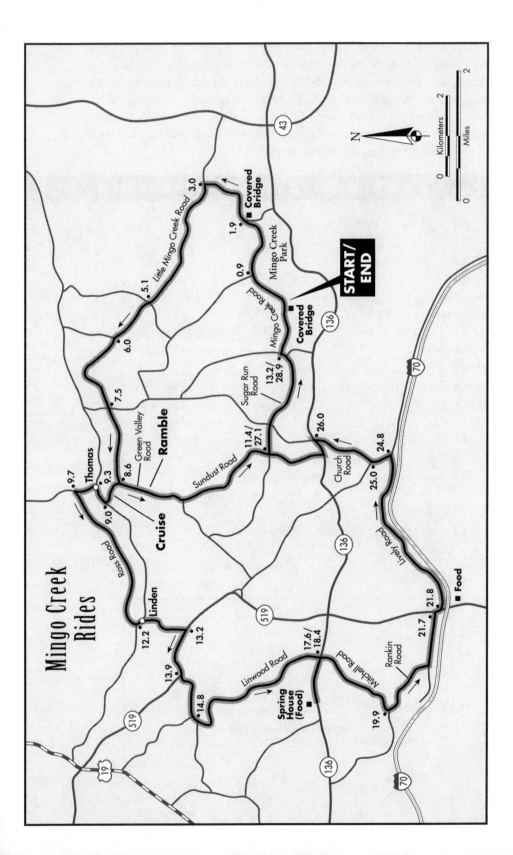

Mingo Creek Rides

Cruise

Ramble

START/END

Covered Bridge

Covered Bridge

Mingo Creek Park

Little Mingo Creek Road

Mingo Creek Road

Sugar Run Road

Green Valley Road

Sundust Road

Church Road

Lively Road

Ross Road

Linwood Road

Mitchell Road

Rankin Road

Thomas

Linden

Spring House (Food)

Food

43

136

70

519

19

136

519

136

70

3.0

1.9

0.9

5.1

6.0

7.5

9.7

9.3

8.6

9.0

11.4/27.1

13.2/28.9

26.0

25.0

24.8

21.8

21.7

19.9

17.6/18.4

14.8

13.9

13.2

12.2

N

Kilometers

Miles

0   2

0   2

0.0 Leave the parking lot the way you came in (through the covered bridge) and turn right onto Mingo Creek Road.

0.2 The Mingo Creek Park Office, on the left, is the best place for information.

0.9 Bear right at the stop sign to remain on Mingo Creek Road.

1.9 At the stop sign continue straight on Mingo Creek Road. The Henry Covered Bridge is on the right.

3.0 Turn left at the stop sign onto State Route 1016/Little Mingo Creek Road.

5.1 At the stop sign continue straight onto Barr Road.

6.0 Bear left at the stop sign onto Munntown Road.

7.5 Continue straight at the stop sign to remain on Munntown Road.

8.6 Bear right to remain on Munntown Road. (*Note:* This is where the shorter ramble goes to the left.)

9.0 Turn right at the stop sign onto State Route 1006/Linden Road.

9.3 Turn left at the stop sign onto State Route 1053/Thomas Road at Thomas Church (on right).

9.7 Turn left onto Ross Road.

12.2 Turn left at the stop sign onto Linden Road; in 0.1 mile turn right onto State Route 1051/Wilson Road.

13.2 Turn right at the stop sign onto PA 519 North.

13.9 Turn left onto Linnwood Road.

14.8 Turn left at the stop sign, then immediately bear left again to remain on Linnwood Road.

17.6 Turn right at the stop sign onto PA 136 West.

18.0 The Spring House is on the right. After your visit, turn left out of the Spring House onto PA 136 East.

18.4 Turn right onto Mitchell Road.

19.9 Turn left at the stop sign onto Rankin Road and enjoy the view and descent.

21.7 Turn right onto PA 519 South.

(continued)

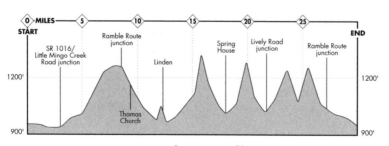

Cruise elevation profile

21.8 Turn left onto Lively Road. (*Note:* Straight ahead on PA 519 is a 7-Eleven and a truck stop diner.)

24.8 Turn left at the stop sign onto State Route 1055/Brownlee Road.

25.0 Bear right onto Church Road.

26.0 At the stop sign turn left onto PA 136 West. Ride with caution for 0.2 mile, then turn right onto Sundust Road.

27.1 Turn right at the stop sign onto State Route 1059/Sugar Run Road. (*Note:* You rejoin the ramble route here.)

28.9 Turn right onto Mingo Creek Road and enter park.

29.1 You have an option here to hop on the bike path, which will take you directly to the ride's end at the parking lot. Otherwise, continue straight.

29.9 Turn right to cycle through the Ebenezer Covered Bridge and to the ride's endpoint.

LOCAL INFORMATION

♦ Washington County Tourism Promotion Agency, 273 South Main Street, Washington, PA 15310; (724) 228–5520 or (800) 531–4114.

LOCAL EVENTS/ATTRACTIONS

♦ Covered Bridge Festival. Held the third weekend of September at various Washington and Greene County covered bridges. Historical exhibits, crafts, food, and entertainment. For information, call the tourist office above.

RESTAURANTS

♦ The Spring House Restaurant and Market, 1531 Route 136, Eighty Four, PA 15330; (724) 228–3339. Working dairy farm offering country-style meals, dairy products, and baked goods.

ACCOMMODATIONS

♦ Inn at Martin Farms, 1989 East Beau Street, Washington, PA 15301; (724) 229–0929. Higher end 1860-era B&B, located about 1 mile west of the Spring House on PA 136.

BIKE SHOP

♦ TRM Cycles, 719 Washington Road, Pittsburgh, PA 15228; (412) 343–6885.

On the ramble route:

◆ Mile 0.0: adjacent to the parking lot
◆ At various locations throughout Mingo Creek Park

On the cruise route:

◆ Mile 0.0: adjacent to the parking lot
◆ At various locations throughout Mingo Creek Park
◆ Mile 18.0: Spring House Restaurant
◆ Mile 21.8: 7-Eleven/truck stop just off route

MAP

◆ *DeLorme Pennsylvania Atlas & Gazetteer,* map 71

Prosperity Challenge

Starting in the small hamlet of Prosperity, this challenge is a rigorous tour of the farms and woodlands of southwest Washington County. Designed for experienced riders, the route offers numerous climbs that will test any cyclist. Take the opportunity to lunch in Claysville before the more difficult second half of the ride. Enjoy several of the county's famed covered bridges and rustic countryside. Conquer some of the area's toughest hills, but enjoy some fabulous vistas and descents as you cycle its low-traffic, rural country roads. Experience a region plain in lifestyle but charming in its simplistic beauty.

The Prosperity Challenge is a rigorous tour of the southwest Washington County countryside. This tour is short on attractions but perfect for what Washington County cycling is all about—low-traffic, quiet country road biking with plenty of hills that challenge. Facilities are limited, so consider picking up supplies in Prosperity at the start or just after the midpoint in Claysville. The route is very rural after Claysville.

The challenge's first quarter offers a pleasant warm-up. Cycling north, the route has just one climb on the way to Taylorstown, and it is a fairly easy one. After a chance to stop at Taylorstown Country Store, you will face a more difficult climb on Reed Road. The descent brings you to Pennsylvania Highway 331 and one of the easier segments of the challenge.

You'll follow PA 331 for about 8 miles as it follows the meandering Brush Run and Buffalo Creek downstream. This stretch is popular with cyclists riding from Washington to Bethany, West Virginia. Enjoy the spin, and conserve your energy for upcoming climbs.

After a left turn onto Dutch Fork Church Road, a tough 2-mile climb starts off gradual but becomes very difficult as you approach the top. Though it's one of the toughest ascents on the route, its isolation and beauty are unrivaled. If you don't feel rewarded by the climb, you will be with the sweeping vistas from atop the ridge you'll cycle for the next several miles before descending to Claysville.

There are several markets and a restaurant in Claysville, where you can fuel up for the rest of the challenge. A succession of tough hills as you leave Claysville elevate you to Good Intent Road and set you up for a fabulous downhill. Undoubtedly the highlight of the challenge is the fast but manageable 4-mile descent past scenic woodlands, pastures, dairy farms, and a covered bridge to the village of Good Intent. Be aware of leaping deer and crossing cattle on this fabulous rural road.

THE BASICS

Start: From the public gravel parking lot along Pennsylvania Highway 18 south of Prosperity.

Length: 54 miles.

Terrain: Moderately hilly. Some long, relaxing stretches with a good number of tough climbs, particularly on the second half. Designed for the experienced, fit cyclist.

Traffic and hazards: Use caution at Mile 24.3, where there are switchbacks on the descent. PA 18 and Pennsylvania Highway 221 carry fast but light traffic. All roads are paved and in good condition.

Getting there: From U.S. Highway 40 in Washington, take PA 18 South for approximately 10 miles to the town of Prosperity. Continue another 0.9 mile to the gravel parking lot on the right side of PA 18. Though no facilities are located here, this is the popular starting point for other Prosperity bike rides.

A stiff 0.75-mile climb after you leave Good Intent brings you to Burnsville Ridge. Some gentle cycling and great views are offered along the ridge, as well as a nice downhill on Rocky Run Road. However, the terrain doesn't let up. A succession of smaller hills and then one long one must be traversed as you make your way northeast back to Prosperity. At Mile 51.6 enjoy the views of the Washington County countryside before one last thrilling 1.5-mile plunge to Prosperity.

LOCAL INFORMATION

♦ Washington County Tourism Promotion Agency, 273 South Main Street, Washington, PA 15301; (724) 228–5520 or (800) 531–4114.

LOCAL EVENTS/ATTRACTIONS

♦ Washington County Agricultural Fair. Mid-August, Washington County Fairgrounds; (724) 225–3151. This annual showcase of agricultural products, exhibits, food, rides, games, and entertainment has been running for more than 200 years.

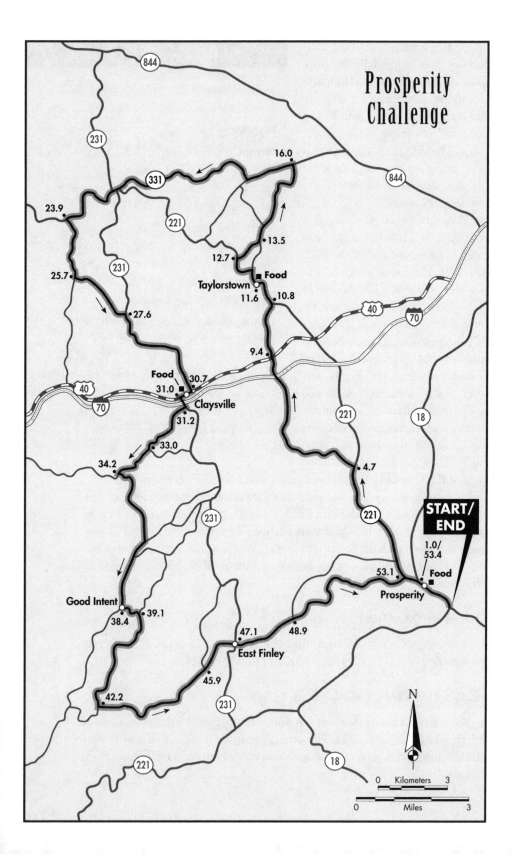

Prosperity Challenge

844

231

16.0

331

221

23.9

12.7
13.5

25.7

231

27.6

Taylorstown ■ Food

11.6   10.8

844

40   70

9.4

Food   30.7
31.0   ■

Claysville

31.2

33.0

34.2

231

221

4.7

18

221

START/
END

1.0/
53.4

53.1   ■ Food

Prosperity

Good Intent   39.1
38.4

47.1   48.9

East Finley

45.9

42.2

231

18

N

0   Kilometers   3

0   Miles   3

0.0 Turn left out of the parking lot onto PA 18 North.

0.9 Jim's Stop & Store is on the right.

1.0 Turn left onto PA 221 North.

4.7 Turn left onto State Route 3009/Cracraft Road, which becomes Sunset Beach Road.

9.4 Continue straight at the stop sign to remain on SR 3009/Sunset Beach Road. Cross US 40. On the left at this intersection is Sunset Beach Swimming Pool, where concessions are available in season.

10.8 Turn left at the stop sign onto PA 221 North.

11.6 Turn right to stay on PA 221 North/Buffalo Creek Road. The Taylorstown Country Store is on the right at this intersection.

12.7 Turn right onto Reed Road.

13.5 Bear left to stay on Reed Road.

16.0 Turn left at the stop sign onto PA 331. Follow for 7.9 miles.

23.9 Make a sharp left onto State Route 3001/Lake Road. Use caution on the upcoming descent.

25.7 Turn left onto State Route 3004/Dutch Fork Church Road.

27.6 Turn right at the stop sign onto Pennsylvania Highway 231 South.

30.7 Turn right at the stop sign onto US 40/Main Street in Claysville. Pop's Place Market and Allum's Restaurant are both located within the next block.

31.0 Turn left onto PA 231 South.

31.2 Turn right onto State Route 3019/Beham Ridge Road.

31.7 Claysville Community Park is on the right. Restrooms and picnicking are available here.

33.0 Bear right at the Dogwood Hills Golf Course.

34.2 Turn left onto State Route 3025/Good Intent Road.

38.4 Turn left in Good Intent to stay on SR 3025/Good Intent Road.

39.1 Turn right at the stop sign onto State Route 3029/Burnsville Ridge Road.

(continued)

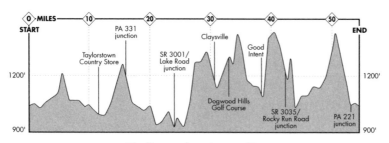

Challenge elevation profile

42.2 Turn left onto State Route 3035/Rocky Run Road just before the white church on the left.

45.9 Bear right to stay on SR 3035/Rocky Run Road.

47.1 Continue straight at the stop sign on SR 3035. Cross PA 231.

48.9 Turn right onto Birch Road, then make the immediate left onto Mt. Zion Road.

53.1 Turn right at the stop sign onto PA 221 South.

53.4 Turn right at the stop sign onto PA 18 South.

54.4 End the ride at the gravel lot on the right.

RESTAURANTS

♦ Allum's Family Restaurant, 153 Main Street, Claysville, PA 15323; (724) 663–7650. Popular hangout conveniently located along the route in Claysville.

ACCOMMODATIONS

♦ The Four Season's Camping Resort, 69 Four Seasons Road, West Finley, PA 15377; (724) 428–4407 or (877) 660–4407. This popular camping resort offers numerous campsites, a hotel, store, swimming pool and many other amenities, and entertainment.

BIKE SHOP

♦ Volpatti's Cycles, 75 West Chestnut Street, Washington, PA 15301; (724) 222–2470.

RESTROOMS

♦ Mile 11.6: Taylorstown Country Store
♦ Mile 30.7: various places in Claysville
♦ Mile 31.7: Claysville Community Park

MAPS

♦ *DeLorme Pennsylvania Atlas & Gazetteer,* maps 70 and 84

Ryerson Station Rides

L ocated in the most southwest reaches of Pennsylvania, the Ryerson Station rides are truly off-the-beaten-path. Both rides start at Ryerson Station State Park with an easy and relaxing ride along its serene sixty-two-acre lake. One long climb will challenge those on the ramble, while the cruise offers an additional 10-mile loop and one additional long climb. The return ride is a relaxing one, following the South Fork of Wheeling Creek as it snakes its way between the county's notorious hills. Recover from the ride with a cool dip in the swimming pool and enjoy the state park's fine picnic facilities.

Tucked neatly into the southwest corner of Pennsylvania, Ryerson Station State Park offers a choice of two beautiful rural rides and plenty of other activities to fulfill your day. Start with a visit to the park office to pick up a map of the state park, which details picnic areas, the campground, hiking trails, and a large, inviting swimming pool.

Ryerson Lake, now called Ronald J. Duke Lake, was formed in 1960 by damming the North Fork of Wheeling Creek. The state park was opened in 1967 and, because of its remoteness, doesn't ever seem crowded. While the lake mainly attracts trout fishermen, the small rustic and isolated campground offers a chance for a dream getaway. The park and surrounding area offer outstanding scenery, an assortment of wildlife, and miles of tree-lined country roads unhampered by traffic.

Two rides are offered from the state park—a short 19-mile ramble and a 29-mile cruise. Both routes share the same roads for 7.6 miles, where you'll slowly gain elevation while following Long Run Creek up the valley. The grade is slight and biking easy for the majority of the way. However, you're quickly

Start: From the Ryerson Station State Park Office/boat launch parking lot.

Length: 19 miles for the ramble; 29 miles for the cruise.

Terrain: The 19-mile ramble is a fairly difficult ride for beginners. Though only containing one climb, it is indeed a long one, and about 1.5 miles are tough. With breaks, beginners should have no problem completing the climb. Once on top, the ramble is fairly easy the rest of the way. The longer cruise version contains one additional hard climb. The cruise route presentation, though short, does provide a respectable workout.

Traffic and hazards: Just after you reach the route's highest elevation, at Mile 7.6, the following descent, whether the ramble or cruise, contains some tight turns that requires good brakes and speed control. Use caution. Toward the end of both routes, be careful riding the short segment of Pennsylvania Highway 21, which carries infrequent but fast traffic.

Getting there: From Waynesburg, travel west following PA 21. Go approximately 20 miles and turn left onto State Route 3022/Bristoria Road, which is also well marked with signs to Ryerson Station State Park. Go 1.3 miles to the park office and boat launch parking lot on the right. Parking is free and plentiful.

reminded that you are in hilly Greene County as you approach the top of the ridge. Mile 7.6 is the highest elevation of either route and also the location of the Centennial Church of God. Take time off the bike here for a deserved rest stop and stroll the cemetery at the back of the church. Views of the countryside from here are spectacular.

Mile 7.6 is also decision time. The shorter ramble bears right here for a thrilling descent and an easy ride back while following the South Fork of Wheeling Creek downstream. The longer cruise route ventures off to explore the far reaches of southwestern Greene County—a region that exemplifies "off-the-beaten-path." Most of the riding is gentle and along streambeds, though one more climb will challenge as you make your way up to Windy Gap. The next descent is a true delight—long, gradual, and lacking in trouble spots. Look for the farm at Mile 18.7 that seems to contain every domesticated animal known to man—and several ones unknown.

The cruise and ramble meet up on Aleppo Road and soon reach Jordan's General Store. Stop in for a snack and say hello to the friendly folk who run the market; it's the only store of any kind on either route. The rest of the tour is a breeze as you continue along winding Aleppo Road, losing elevation until you reach PA 21. Use caution on this short 0.8-mile segment; traffic can be a little fast. Approaching the park office, note the turnoff to the right at Mile 18.5/28.5. The Maple Grove Picnic Area and swimming pool are just 0.4 mile up this road. The pool, concessions, picnic tables, and grassy lake shoreline are just the ticket for a refreshing recovery from your ride.

LOCAL INFORMATION

♦ Ryerson Station State Park, 361 Bristoria Road, Wind Ridge, PA 15380; (724) 428–4254.

LOCAL EVENTS/ATTRACTIONS

♦ Arts in the Park. Held last weekend in September at Ryerson Station State Park by the Aleppo Grange and community volunteers. Historical reenactments, wagon rides, food, crafts, games, and music. Call (724) 428–3729 for information.

RESTAURANTS

♦ Burn's Delight, Route 21, Wind Ridge, PA 15380; (724) 428–4363. Local favorite located 2 miles before the state park entrance on PA 21.

ACCOMMODATIONS

♦ Ryerson Station State Park, 361 Bristoria Road, Wind Ridge, PA 15380. Primitive sites, electric sites, and several cottages. Very reasonable. Reserve by calling (888) PA–PARKS (888–727–2757).

Our horned friend in Greene County.

BIKE SHOP

♦ None in the county.

RESTROOMS

♦ Mile 0.0: in the park office
♦ Mile 10.3/20.3: Jordan's General Store

MAP

♦ *DeLorme Pennsylvania Atlas & Gazetteer,* map 84

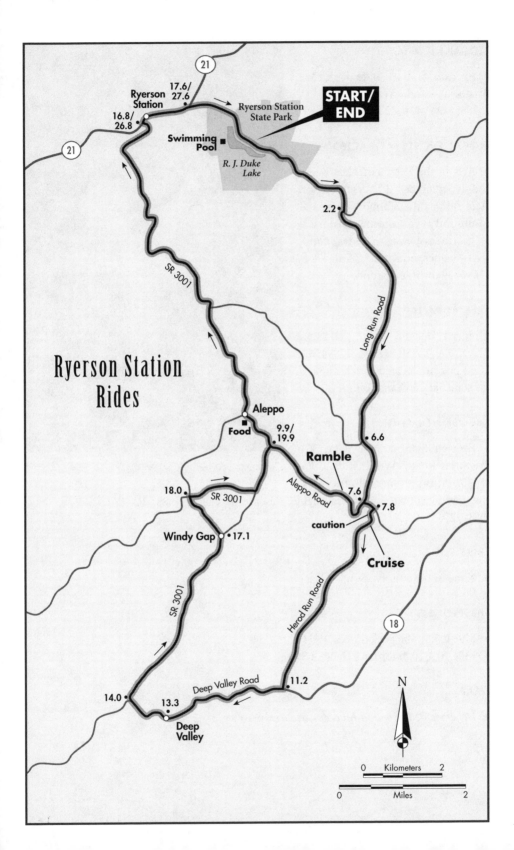

Ryerson Station
Rides

21

17.6/
27.6
Ryerson
Station

16.8/
26.8

21

START/
END

Ryerson Station
State Park

Swimming
Pool

R. J. Duke
Lake

2.2

SR 3001

Long Run Road

Aleppo

Food

9.9/
19.9

Ramble

6.6

18.0

SR 3001

Aleppo Road

7.6

7.8

caution

Windy Gap

17.1

Cruise

SR 3001

Herod Run Road

18

11.2

14.0

13.3

Deep Valley Road

Deep
Valley

N

0   Kilometers   2

0   Miles   2

0.0 Turn right out of the parking lot onto SR 3022/Bristoria Road.

2.2 Turn right onto State Route 3005/Long Run Road.

6.6 At the top of the hill, bear left to stay on SR 3005/Long Run Road.

7.6 Turn right at the stop sign onto State Route 3001/Aleppo Road. The Centennial Church of God is located here. (*Note:* The cruise turns left here for the longer route.)

9.9 Continue straight. (*Note:* The cruise joins from the left.)

10.3 Jordan's General Store is on the left.

16.8 Turn right at the stop sign onto PA 21/Furman Highway. Ride with caution.

17.1 The Crow's Nest Restaurant is on the left.

17.6 Turn right onto SR 3022/Bristoria Road.

18.5 Continue straight. Note the park road to the right; it leads to the picnic area and swimming pool.

18.9 End the ride back at the park office.

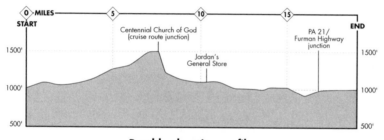

Ramble elevation profile

0.0 Turn right out of the parking lot onto SR 3022/Bristoria Road.

2.2 Turn right onto State Route 3005/Long Run Road.

6.6 At the top of the hill, bear left to stay on SR 3005/Long Run Road.

7.6 Bear left onto SR 3005 at the Centennial Church of God. (*Note:* The ramble turns right at this intersection for the shorter route.)

7.8 Turn right onto SR 3005/Herod Run Road. Caution on the descent—switchbacks.

11.2 Turn right at the stop sign onto State Route 3010, which becomes Deep Valley Road.

13.3 Continue straight as SR 3010 joins State Route 3001.

(continued)

14.0 Bear to the right onto SR 3001 (SR 3010 goes left).

17.1 Bear left to stay on SR 3001 at Windy Gap.

18.0 Turn right to stay on SR 3001.

18.7 Continue straight, but check out the interesting farm to the left.

19.9 Turn left at the stop sign onto SR 3001/Aleppo Road. (*Note:* The cruise joins the ramble route at this point.)

20.3 Jordan's General Store is on the left.

26.8 Turn right at the stop sign onto PA 21/Furman Highway. Ride with caution.

27.1 The Crow's Nest Restaurant is on the left.

27.6 Turn right onto SR 3022/Bristoria Road.

28.5 Continue straight. Note the park road to the right; it leads to the picnic area and swimming pool.

28.9 End the ride back at the park office.

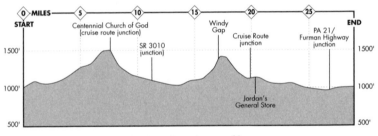

Cruise elevation profile

Greene County Country Cruise

The Greene County Country Cruise is a rural and moderately hilly ride through southwest Pennsylvania's picturesque countryside. Cycle through miles of pastures and farms boasting stone homes and Mail Pouch barns. With long, flat, relaxing stretches along popular trout streams, the cruise challenges with several granny-gear climbs that eventually reward with stunning ridge vistas. Spend a weekend in one of Waynesburg's charming Victorian B&Bs and enjoy the Ryerson Station rides on your second day. Time your visit to Waynesburg for July 29 and enjoy the town's "Rain Day" festival. The townsfolk guarantee you a wet ride.

Greene County is located in the far southwest corner of Pennsylvania. With a county population of only 40,000 stretched out over 400,000 green rolling acres, Greene County is an outdoor enthusiast's wonderland. Miles of traffic-free country roads await the cyclist. Besides this challenge and the Ryerson Ramble included in this book, the Greene County Tourism Promotion Agency publishes a cycling map detailing six other great rides. Pick up that map and other information on the county at the chamber of commerce office in the county seat of Waynesburg.

When planning your bike outing to Waynesburg, you might not want to consider July 29—unless you enjoy cycling in the rain. Waynesburg celebrates Rain Day with a street fair in the heart of town with lots of food, crafts, and entertainment. Rain Day has the distinction of having rain fall in Waynesburg 107 times out of the past 127 years, and each year media from across the country flood the town to cover the event. This makes me wonder if the town's

Start: From the parking lot just east of Ruff Creek General Store.

Length: 38 miles.

Terrain: Moderately hilly. Several challenging hills with lots of flat, relaxing roads in between.

Traffic and hazards: Use caution on the outskirts of Waynesburg, where traffic is heavier. Traffic is very light throughout the challenge, but use caution on Pennsylvania Highways 21 and 221, where traffic is fast. Use caution descending Denny Hill Road at Mile 30.1; there are several tight turns.

Getting there: Coming from the north, take Interstate 79 South to exit 19, Ruff Creek (PA 221). At the end of the ramp, turn left onto U.S. Highway 19 South and go 0.2 mile to the junction with PA 221. Turn left onto PA 221 South. The Ruff Creek General Store is immediately on the right. Pass the store and park in the gravel lot on the right. Restrooms are available at the store.

schedule of activities would be canceled due to *good* weather.

Thanks to Ken Mason, former Greene County resident and current Ride Captain of the Western Pennsylvania Wheelmen, for submitting this ride. Ken still loves the rolling hills and rural nature of Greene County and enjoys leaving the busy Pittsburgh suburbs to lead rides for the WPW several times a year.

You can pick up the supplies you need at the Ruff Creek General Store. You'll have another opportunity outside Waynesburg as the route skirts the city to avoid the downtown shopping district. There are no major attractions along this countryside tour, as with any bike route in Greene County. Forested state game lands encompass part of the route; farms and pasturelands dominate the remainder. In fact, more sheep are raised in Greene County than any other county in the state. You'll pass several small towns along the route, but most will be missed with a blink of the eye.

Large portions of the route follow streambeds as they snake their way between the county's notorious hills. Enjoy these long stretches of flat cycling, and conserve your energy for the hills you'll encounter in between. Though some of the hills are long and challenging, the route overall is not extremely difficult. For those not accustomed to Western Pennsylvania's hills, the route may be better classified as a moderate challenge. Flatlanders need to allow more time and carry sufficient water and fuel.

After the ride consider spending time in Waynesburg. Home to Waynesburg College, a Christian liberal arts college founded in 1849, the town has a lot of vitality for its small size. Part of downtown has been declared a Historic District and includes numerous Victorian buildings; many converted into small specialty shops and boutiques. Pick up a town walking map at the chamber of commerce and be charmed by the town's turn-of-the-twentieth-century architecture.

LOCAL INFORMATION

♦ Waynesburg Area Chamber of Commerce, 19 South Washington Street, Suite 100, Waynesburg, PA 15370; (724) 627–5926.

LOCAL EVENTS/ATTRACTIONS

♦ Annual Rain Day Festival. Held annually July 29 in downtown Waynesburg. Street festival with lots of food, crafts, games, and entertainment. Call the Special Events Commission at (724) 627–8111 for information. Free admission—but pack an umbrella.

RESTAURANTS

♦ Laverne's Place, 934 Jefferson Road, Waynesburg, PA 15370; (724) 883–2643. Makes for a good lunch spot along the cruise route.
♦ Groovy's American Cafe, 46 South Morris Street, Waynesburg, PA 15370; (724) 627–5045. Popular downtown Waynesburg café housed in restored century-old building.

Hills and great vistas are common throughout Greene County.

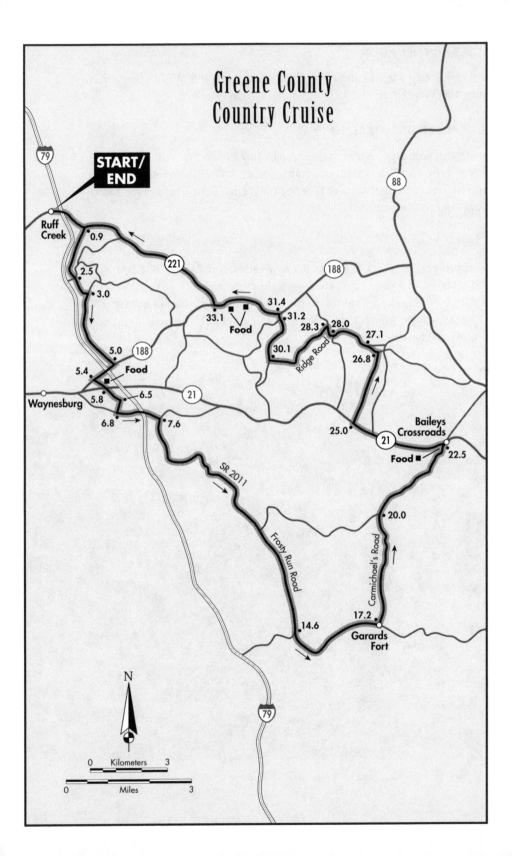

Greene County
Country Cruise

START/END

79

Ruff
Creek

0.9

2.5

3.0

221

188

31.4

33.1   31.2

Food   28.3   28.0

30.1   27.1

Ridge Road   26.8

5.0

188

5.4   Food

Waynesburg

5.8   6.5   21

6.8   7.6

25.0

Baileys
Crossroads

21

Food

22.5

SR 2011

20.0

Frosty Run Road

Carmichael's Road

14.6   17.2

Garards
Fort

88

N

0   Kilometers   3

0   Miles   3

0.0 Turn right out of the parking lot onto PA 221 South.

0.9 Make a sharp right onto Green Valley Road.

2.5 Continue straight at stop sign on unmarked road.

3.0 Turn right at the T intersection on another unmarked road. You'll be cycling parallel to Interstate 79 on your right.

5.0 Turn right at the stop sign onto Pennsylvania Highway 188/Jefferson Road.

5.4 Turn left onto Elm Drive just after a narrow bridge.

5.8 Continue straight at the stoplight on Elm Drive. Use caution crossing busier PA 21. Several food stores and restaurants are located at this intersection.

6.5 Turn right at the stop sign onto Willow Road.

6.8 Turn left at the stop sign onto Rolling Meadows Road.

7.6 Turn right onto State Route 2011/Coal Lick Road. Continue on PA 2011 for 7 miles.

14.6 Continue straight on SR 2011 toward Garards Fort.

17.2 Turn left onto State Route 2017/Carmichael's Road.

20.0 Bear right to stay on SR 2017.

22.5 Turn left at the stop sign onto PA 21. Expect faster traffic but a nice shoulder. Pat's Pub & Restaurant is at this intersection.

25.0 Turn right onto State Route 1017/Kovalcheck Road, which becomes Sugar Run Road.

26.8 Turn left onto Reynolds Road. Gear down for a steep climb. Be sure to stop before the top and look back to enjoy the view of the sheep farms nestled in the valley.

27.1 Turn left onto State Route 1002 (unmarked road).

28.0 Turn right at the stop sign onto State Route 1011.

28.3 Turn left onto Ridge Road. Enjoy more great views from the ridge.

30.1 Turn right onto unmarked Denny Hill Road at the top of the hill. Use caution on your descent—there are several tight turns.

(continued)

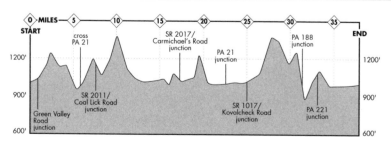

Cruise elevation profile

31.2 Bear right at the stop sign onto Icebox Road.

31.4 Turn left at the stop sign onto PA 188.

32.5 The *77 Market* is on the left.

32.9 Laverne's Place restaurant is on the right.

33.1 Turn right onto PA 221 North.

37.9 Turn left into the Ruff Creek General Store parking lot.

ACCOMMODATIONS

♦ Denny House B&B, 145 West High Street, Waynesburg, PA 15370; (724) 627–9190. This elegant Victorian B&B has become a Waynesburg landmark. Moderate.

♦ Super 8 Motel, 100 Stanley Drive, Waynesburg, PA 15370; (724) 627–8880 or (800) 800–8000. Budget motel located steps from the route.

BIKE SHOP

♦ None in the county.

RESTROOMS

♦ Mile 0.0: Ruff Creek General Store
♦ Mile 5.8: various locations at the PA 21 intersection
♦ Mile 22.5: Pat's Pub & Restaurant
♦ Mile 32.9: Laverne's Place

MAP

♦ *DeLorme Pennsylvania Atlas & Gazetteer*, map 85

Twin Lakes Cruise

Starting at the popular Twin Lakes Park in Westmoreland County, the Twin Lakes Cruise takes cyclists on a roller-coaster ride through the notorious hills of southwest Pennsylvania. Enjoy fabulous views of lush valleys and the looming Laurel Highlands. Stop for a swim at the Keystone State Park beach, or relax at one of many picnic sites along the scenic lake. Confront more hills on your return to Twin Lakes, but also glide past meticulously kept farms on quiet country roads. Keep your legs pumping after your ride as you propel around Lower Lake in a rented paddleboat. Visit in early July and discover why the Westmoreland Arts and Heritage Festival is rated one of the best in the United States.

This short little cruise packs a lot of Western Pennsylvania punch. Though close to Greensburg, the Twin Lakes Cruise remains rural throughout. Due to its terrain, however, it's not recommended for those looking for an easy, relaxing day in the saddle. In fact, a good portion of the time will find you climbing out of the saddle.

Traffic is light and the scenery extraordinary in these parts of Westmoreland County. Many of your climbs will be rewarded with fabulous vistas out over the green, rolling countryside, with towering Chestnut Ridge looming in the distance to the east.

Your destination today is Keystone State Park, a compact multiuse park with a small lake, located conveniently at the midpoint of the cruise. The park

Start: From Twin Lakes County Park.

Length: 24 miles.

Terrain: Though relatively short, the cruise's difficulty arises from its rugged terrain—typical of most of Western Pennsylvania, it includes numerous short, steep hills.

Traffic and hazards: Use caution on the short segments of Pennsylvania Highway 981, where traffic is fast.

Getting there: From Greensburg follow U.S. Highway 30 East to the Westmoreland Mall. Continue another 1.7 miles (just past the Holiday Inn Express) and turn left at the stoplight onto Lewis Road. Go 1.2 miles, then jog right, then left onto State Route 1049. Continue 0.2 mile to the Tamarack parking lot on the left (also signed PAVILION #1). Plenty of free parking.

offers a campground and several modern cabins, which would also make for an ideal overnight stay. The seventy-eight-acre lake is popular for fishing, picnicking, and swimming from the sandy beach on its northeastern shore. A concession stand here should meet the needs of a thirsty cyclist.

The ride back to Twin Lakes is more of the same—quiet country roads with several stubborn hills. Once back at Twin Lakes, consider stopping at the Boathouse, where you can rent canoes, rowboats, or paddleboats by the hour. If you enjoy fishing, the trout-stocked lakes are extremely popular during the April trout season and have outstanding shore access and fishing locations. If you need more exercise, a trail encircles the lakes, while others explore the woodlands throughout the picturesque park. Consider a visit in early July, when the Westmoreland Arts and Heritage Festival is in swing. This annual event, held at Twin Lakes, is nationally recognized as one of the top one hundred festivals in North America.

LOCAL INFORMATION

♦ Laurel Highlands Visitors Bureau, 120 East Main Street, Ligonier, PA 15658; (724) 238–5661.
♦ Keystone State Park, RD 2, Box 101, Derry, PA 15627; (724) 668–2939 (park office); (724) 668–2566 (visitor center).

LOCAL EVENTS/ATTRACTIONS

♦ Westmoreland Arts and Heritage Festival. Held at Twin Lakes Park for four days in early July; (724) 834–7474. Includes more than a hundred live performances, 200 arts and crafts exhibitors, ethnic foods, and heritage and history demonstrations. Free admission.

RESTAURANTS

♦ No restaurants along the route but a wide variety along PA 30 between Greensburg and Latrobe.

ACCOMMODATIONS

♦ Keystone State Park, RR 2, Box 101, Derry, PA 15627. Campground and cabins. Very reasonable. Reserve by calling (888) PA–PARKS (888–727–2757).
♦ Holiday Inn Express, Route 30 East, Greensburg, PA 15601; (724) 838–7070. Moderate chain hotel close to Twin Lakes Park.

CRUISE MILES AND DIRECTIONS

0.0 Turn left out of the parking lot onto SR 1049.

0.3 The Boathouse is to the left. Concessions and restrooms are available.

0.6 Turn left onto State Route 1051/Twin Lakes Road.

0.9 Turn right to remain on SR 1051.

1.4 Turn left at the stop sign onto State Route 1028.

2.2 Turn right onto State Route 1053/Cameo Lane.

3.2 Turn right at the stop sign onto U.S. Highway 119 North.

3.5 Turn right onto State Route 1032/Calvary Hill Road.

6.3 Turn left onto State Route 1022; in 0.1 mile turn right onto Butz Road, which eventually becomes McChesney Road.

9.1 Bear left and cross the bridge onto Township Road 881.

9.5 Turn right at the stop sign onto PA 981. *Caution:* faster traffic.

10.9 Turn left onto Slag Road. In 0.7 mile enter Keystone State Park.

11.8 A park contact station in on the right; pick up information if desired.

12.6 Turn right at the stop sign onto State Route 1018. Walt's Dairy Bar is on the left.

13.0 The state park beach and a concession stand are on the right; the park office is on the left. There are lots of picnic facilities in this area.

14.0 Turn right at the stop sign onto State Route 1031.

15.5 Turn left at the stop sign onto PA 981.

16.2 Turn right onto Derbytown Road.

17.3 Turn right at the stop sign onto McFarland Road.

17.6 Turn left at the stop sign onto Longs Road.

18.4 Turn right at the stop sign onto SR 1022.

20.2 Turn left onto SR 1028.

(continued)

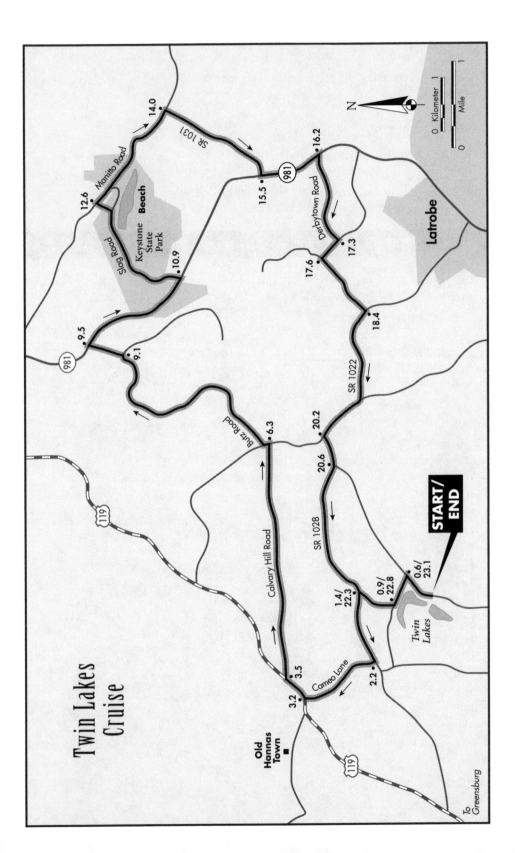

Twin Lakes Cruise

SR 1031

SR 1022

Derbytown Road

Slag Road

Manitto Road

Buzz Road

Calvary Hill Road

SR 1028

Cameo Lane

Keystone State Park

Beach

Latrobe

Old Hannas Town

Twin Lakes

START/ END

To Greensburg

N

0 Kilometer 1

0 Mile 1

14.0
12.6
10.9
9.5
9.1
15.5
16.2
17.6
17.3
18.4
20.2
20.6
6.3
3.5
3.2
2.2
1.4/ 22.3
0.9/ 22.8
0.6/ 23.1

981
981
119
119

20.6 Turn right to remain on SR 1028.

22.3 Turn left onto SR 1051.

22.8 Turn left to remain on SR 1051.

23.1 Turn right onto SR 1049.

23.7 End the ride back at the Tamarack parking lot.

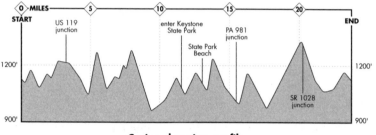

Cruise elevation profile

BIKE SHOP

♦ A & A Cycles, RD 9, Box 496, Latrobe, PA 15650; (724) 537–7393.

RESTROOMS

♦ Mile 0.0: Twin Lakes Park
♦ Mile 13.0: various locations in Keystone State Park

MAP

♦ *DeLorme Pennsylvania Atlas & Gazetteer,* map 72

Ligonier Rides

Located in the heart of the Laurel Highlands, Ligonier is one of Pennsylvania's best small towns. Four rides are offered from this appealing town so that everyone can enjoy cycling this spectacular region, regardless of ability. An 11-mile easy out-and-back ramble winds its way along Loyalhanna Creek to Rector and includes an option to cycle up to Linn Run State Park. The 30-mile cruise explores more of the woodlands and meticulously kept farms south of the town and includes several heart-pumping hills. The 41-mile challenge turns north to the Tubmill Reservoir for a roller-coaster ride teeming with wildlife. The 65-mile classic is a combination of the challenge and the cruise that will test even the fittest cyclists. Regardless of which route you choose, plan to spend time after your ride in charming Ligonier to experience its sophisticated and hospitable character.

Nestled in a valley between Chestnut Ridge to the west and Laurel Mountain to the east is the jewel of the Laurel Highlands, Ligonier. Quaint shops and cozy restaurants give the town a turn-of-the-twentieth-century flavor, highlighted by a charming bandstand in the middle of the town square affectionately known as "The Diamond." Not only is Ligonier a pleasant town to stroll, but it serves as an excellent base for further exploration of the Laurel Highlands.

Though none of the four rides featured from Ligonier ascend the above-mentioned ridges, the 10-mile-wide valley between them is indeed hilly. The region is entirely in the "highlands," and only the ramble manages to escape a large hill—by doing an out-and-back.

The ramble's best cycling comes after it crosses US 30 onto PA 381. The terrain is very mild all the way to Rector and borders the private and exclusive Rolling Rock Country Club. When you reach Rector, the Mountain Market makes a convenient break from your bike. If you're feeling energetic, consider cycling past the store on Linn Run Park Road and up the hill to Linn Run State Park. It's approximately 2 miles at a grade of 2 to 3 percent. The small but absolutely gorgeous state park has numerous picnic spots nestled along Linn Run and among a mixed evergreen and hardwood forest. Check out Adams Falls and several of the short hiking trails. The 2-mile gentle climb is worth the effort—and you get to ride back down. Unfortunately, but necessarily to maintain an easy route, the ramble follows the same route back to town.

The cruise route starts out with a few hills but soon drops down to Fourmile Run for an extremely beautiful and easy spin along the winding stream. After a tough climb to PA 711 near Stahlstown, the cruise drops back down to Rector to follow the ramble route back to Ligonier. Though relatively short, the cruise packs a punch, with several good climbs and descents plus splendid scenery throughout.

The challenge route heads north and takes in Tubmill Reservoir and Mirror Lake before heading south back to Ligonier. The terrain is moderately hilly (you don't climb either ridge), but the challenge comes with the constantly rolling terrain. Relief comes near Tubmill Reservoir, where you'll follow Tubmill Creek downstream for about 9 easy miles. When you get to Mile 37.9,

THE BASICS

Start: All four rides start on North Walnut Street in Ligonier, in front of the Pennsylvania Armory.

Length: 11 miles for the out-and-back ramble; 30 miles for the cruise; 41 miles for the challenge; 65 miles for the classic.

Terrain: The ramble is relatively mild. Though there are some short hills, the terrain and the short distance make it suitable for anyone. The cruise contains several climbs that will challenge and several flat segments that provide welcome relief. The challenge and classic routes involve considerable climbing and are suitable only for fit cyclists.

Traffic and hazards: Use caution on the very short segments on U.S. Highway 30; particularly at the intersection with Pennsylvania Highway 381. Traffic is relatively light throughout. Use caution on all descents; some have tighter than normal turns.

Getting there: From the stoplight on US 30, take Pennsylvania Highway 711 North about 0.1 mile into Ligonier. Turn left onto West Main Street (you'll need to jog around the traffic circle). Go about 0.4 mile and turn right onto North Walnut Street. Continue a few hundred yards or so and park along the right-hand side of the street in front of the Pennsylvania Armory. There is plenty of free parking available.

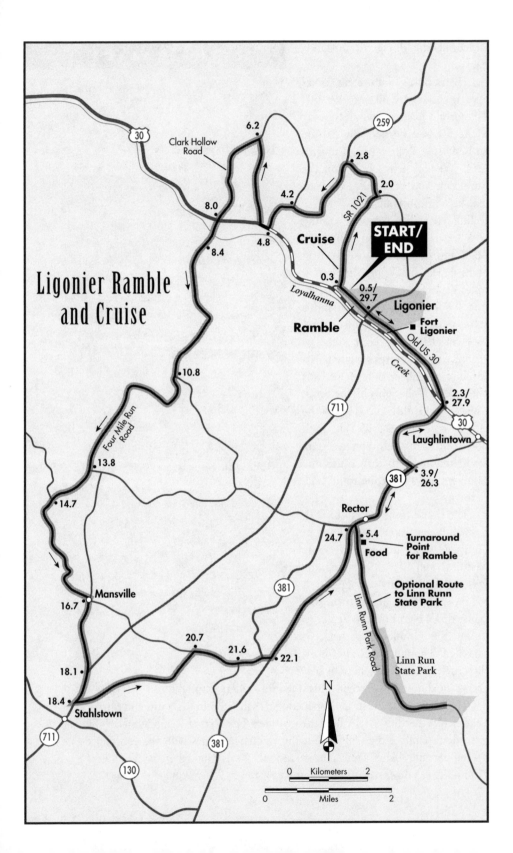

Ligonier Ramble and Cruise

US 30

259

Clark Hollow Road

6.2

2.8

SR 1021

4.2

2.0

8.0

4.8

8.4

Cruise

START/
END

0.3

0.5/
29.7

Loyalhanna

Ligonier

■ Fort
Ligonier

Ramble

Old US 30

Creek

711

2.3/
27.9

30

10.8

Laughlintown

Four Mile Run Road

13.8

381

3.9/
26.3

14.7

Rector

24.7

5.4
Food

**Turnaround
Point
for Ramble**

**Optional Route
to Linn Runn
State Park**

381

Linn Runn Park Road

Mansville

16.7

**Linn Run
State Park**

20.7

21.6

22.1

N

18.1

18.4 **Stahlstown**

711

381

130

0   Kilometers   2

0   Miles   2

you can decide if you want to finish in about 3 miles—or in another 24 by doing the classic. The classic route is simply a combination of the Loyalhanna Cruise and the Tubmill Challenge loops for a 65-mile dream ride. Due to the amount of climbing involved, I recommend a weekend stay in Ligonier and doing the challenge and cruise routes on successive days. You'll have two wonderful days of cycling and plenty of time to enjoy one of Pennsylvania's best small towns.

RAMBLE MILES AND DIRECTIONS

0.0 Head back to West Main Street and turn left at the stop sign toward downtown Ligonier.

0.5 Continue straight on East Main Street, crossing PA 711. You'll need to jog around the traffic circle.

0.8 At the top of a rise, bear left onto Old U.S. Highway 30.

2.3 Bear left onto US 30, then make the immediate right onto PA 381 South. Use caution at this intersection.

3.9 Bear right to remain on PA 381 South.

5.4 Turn left onto State Route 2043/Linn Run Park Road. On the left will be the Mountain Market, which is also your turnaround point. To visit Linn Run State Park, continue up SR 2043/Linn Run Park Road for approximately 2 miles. Otherwise, retrace your route back to Ligonier.

10.8 End the ride back at the armory.

CRUISE MILES AND DIRECTIONS

0.0 Head back to West Main Street and turn right at the stop sign.

0.3 Turn right onto State Route 1021 just after the Mobil station.

2.0 Bear left to stay on SR 1021.

2.8 Turn left at the stop sign onto Pennsylvania Highway 259 South.

4.2 Bear left to remain on PA 259 South.

4.8 Turn right at the stop sign onto US 30 West. Continue for 0.1 mile, and turn right onto Orme Road. Ride with caution on US 30.

6.2 Turn left at the yield sign onto Clark Hollow Road.

8.0 Continue straight at the stop sign on Clark Hollow Road. Use caution crossing US 30.

8.4 Turn left at the stop sign after the bridge onto State Route 2043.

10.8 Turn right onto State Route 2037/Four Mile Run Road.

13.8 Turn right to remain on SR 2037.

(continued)

14.7 Turn left at the stop sign onto State Route 2033.

16.7 After the road bends to the right, go straight onto State Route 2031. (SR 2033 goes left.)

18.1 Turn right at the stop sign onto PA 711 South.

18.4 Turn left onto Hauge Hood Road. This is the second left after you get on PA 711.

20.7 Turn right at the stop sign onto Seaton Road.

21.6 Continue straight at the stop sign as the road becomes State Route 2039/Seaton Road.

22.1 Turn right at the stop sign onto PA 381 South, then make the immediate left onto Weaver Mill Road.

24.7 Turn right onto PA 381 North.

24.8 Continue straight on PA 381 North. (*Note:* The Mountain Market is off to your right on Linn Run Park Road. If you want to bike up to Linn Run State Park, continue past the store for approximately 2 miles.)

26.3 Bear left at the stop sign to remain on PA 381 North.

27.9 Turn left at the stop sign onto US 30 West. Use caution here. Immediately make a soft right onto Old U.S. Highway 30. (*Note:* Do not take the first sharp right up the hill [Mable Street].)

29.4 Continue straight at the stop sign, merging onto East Main Street.

29.7 Continue straight at the traffic circle onto West Main Street. You must jog around circle.

30.1 Turn right onto North Walnut Street.

30.2 End the ride back at the Armory.

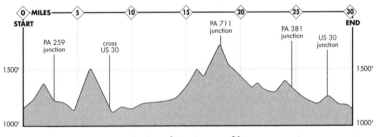

Cruise elevation profile

LOCAL INFORMATION

♦ Laurel Highlands Visitors Bureau, 120 East Main Street, Ligonier, PA 15658; (724) 238–5661.

The town square in one of everyone's favorite small towns, Ligonier.

LOCAL EVENTS/ATTRACTIONS

♦ Fort Ligonier Days. Midtown Ligonier, usually second weekend in October. Information c/o Ligonier Valley Chamber of Commerce, 120 East Main Street, Ligonier, PA 15658; (724) 238–4200. Very popular three-day festival commemorating the Battle of Fort Ligonier. Excellent entertainment schedule, battle reenactments, food, parade, craft booths, and sidewalk sales.

RESTAURANTS

♦ Ligonier Tavern, 137 West Main Street, Ligonier, PA 15658; (724) 238–4831. Great location in the heart of town. Highly recommended for lunch or dinner after your ride. Open daily.
♦ Diamond Cafe, 109 West Main Street, Ligonier, PA 15658; (724) 238–3111. Great place to start your day. Located on the "diamond."

ACCOMMODATIONS

♦ Campbell House B&B, 305 East Main Street, Ligonier, PA 15658; (724) 238–9812 or (888) 238–9812. Offers higher end guest rooms and more economical efficiency motel-type rooms.

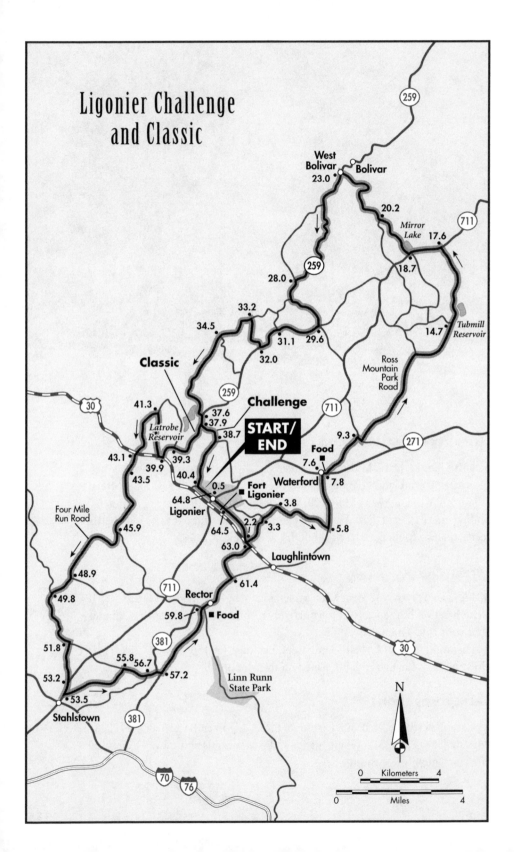

Ligonier Challenge and Classic

West Bolivar
23.0
Bolivar

20.2

Mirror Lake 17.6

18.7

(259)

(711)

(259)

28.0

33.2

34.5

31.1 29.6

32.0

Tubmill Reservoir 14.7

Ross Mountain Park Road

Classic

(259)

(30)

41.3

37.6
37.9

Challenge

START/END

9.3

(711)

(271)

Latrobe Reservoir

38.7

Food

43.1

39.3

40.4

7.6

39.9

43.5

0.5

Fort Ligonier

Waterford 7.8

64.8

Ligonier

3.8

Four Mile Run Road

45.9

64.5

2.2

3.3

5.8

63.0

Laughlintown

48.9

(711)

49.8

Rector

61.4

59.8 **Food**

51.8

(381)

55.8 56.7

57.2

Linn Runn State Park

(30)

53.2

53.5

Stahlstown

(381)

N

(70)

(76)

0   Kilometers   4

0   Miles   4

◆ Ramada Inn Historic Ligonier, 216 West Loyalhanna, Street, Ligonier, PA 15658; (724) 238–9545. Moderately priced hotel with great location and amenities.

BIKE SHOP

◆ Speedgoat Bicycles, Route 30 East, Laughlintown, PA 15655; (724) 238–7181.

RESTROOMS

On the ramble route:
◆ Mile 0.5: various locations in Ligonier
◆ Mile 5.4: Mountain Market

On the cruise route:
◆ Mile 0.0: downtown Ligonier
◆ Mile 24.8: Mountain Market

On the challenge route:
◆ Mile 0.5: various locations in Ligonier
◆ Mile 7.8: BP station

On the classic route:
◆ Mile 0.5: various locations in Ligonier
◆ Mile 7.8: BP station
◆ Mile 59.9: Mountain Market

MAPS

◆ *DeLorme Pennsylvania Atlas & Gazetteer*, maps 72 and 73

CHALLENGE MILES AND DIRECTIONS

0.0 Head back to West Main Street and turn left at the stop sign toward downtown Ligonier.

0.5 Continue straight on East Main Street, crossing PA 711. You'll need to jog around the traffic circle.

0.8 At the top of a rise, bear left onto Old U.S. Highway 30.

2.2 Turn left onto Thomas Road.

3.3 Bear right onto Hermitage School Road.

3.8 Turn right at the stop sign onto State Route 1010; in 0.1 mile bear right to remain on SR 1010.

5.8 Turn left at the stop sign onto State Route 1023.

7.6 Turn right at the stop sign onto Pennsylvania Highway 271 North.

(continued)

7.8 Turn left onto Harvey Road. There is a BP service station and market on the left.

9.3 Turn right at the stop sign onto Turkey Run Road; in 0.2 mile turn left onto State Route 1007/Ross Mountain Park Road.

14.7 Bear right to stay on SR 1007.

15.0 Tubmill Reservoir is on the right.

17.6 Turn left at the stop sign onto PA 711 South.

18.1 The Frosty Way ice-cream stand is on the left.

18.7 Turn right onto State Route 1006 at Mirror Lake.

20.2 Continue straight to remain on SR 1006.

23.0 Turn left at the stop sign onto Pennsylvania Highway 259 South.

28.0 Bear left to stay on PA 259 South.

29.6 Turn right at the stop sign to remain on PA 259 South.

31.1 Turn left to remain on PA 259 South.

32.0 Turn right onto State Route 1008/Derry Ridge Road.

33.2 Turn left to stay on SR 1008.

34.5 Continue straight onto Austraw Road.

37.6 Turn right at the stop sign onto PA 259 South.

37.9 Turn left onto State Route 1021. (*Note:* If you decide to do the classic route, you would continue straight here.)

38.7 Turn right at the stop sign to remain on SR 1021.

40.4 Turn left at the stop sign onto State Route 1046, which becomes West Main Street.

40.6 Turn left onto North Walnut Street.

40.7 End the ride back at the armory.

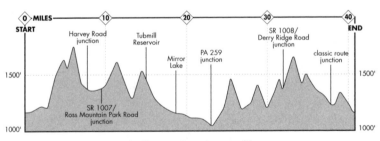

Challenge elevation profile

0.0 Head back to West Main Street and turn left at the stop sign toward downtown Ligonier.

0.5 Continue straight on East Main Street, crossing PA 711. You'll need to jog around the traffic circle.

0.8 At the top of a rise, bear left onto Old U.S. Highway 30.

2.2 Turn left onto Thomas Road.

3.3 Bear right onto Hermitage School Road.

3.8 Turn right at the stop sign onto State Route 1010; in 0.1 mile bear right to remain on SR 1010.

5.8 Turn left at the stop sign onto State Route 1023.

7.6 Turn right at the stop sign onto Pennsylvania Highway 271 North.

7.8 Turn left onto Harvey Road. There is a BP service station and market on the left.

9.3 Turn right at the stop sign onto Turkey Run Road; in 0.2 mile turn left onto State Route 1007/Ross Mountain Park Road.

14.7 Bear right to stay on SR 1007.

15.0 Tubmill Reservoir is on the right.

17.6 Turn left at the stop sign onto PA 711 South.

18.1 The Frosty Way ice-cream stand is on the left.

18.7 Turn right onto State Route 1006 at Mirror Lake.

20.2 Continue straight to remain on SR 1006.

23.0 Turn left at the stop sign onto Pennsylvania Highway 259 South.

28.0 Bear left to stay on PA 259 South.

29.6 Turn right at the stop sign to remain on PA 259 South.

31.1 Turn left to remain on PA 259 South.

32.0 Turn right onto State Route 1008/Derry Ridge Road.

33.2 Turn left to stay on SR 1008.

34.5 Continue straight on Austraw Road.

37.6 Turn right at the stop sign onto PA 259 South.

37.9 Continue straight on PA 259 South. (*Note:* The challenge route turns left here on State Route 1021.)

39.3 Bear left to remain on PA 259 South.

39.9 Turn right at the stop sign onto US 30 West. Continue for 0.1 mile, and turn right onto Orme Road. Ride with caution on US 30.

41.3 Turn left at the yield sign onto Clark Hollow Road.

43.1 Continue straight at the stop sign onto Clark Hollow Road. Use caution crossing US 30.

(continued)

43.5 Turn left at the stop sign after the bridge onto State Route 2043.

45.9 Turn right onto State Route 2037/Four Mile Run Road.

48.9 Turn right to remain on SR 2037.

49.8 Turn left at the stop sign onto State Route 2033.

51.8 After the road bends to the right, go straight on State Route 2031. (SR 2033 goes left.)

53.2 Turn right at the stop sign onto PA 711 South.

53.5 Turn left onto Hauge Hood Road. This is the second left after you get on PA 711.

55.8 Turn right at the stop sign onto Seaton Road.

56.7 Continue straight at the stop sign as the road becomes State Route 2039/Seaton Road.

57.2 Turn right at the stop sign onto PA 381 South, then make the immediate left onto Weaver Mill Road.

59.8 Turn right onto PA 381 North.

59.9 Continue straight on PA 381 North. (*Note:* The Mountain Market is off to your right onto Linn Run Park Road. If you want to bike up to Linn Run State Park, continue past the store for approximately 2 miles.)

61.4 Bear left at the stop sign to remain on PA 381 North.

63.0 Turn left at the stop sign onto US 30 West. Use caution here. Immediately make a soft right onto Old US 30. (*Note:* Do not take the first sharp right up the hill [Mable Street].)

64.5 Continue straight at the stop sign, merging onto East Main Street.

64.8 Continue straight at the traffic circle onto West Main Street. You must jog around circle.

65.2 Turn right onto North Walnut Street.

65.3 End the ride back at the armory.

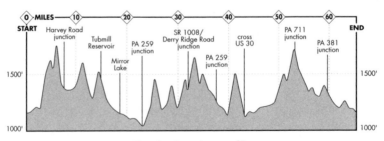

Classic elevation profile

Somerset Miracle Cruise

*T*he Somerset Miracle Cruise is a moderately hilly ride through the picturesque farmlands of Somerset County. Start your day with a visit to the Somerset Historical Center, a museum depicting southwestern Pennsylvania rural life that also serves as the ride's starting point. Stop for lunch at one of several inviting restaurants in Jennerstown, or make reservations for evening dinner and theater at the Green Gables Restaurant and Mountain Playhouse. Cycle past the Quecreek Mine and farm site, where nine miners were miraculously rescued in July 2002. End your fulfilling day with a visit to nearby Shanksville, solemn site of the September 11, 2001, crash of United Airlines Flight 93.

Somerset County was formed in 1795 and can best be classified as mountainous and rural. More than 1,000 farms dot the county's landscape. The majority are Century Farms—that is, they have been in the same family for more than one hundred years. The county is rich in natural resources, with coal and lumber playing key roles in the region's development. During the 1920s Somerset County was the largest coal-producing county in the world.

The Somerset Cruise takes off from the Somerset Historical Center. This museum portrays southwestern Pennsylvania rural life with captivating exhibits and re-created buildings. On display are a 1770 farmstead, an 1800 log farmhouse and barn, a covered bridge, maple sugar camp, and other tools, furnishings, and equipment. The museum is definitely worth your time before or after your cruise.

One of many Mail Pouch barns in rural Pennsylvania.

The first half of the cruise takes you north, cycling at the base of towering Laurel Hill. You never have to climb the ridge, but you do encounter a succession of roller-coaster hills that will indeed test you. Traffic is extremely light all the way to the ride's midpoint at PA 985. After a short, flat segment on PA 985 along Bens Creek, a stiff 1.5-mile climb challenges you on Brehm Road. Once on top, the terrain eases as you glide by several dairy farms on the way to Jennerstown.

Besides a motor speedway, Jennerstown is home to a number of interesting establishments. Before you reach US 30, the Mountain Playhouse and Green Gables Restaurant will be on the left, not exactly a place for a bicycling rest stop. Consider spending an evening here for an excellent dinner and professional theater. The Mountain Playhouse has being staging plays for more than sixty years in the wonderful setting of a restored gristmill. For dining call (814) 629–9201, ext. 103; for theater call (814) 629–9201, ext. 290.

After you turn left onto US 30, several convenience stores are available as well as several more B&Bs and restaurants. Continue for about a mile with caution along busy US 30 and turn off onto State Route 4023. Continue south through more farmland and gentler terrain. At Mile 29.0 note the mine entrance on the right. Though it's private and not open to the public, passing the Quecreek Mine will send chills down the spine of anyone who followed the events of July 2002. Nine miners were miraculously rescued after being trapped deep in a partially flooded chamber for seventy-four hours. Hop back on your bike and continue the climb for another notable stop just up the road.

When you reach the intersection with PA 985 at Mile 29.7, you need to turn left to return to the historical center. However, if you continue straight on Haupt Road for just a few hundred yards, you can visit the site where rescuers bored more than several hundred feet to reach the trapped miners. Against improbable odds, rescuers were able to locate, drill, and lower a capsule that hoisted the miners to safety one by one. The event captured the attention and prayers of the world, and the bravery of the Quecreek Nine and the teamwork and undaunted efforts of the rescuers truly represent the strength and character of our great nation. Very simply, it was America at its finest.

The town of Somerset contains quite a few B&Bs and a variety of restaurants. Head to the town center at the intersection of Main Street and Center Avenue for a spruced-up look that still maintains small-town charm. For a local tradition, follow Route 31 West for 6 miles to the Oakhurst Tea Room. This popular smorgasbord, boasting "everything homemade," brings them in by the busloads.

Stop in the chamber of commerce office for directions to nearby Shanksville. Located about 10 miles northeast of Somerset, it was near Shanksville that United Flight 93 crashed on September 11, 2001. A memorial has been established at the site where visitors have left flags, cards, flowers, and messages that honor the men and women who died that day. A visit to the site is an emotional experience—one that may take your breath away. But although the site does remind of our country's tragic loss, it is more a symbol of the never-ending pride and hope of Americans.

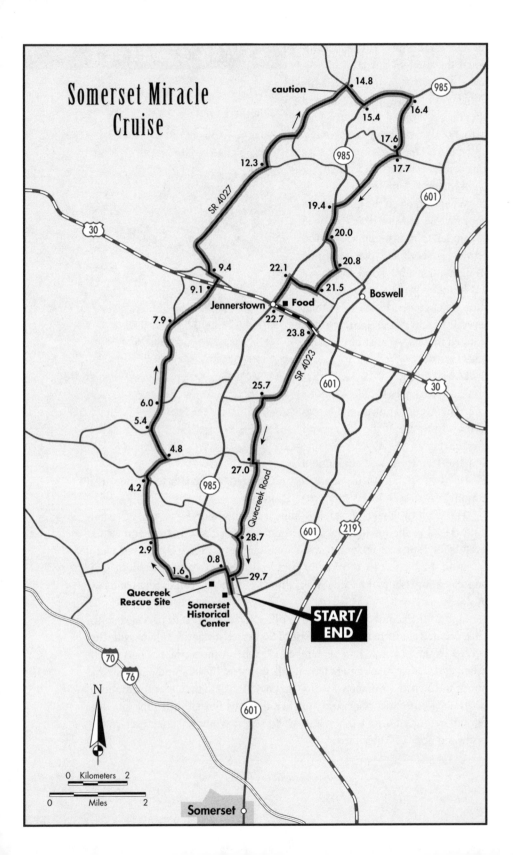

Somerset Miracle Cruise

caution

14.8
15.4
16.4
17.6
17.7
985
985
12.3
601
SR 4027
19.4
20.0
30
20.8
9.4
22.1
21.5
9.1
Boswell
Jennerstown ▪ Food
7.9
22.7
23.8
SR 4023
25.7
601
30
6.0
5.4
27.0
4.8
Quecreek Road
985
4.2
28.7
2.9
601
219
0.8
1.6
29.7
Quecreek
Rescue Site
Somerset
Historical
Center
START/
END
70
76
N
0   Kilometers   2
0   Miles   2
601
Somerset

0.0 Turn left out of Somerset Historical Center parking lot onto PA 985 North.

0.8 Turn left onto State Route 4015/Casebeer Church Road.

1.6 Turn right onto Faidley Road just past an unpaved road that also goes right.

2.9 Continue straight at the stop sign onto Flannery Road.

4.2 Bear left at the stop sign onto State Route 4002. In 0.1 mile bear right onto Barnett Road.

4.8 Turn left onto Yoder Road.

5.4 Bear right at the stop sign onto State Route 4013.

6.0 Continue straight on SR 4013/Keysertown Road.

7.9 Turn right onto Willison Road.

9.1 Go straight at the stop sign to stay on Willison Road and cross US 30. In 0.1 mile, turn left at the stop sign onto State Route 4027.

9.4 Bear right at the stop sign to stay on SR 4027/Klines Mill Road.

12.3 Turn left onto SR 4027/Roaring Road.

14.5 *Caution:* There is a one-lane bridge at the bottom of the hill.

14.8 Turn right at the stop sign to remain on SR 4027/Roaring Run Road.

15.4 Turn left at the stop sign onto PA 985 North/Somerset Pike. Expect more traffic for the next mile.

16.4 Turn right onto Brehm Road. Good climb ahead.

17.6 Bear left at the top of the hill to stay on Brehm Road.

17.7 Turn right onto Speigle Road. Continue straight all the way to PA 985. The road becomes Rolling Hill Road.

19.4 Turn left onto PA 985 South.

20.0 Turn left onto Clay Hill Road.

20.8 Turn right onto Four Seasons Road.

21.5 Turn right at the stop sign onto Mountain Road.

22.1 Turn left at the stop sign onto PA 985 South/Somerset Pike. In 0.2 mile the Mountain Playhouse and the Green Gables Restaurant will be on the left.

(continued)

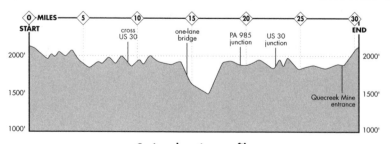

Cruise elevation profile

22.7 Turn left at the stoplight onto US 30. Use caution while cycling this segment— there is an adequate shoulder. There are several convenience stores, B&Bs, and restaurants at this intersection and along US 30.

23.8 Turn right onto SR 4023/Million Dollar Highway.

25.7 Turn left onto SR 4015/Watson Avenue.

27.0 Turn left at the stop sign onto SR 4015/4006/Acosta Road. Then make the immediate right onto SR 4015/Quecreek Road.

28.7 Turn left at the stop sign to stay on SR 4015/Quecreek Road. In 0.25 mile look for the Quecreek Mine entrance on the right. Be aware that it is private property.

29.7 Turn left at the stop sign onto PA 985 South. (*Note:* If you continue straight on Haupt Road and go several hundred yards, you can visit the farm site where the miners were rescued from the July 2002 mine accident at Quecreek.)

30.3 Turn right to end the ride back at the Somerset Historical Center.

LOCAL INFORMATION

♦ Somerset County Chamber of Commerce, 601 North Center Avenue, Somerset, PA 15501; (814) 445–6431.

LOCAL EVENTS/ATTRACTIONS

♦ Mountain Craft Days. Held during the first weekend after Labor Day on the grounds of the Somerset Historical Center; (814) 445–6077. More than 125 craftspeople demonstrate the skills of pioneer ancestors. Early American food, entertainment, children's activities.

RESTAURANTS

♦ Oakhurst Tea Room, 2409 Glades Pike, Somerset, PA 15501; (814) 443–2897. Famous for its smorgasbord.

♦ Brandywine Restaurant, 1649 Pitt Street, Jennerstown, PA 15547; (814) 629–5518. Open daily. Conveniently located on the cruise route in Jennerstown.

♦ The Summit Diner, 791 North Center Avenue, Somerset, PA 15501; (814) 445–7154. Old fashioned small-town diner; popular with everyone. Great place to start your day.

ACCOMMODATIONS

♦ The White Star B&B Inn, 1640 Lincoln Highway, P.O. Box 284, Jennerstown, PA 15547; (814) 629–5200. Attractive lodging located on the cruise route in Jennerstown. Moderate.

♦ Somerset Country Inn B&B, 329 North Center Avenue, Somerset, PA 15501; (814) 443–1005. Circa 1860 Victorian farmhouse located half a block from the town center. Moderate.

BIKE SHOP

♦ Mountain Sports, Inc, 750 North Center Avenue, Somerset, PA 15501; (814) 445–2115.

RESTROOMS

♦ Mile 0.0: Somerset Historical Center
♦ Mile 22.7: various convenience stores and restaurants in Jennerstown

MAP

♦ *DeLorme Pennsylvania Atlas & Gazetteer,* map 73

Ohiopyle Rides

O hiopyle offers the cyclist three exciting tours of the Youghiogeny River gorge and surrounding Laurel Highlands. The easy out-and-back ramble follows the gorgeous Youghiogeny Rail-Trail to Confluence, where the ramble can be extended with a short road ride to the picture-perfect Lower Humbert Covered Bridge. The challenge and classic routes offer numerous difficult climbs throughout the Laurel Highlands that will test even the fittest cyclist. Plan your classic ride as a two-day outing and camp for the night in peaceful Laurel Hill State Park. Cruise Indiantown Road, one of the premier biking roads in Somerset County. Enjoy lunch at the cyclist-friendly River's Edge Cafe overlooking the cool Yough River. Spend additional time in Ohiopyle and test your nerves with a white-water rafting trip down the Yough's Class III and IV rapids. Relax the pace with a visit to Fallingwater, architect Frank Lloyd Wright's masterpiece built over a waterfall and one of the most famous private homes ever built.

Ohiopyle has always been my favorite place in Pennsylvania. Its name derived from an Indian word meaning "white, frothy water," the town of Ohiopyle and the surrounding 19,000-acre state park offer thrilling recreational pursuits as well as striking scenic beauty. Perhaps best known for white-water rafting, the Youghiogeny (*Yaw-ki-GAY-nee*) River cuts through the Laurel Highlands and provides some of the best white-water boating in the eastern United States. While the middle Yough (*Yawk*) provides Class I and II rapids and gentler boating, the lower Yough contains numerous Class III and IV rapids that are best attempted with guided outfitters.

George Washington was searching for a water route to Fort Duquesne (now Pittsburgh) when he came across the waterfalls at Ohiopyle. The falls that forced Washington on a different route are now the central attraction of visitors to Ohiopyle State Park. Concessions, picnic areas, and observation platforms are provided to enjoy the falls, which pack them in on summer weekends. After your ride, take time to enjoy the falls and the park, located just a short stroll from the visitor center.

In addition to white-water boating and rail-trails, the Ohiopyle area also boasts rugged mountain bike trails, 70 miles of hiking trails, waterfalls, camping, equestrian trails, excellent wilderness trout fishing, a number of interesting B&Bs, and a youth hostel. With all the beauty and recreational activities Ohiopyle has to offer, you might not want to leave. But by taking one of these Ohiopyle bike tours, you'll discover that surrounding Fayette and Somerset Counties are equally rewarding.

All three tours start from the Ohiopyle State Park Visitor Center. The ramble basically follows the Youghiogeny Rail-Trail upstream to Confluence. Perhaps the most scenic stretch of biking in the entire state, the trail is very secluded. No roads parallel or cross the trail, so be sure you carry the necessary supplies. If you do get in trouble, wait it out. The trail is very popular, and even during midweek there are other users who can offer assistance.

THE BASICS

Start: From the Ohiopyle State Park Visitor Center.

Length: 22 to 30 miles for the ramble; 42 miles for the challenge; 65 miles for the classic.

Terrain: The ramble is primarily on the rail-trail, with an easily manageable 1 percent grade. The ramble's road portion has similar terrain and is very suitable for beginners. Both the challenge and classic routes contain long, steep hills and higher-use state roads and should be attempted only by experienced, fit cyclists.

Traffic and hazards: Pennsylvania Highways 653 and 281 on the challenge and classic routes have fast traffic, though it is light. The entire challenge and classic routes are paved. Use caution on the descents; many contain tight turns. The ramble requires more than 20 miles of cycling on an unpaved rail-trail. I recommend using mountain bike–sized or hybrid tires of 28mm or wider when cycling any unpaved rail-trail.

Getting there: From Uniontown take U.S. Highway 40 East approximately 12 miles. Turn left onto Pennsylvania Highway 381 North and go about 6.8 miles to Ohiopyle. Turn right onto Sheridan Street just before the bridge over the Youghiogeny River. Go 1 block to the Train Station/Ohiopyle State Park Visitor Center on the left. Free parking. Water and restrooms are available.

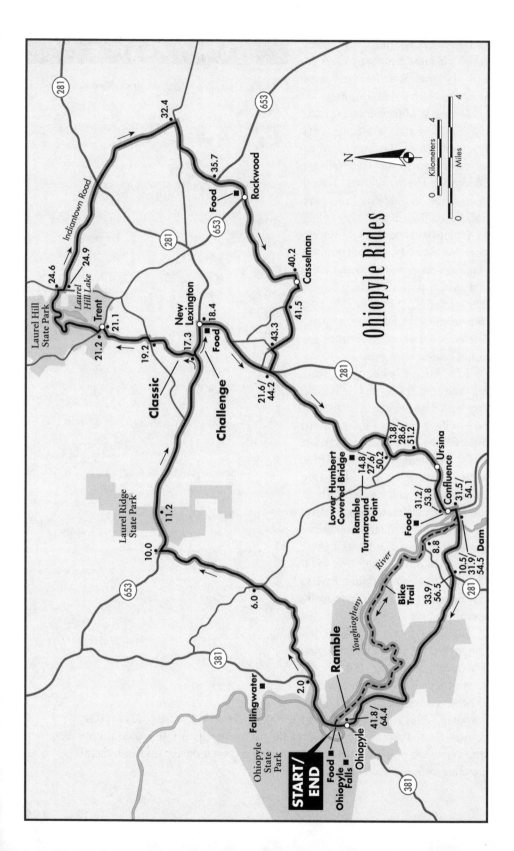

Ohiopyle Rides

0.0 Head right out of the Train Station/Visitor Center, following the rail-trail upriver.

8.8 This area is called the Ramcat Launch Area. Restrooms are located here, as well as concessions in season. Continue straight on the gravel road to remain on the trail.

10.5 Turn left and cross the bike/pedestrian bridge over the Yough River. After the bridge, turn left onto River Road. In 0.1 mile Danny's Place Restaurant is on the right.

10.8 Turn right at the stop sign onto Yough Street. (*Note:* The River's Edge B&B and Cafe is located on the left at this intersection. Besides being a very good restaurant, it also serves as the turnaround point for the 22-mile ramble.) For the 30-mile ramble, continue on Yough Street.

10.9 At the end of Yough Street, cross the second bike/pedestrian bridge. After the bridge bear to the right onto Ross Street.

11.0 Turn right at the stop sign onto Huchart Street and then make an immediate left onto Logan Place. The Confluence Town Park and a gazebo will be on the left. Continue straight as the road becomes PA 281 North, which you must follow for several miles.

13.8 Turn left onto Humbert Road.

14.8 Arrive at the Lower Humbert Covered Bridge. This is the turnaround point for the ramble. Reverse your route back to Ohiopyle for a 29.6-mile round-trip.

29.6 Arrive back at the Ohiopyle Train Station/Visitor Center.

0.0 Leaving the Train Station/Visitor Center, turn right onto Sheridan Street. Go 1 block and turn right onto PA 381 North/Main Street. The Falls Market is located at this intersection. In 0.1 mile, the Youth Hostel is located on the left.

2.0 Turn right onto State Route 2017/Maple Summit Road. The High Waters Grill is located at this intersection.

6.0 Turn left to stay on SR 2017. In 0.25 mile bear right to remain on SR 2017. In 1 mile the windmill farm on the right makes a nice photo op.

10.0 Turn right at the stop sign onto PA 653/Jim Mountain Road.

11.2 Laurel Ridge State Park Office is on the right. Water, picnic facilities, and restrooms are located within the park.

18.4 Turn right at the stop sign onto PA 281 South. New Lexington Market is at this intersection.

(continued)

21.6 Turn right onto State Route 3007/Humbert Road.

27.6 The Lower Humbert Covered Bridge is on the right.

28.6 Turn right at the stop sign onto PA 281 South/Kingwood Road.

31.2 Turn left onto PA 281 South/Oden Street at the Community Center on the right.

31.5 Turn right onto PA 281 South/Robert Brown Road.

31.9 Continue straight on PA 281 South to take the hilly road segment back to Ohiopyle. For the easier trail ride back, turn right here onto the trail and follow it approximately 10.7 miles back to Ohiopyle. For camping, turn left here into the Youghiogeny Outflow Camping area.

32.0 Suder's Soft Freeze is on the left.

33.9 Turn right onto Sugar Loaf Road. Use caution on the steep descents.

41.8 Turn right at the stop sign onto PA 381 North.

41.9 The Ohiopyle Falls are located on the left.

42.0 Turn right onto Sheridan Street and then turn left into the visitor center lot.

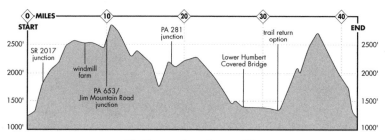

Challenge elevation profile

0.0 Leaving the Train Station/Visitor Center, turn right onto Sheridan Street. Go 1 block and turn right onto PA 381 North/Main Street. The Falls Market is located at this intersection. In 0.1 mile the Youth Hostel is located on the left.

2.0 Turn right onto State Route 2017/Maple Summit Road. The High Waters Grill is located at this intersection.

6.0 Turn left to stay on SR 2017. In 0.25 mile bear right to remain on SR 2017. In 1 mile the windmill farm on the right makes a nice photo op.

10.0 Turn right at the stop sign onto PA 653/Jim Mountain Road.

11.2 Laurel Ridge State Park Office is on the right. Water, picnic facilities, and restrooms are located within the park.

17.3 Turn left onto State Route 3033/Barron Church Road.

(continued)

19.2 Bear right where Rean Road joins from the left to stay on SR 3033. Then, immediately bear left to stay on SR 3033 where Rean Road leaves to the right.

21.1 Turn left at the stop sign onto State Route 3029/Copper Kettle Highway. The Trenthouse Inn B&B is located at this intersection.

21.2 Turn right into Laurel Hill State Park. In 0.25 mile the park office and visitor center will be on the left. Just after that, there is a campground on the left.

21.8 Laurel Hill Lake and several picnic areas are on the right.

24.2 Another park office is on the left.

24.6 Exit the park and turn right onto State Route 3037/Trent Road.

24.9 Turn left onto State Route 3010/Indiantown Road and continue straight on SR 3010 for 7.5miles.

32.4 Turn right at the stop sign onto State Route 3015/Water Level Road.

35.7 Continue straight at the stop sign on Main Street in Rockwood. There are quite a few stores, restaurants, and B&Bs in Rockwood.

36.4 Continue straight on State Route3006/Main Street. If you desire a hill-free ride back to Ohiopyle, you can make a left here onto Bridge Street, go 0.1 mile, and turn right into the Rockwood trailhead of the Allegheny Highlands Trail. This trail follows the Casselman River downstream to Confluence, where it then follows the Youghiogeny River back to Ohiopyle.

40.2 Bear right onto Casselman Road.

41.5 Turn left onto State Route 3007/Casselman Road.

43.3 Turn left to stay on SR 3007/Casselman Road.

44.2 Go straight (actually slightly left) on SR 3007/Humbert Road after crossing PA 381.

50.2 The Lower Humbert Covered Bridge is on the right.

51.2 Turn right at the stop sign onto PA 281 South/Kingwood Road.

53.8 Turn left onto PA 281 South/Oden Street at the Community Center on the right.

54.1 Turn right PA 281 South/Robert Brown Road.

54.5 Continue straight on PA 281 South to take the hilly road segment back to Ohiopyle. For the easier trail ride back turn right here onto the trail and follow

(continued)

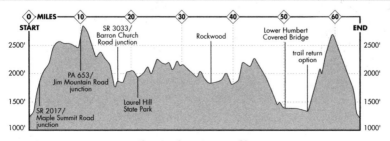

Classic elevation profile

it approximately 10.7 miles back to Ohiopyle. For camping, turn left here into the Youghiogeny Outflow Camping area.

54.6 Suder's Soft Freeze is on the left.

56.5 Turn right onto Sugar Loaf Road. Use caution on the steep descents.

64.4 Turn right at the stop sign onto PA 381 North.

64.5 The Ohiopyle Falls are located on the left.

64.6 Turn right onto Sheridan Street and then turn left into the visitor center lot.

When you reach Confluence, consider lunch at my favorite restaurant there, the River's Edge B&B/Cafe. Most of the clientele on weekends are bicyclists, so you won't be out of place in cycling attire. Try for a table on the wraparound porch, where you can overlook their attractive flower garden while watching trout fishermen casting flies on the frothy Yough.

Most cyclists turn around at Confluence and head back down the trail for a 22-mile round-trip. However, consider lengthening your ramble by 8 miles and follow PA 281 to the north. You're only on PA 281 for 2.5 miles, and there is a wide shoulder. Another mile of country road alongside grazing cattle brings you to Lower Humbert Covered Bridge. The Queen Post Truss–type bridge was built in 1891 and spans Laurel Hill Creek. The bridge makes a wonderful rest stop, photo op, and turnaround point for the longer-version ramble.

Both the challenge and classic routes share the same roads for the first 17 miles. There's an extraordinary amount of climbing as you make your way up to Laurel Ridge. You can break at Laurel Ridge State Park at Mile 11.0, but the facilities there are limited to restrooms and water. The state park stretches through five counties but mainly features the 70-mile-long Laurel Highlands Hiking Trail. At Mile 17.3 you need to decide whether to bike the classic or shorter challenge route.

The classic route turns north and winds its way to Laurel Hill State Park. Camping is available in this state park, and a B&B is located along the route

A restored trail station houses the visitor center along the Yough Trail in Ohiopyle.

The Lower Humbert Covered Bridge near Confluence.

just before the entrance, in case you're planning a two-day outing. After leaving the park, the route follows some of the best cycling roads in Somerset County. The town of Rockwood is conveniently located along the Casselman River and the Allegheny Highlands Trail. Besides several stores and B&Bs, Rockwood offers tired cyclists an opportunity to hop on the rail-trail for an easy spin back to Ohiopyle.

The challenge and classic routes meet up again at Mile 21.6/44.2 and follow the same roads back to Ohiopyle. First enjoy the long descent to the Yough River at Confluence, where you can find a variety of places for a rest stop. At Mile 31.9/54.5 you face another route decision. Turning right to hop on the nearly flat Yough Trail for the return ride would be taking the easy way out. But taking the road route back to Ohiopyle would mean facing another extremely difficult mountain climb. Options abound in the Ohiopyle area. Whichever you choose, you're guaranteed a spectacular ride.

To top off you visit to the Ohiopyle region, consider a visit to Frank Lloyd Wright's Fallingwater. Located about 3.5 miles north of Ohiopyle on PA 381,

Frank Lloyd Wright's masterpiece Fallingwater.

Fallingwater was built for Pittsburgh businessman Edgar J. Kaufmann. One of the most famous private residences ever built, the home is dramatically cantilevered over a waterfall and mountain stream in a harmonious union of nature and art. Wright's masterpiece is now entrusted to the Western Pennsylvania Conservancy, which operates regular in-depth children's and special curator staff tours.

LOCAL INFORMATION

♦ Ohiopyle State Park, P.O. Box 105, Sheridan Street, Ohiopyle, PA 15470; (724) 329–8591.

LOCAL EVENTS/ATTRACTIONS

♦ Frank Lloyd Wright's Fallingwater, one of architect Wright's most acclaimed works. Route 381, P.O. Box R, Mill Run, PA 15464; (724) 329–8501. Admission $10 to $15, depending on time; reservations are usually a must.
♦ Youghiogeny River White-water Rafting. Call the park office at (724) 329–8591 to arrange launch permits for private trips. For guided trips call one of several licensed outfitters in Ohiopyle. Here are two: Laurel Highlands River Tours, 4 Sherman Street, Ohiopyle, PA 15470; (800) 472–3846. White Water Adventurers, 6 Negley Street, Ohiopyle, PA 15470; (800) 992–7238.

RESTAURANTS

♦ River's Edge B&B/Cafe, 203 Yough Street, Confluence, PA 15424; (814) 395–5059. Great place for lunch and a break from the bike. Try for a porch table.
♦ Fox's Pizza Den, 15 Sherman Street, Ohiopyle, PA 15470; (724) 329–1111. Casual spot for sandwiches and pizza; popular with cyclists.

ACCOMMODATIONS

♦ River's Edge B&B/Cafe, 203 Yough Street, Confluence, PA 15424; (814) 395–5059. Great food and location overlooking the Yough River. Moderate.
♦ Yough Plaza Motel, P.O. Box 31, Ohiopyle, PA 15470; (800) 992–7238. Moderate motel just steps away from the ride's start.

BIKE SHOP

♦ Ohiopyle Recreational Rentals, Main Street, PA 381, Ohiopyle, PA 15470; (724) 329–8810.

RESTROOMS

On the ramble route:
♦ Mile 0.0: Train Station/Visitor Center
♦ Mile 8.8: Ramcat Launch Area
♦ Mile 10.8: River's Edge B&B/Cafe
♦ Mile 11.0: various places in Confluence

On the challenge route:
♦ Mile 0.0: Train Station/Visitor Center
♦ Mile 2.0: High Waters Grill
♦ Mile 11.2: Laurel Ridge State Park
♦ Mile 18.4: New Lexington Market
♦ Mile 31.2: various places in Confluence

On the classic route:
♦ Mile 0.0: Train Station/Visitor Center
♦ Mile 2.0: High Waters Grill
♦ Mile 11.2: Laurel Ridge State Park
♦ Mile 21.2: Laurel Hill State Park Office
♦ Mile 24.2: Laurel Hill State Park Office
♦ Mile 35.7: various locations in Rockwood
♦ Mile 53.8: various locations in Confluence

MAPS

♦ *DeLorme Pennsylvania Atlas & Gazetteer*, maps 73, 86, and 87

Bedford County Rides

T hree rides of varying lengths and ability levels are featured in Bedford County. The 16-mile out-and-back ramble is a flat ride that starts in Osterburg and passes several of Bedford County's renowned covered bridges. Take a short detour to visit the Reynoldsdale Fish Culture Station and learn how trout are raised for stocking our streams. The 18-mile cruise and the 41-mile challenge start in downtown Bedford and cover a little more ground—and hills. After a quick exit from downtown, both rides offer miles of low-traffic and great-scenery roads through picturesque farmlands. Complement your ride with a walking tour of Historic Downtown Bedford, featuring a remarkably slower pace of life. Step back in time with a stay at the historic Jean Bonnet Tavern, serving travelers like you for 240 years.

Bedford County's motto, "Return to Life's Simpler Pleasures," will pretty much sum up your visit here. Built along a Native American path, the town of Bedford developed around Fort Bedford, built in 1758 by the British as a supply fort and to provide protection against Indian attacks. It became an important trading post and served as a strategic base for the establishment of an east-west thoroughfare during the French and Indian War.

Fort Bedford no longer exists, but the Fort Bedford Museum includes a scale model of the fort and other exhibits that help create the atmosphere of the pioneer days on Pennsylvania's western frontier. The Walking Tour of Historic Downtown Bedford takes in the museum as well as many other historical sites in this now peaceful town. Walking in Bedford is a delight; there are numerous

Start: The challenge and the cruise start from a parking lot on Penn Street, just behind the County Courthouse in downtown Bedford. The ramble begins in downtown Osterburg.

Length: 16 miles for the ramble; 18 miles for the cruise; 41 miles for the challenge.

Terrain: The ramble is relatively flat. There are several rollers, but they are well within the capability of beginners. The cruise has several good climbs that will provide some challenge to this relatively short ride. The challenge route has additional climbs and plenty of roller-coaster hills, but at just 41 miles it is one of the easier challenges in this book.

Traffic and hazards: Several of the descents have some tight turns to negotiate. Overall, traffic is light. There are no areas of caution on the ramble route. Use caution on the short segments on U.S. Highway 220 leaving and reentering Bedford. Use caution at Mile 17.0 on the cruise and Mile 39.3 on the challenge; there is a sharp turn on a descent with a stop sign at the bottom of the hill. Be very careful. If you fail to stop, you enter into the cross-traffic of busy US 220.

Getting there: For the cruise and challenge, take U.S. Highway 30 Business into downtown Bedford. Turn right at the stoplight if coming from the west (or left if coming from the east) onto South Juliana Street. Go 1 block and turn right on Penn Street. (The Bedford Visitor Center will be on the left as you drive down Juliana Street.) After turning onto Penn, go past the County Courthouse on the left and turn left onto Lafayette Street. Park in the free public lot on the right side of Lafayette—the lots on the left side of the alley are reserved for employees.

For the ramble, take Interstate 99 North from Bedford. Go approximately 9 miles and take the exit for Pennsylvania Highway 869 West. Follow PA 869 West for 1.75 miles to Osterburg. The Osterburg Country Store will be on the left. There is limited street parking near the store or on several side streets in town.

shops and boutiques and enticing restaurants. The town, like the bike ride through the county, is best experienced at a slower pace.

The Bedford area offers three rides. The ramble starts and ends in Osterburg, a short drive out of Bedford to the north. Starting there, cyclists can enjoy several of Bedford County's celebrated covered bridges and beautiful farmlands while remaining on fairly flat terrain. The ride is an out-and-back that is big on scenery and short on hills.

Pick up your supplies at the Osterburg Country Store and within 2 miles you're at the first covered bridge. Not much information is available on the Bowser Bridge's background, and it is perhaps one of the less picturesque of the

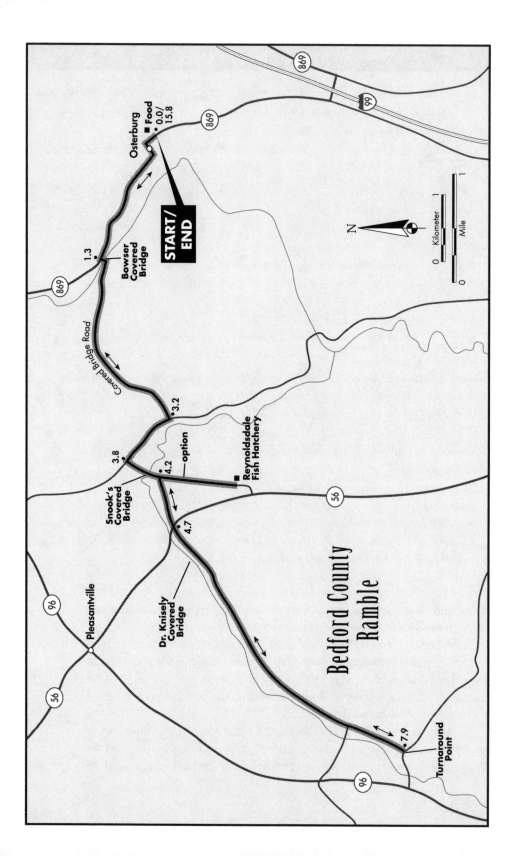

Osterburg
■ Food ● 0.0/
15.8

START/
END

● 1.3
Bowser
Covered
Bridge

Covered Bridge Road

● 3.2
option

● 3.8
Snook's
Covered
Bridge

● 4.2

Reynoldsdale
Fish Hatchery

● 4.7

Dr. Knisely
Covered Bridge

Pleasantville

Bedford County
Ramble

● 7.9
Turnaround
Point

N

Kilometer

Mile

0.0 From the Osterburg Country Store, head west on PA 869. Follow PA 869 as it winds through the town.

1.3 Turn left onto Covered Bridge Road. The Bowser Covered Bridge is located here.

3.2 Turn right at the stop sign onto Gordon Hall Road.

3.8 Turn left onto Fish Hatchery Road.

4.2 Turn right onto Chestnut Ridge Market Road just after you pass through the Snook's Covered Bridge. (*Note:* For a detour to the Reynoldsdale Fish Culture Station, continue straight on Fish Hatchery Road and go 0.75 mile to the fish hatchery.)

4.7 At the stop sign continue straight on Dunning Creek Road. Cross Pennsylvania Highway 56.

4.9 The Dr. Knisely Covered Bridge is located on the right.

7.3 The Ryot Covered Bridge, destroyed by arson, was located here on the right.

7.9 Once you reach State Route 4026/Crissman Road, turn around and reverse your route back to Osterburg.

15.8 End the ride back at the Osterburg Country Store.

county's bridges. Continue another 3 miles to cycle through Snook's Bridge, a Burr Truss–design built in 1883. There's a great photo op after you bike through the bridge.

Just after the Snook's Bridge, turn right onto Chestnut Ridge Market Road to stay on the route. If you want to visit the Reynoldsdale Fish Culture Station, continue straight on Fish Hatchery Road for 0.75 mile to the fish hatchery. The hatchery mainly raises and stocks trout, but there is also a little museum with fish, reptile, and ecosystem displays. A picnic area at the hatchery rounds out a perfect rest break from your tour.

Within another mile you'll pass the Dr. Knisely Covered Bridge. Another Burr Truss Arch bridge, it was built in 1867. It is privately owned and cannot be traversed, but the views of the bridge and surrounding countryside are incredible.

Down the road, the Ryot Covered Bridge was destroyed by an arsonist in summer 2002. Fortunately, the county plans to rebuild the bridge. Continue another 0.6 mile until you hit Crissman Road. This is the turnaround point for the ramble. If you're intent on fashioning a loop back to Osterburg, you can do so by turning left here, climbing Chestnut Ridge, and following the challenge route. Just keep in mind that the hills you will encounter will affect the casual nature of this ride.

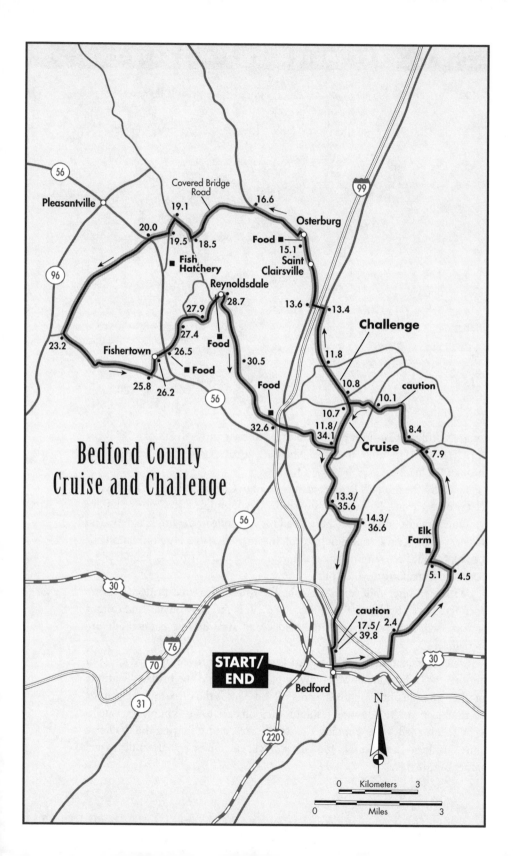

Bedford County
Cruise and Challenge

0.0 Turn right out of the parking lot onto Penn Street. Go 1.5 blocks and turn left at the stoplight onto Richard Street. Continue with caution through town.

0.4 Turn right onto SR 1001/Sunnyside Road. There is an Exxon Mini Mart on the left.

2.4 Turn right onto Deibert Road.

4.5 Turn left onto Rabbit Lane.

5.1 Turn right at the stop sign onto SR 1001/Imlertown Road. The Keystone Elk Farm is located here.

7.9 Turn right at the stop sign onto State Route 1014, then in 0.1 mile turn left onto Shoemaker Road.

8.4 Turn right onto State Route 1018/Yount Road. Be aware of a steep climb ahead.

9.6 Continue straight. Use caution on the descent; there are several tight turns.

10.1 Continue straight at the stop sign on SR 1018.

10.7 Turn left onto SR 1001 to remain on the cruise route. (*Note:* The challenge route turns right here to continue to Osterburg.)

11.8 Continue straight on SR 1001. *Note:* This is where the challenge route reenters the cruise route.

13.3 Turn left at the stop sign onto SR 1014.

14.3 Turn right at the stop sign onto Briar Valley Road.

17.0 *Caution:* Steep descent and stop sign ahead. Check brakes and control your speed.

17.5 Turn left onto US 220. More traffic but adequate shoulder. Road becomes Richard Street in town.

18.2 Turn right at the stoplight onto Penn Street.

18.3 Turn left onto Lafayette and into parking lot.

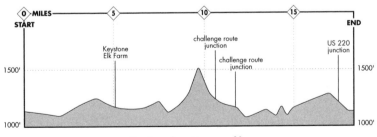

Cruise elevation profile

0.0 Turn right out of the parking lot onto Penn Street. Go 1.5 blocks and turn left at the stoplight onto Richard Street. Continue with caution through town.

0.4 Turn right onto SR 1001/Sunnyside Road. There is an Exxon Mini Mart on the left.

2.4 Turn right onto Deibert Road.

4.5 Turn left onto Rabbit Lane.

5.1 Turn right at the stop sign onto SR 1001/Imlertown Road. The Keystone Elk Farm is located here.

7.9 Turn right at the stop sign onto State Route 1014, then in 0.1 mile turn left onto Shoemaker Road.

8.4 Turn right onto State Route 1018/Yount Road. Be aware of a steep climb ahead.

9.6 Continue straight. Use caution on the descent; there are several tight turns.

10.1 Continue straight at the stop sign on SR 1018.

10.7 Turn right onto SR 1001 to remain on the challenge route. (*Note:* The cruise route turns left here for a short way back to Bedford.)

10.8 Turn left onto Willow Brook Lane where SR 1001 goes to the right. Use caution on the steep climb and descent ahead.

11.8 Turn left onto Oppenheimer Road. Then immediately bear right onto Kaufman Hollow Road.

13.4 Turn left at the stop sign onto PA 869 West/Brumbaugh Road. Use caution here at the I–99 interchange.

13.6 Turn right at the stop sign onto PA 869 West/William Penn Road.

15.0 There is a Sunoco Station and a market on the left.

15.1 Bear left to stay on PA 869 West.

15.3 The Osterburg Country Store is on the left. (*Note:* This is the starting point for the ramble. Continue west on PA 869, following it as it winds through the town.)

16.6 Turn left onto Covered Bridge Road. The Bowser Covered Bridge is located here.

18.5 Turn right at the stop sign onto Gordon Hall Road.

19.1 Turn left onto Fish Hatchery Road.

19.5 Turn right onto Chestnut Ridge Market Road just after you pass through the Snook's Covered Bridge. (*Note:* For a detour to the Reynoldsdale Fish Culture Station, continue straight on Fish Hatchery Road and go 0.75 mile to the fish hatchery.)

(continued)

20.0 At the stop sign continue straight on Dunning Creek Road. Cross Pennsylvania Highway 56.

20.2 The Dr. Knisely Covered Bridge is located on the right.

22.6 The Ryot Covered Bridge, destroyed by arson, was located here on the right.

23.2 Turn left onto State Route 4026/Crissman Road.

25.8 Turn left at the stop sign onto State Route 4003/Valley Road.

26.2 Turn right onto State Route 4028/Old Town Road. (*Note:* This is the *second* SR 4028 that goes right. It's located about 75 yards beyond the first SR 4028.)

26.5 Continue straight at the stop sign on Hammond Hill Road and cross PA 56. The Fishertown Country Store is located on the right at this intersection.

27.4 Continue straight on Sawmill Road.

27.9 Turn left at the stop sign onto State Route 4015/Adams Run Road.

28.7 Turn right at the stop sign onto State Route 4032/Reynoldsville Road. Judy's Market is on the left at this intersection. Cross the bridge and continue straight on State Route 4019.

30.5 Bear left to stay on SR 4019/Pine Grove Church Road. *Caution:* Do not take the sharp left.

32.6 Go straight at the stop sign on Hoagland Road. Fisher's Country Store is on the left at this intersection.

34.1 Turn right at the stop sign onto SR 1001. (*Note:* The cruise route joins the challenge route here from the left.)

35.6 Turn left at the stop sign onto SR 1014.

36.6 Turn right at the stop sign onto Briar Valley Road.

39.3 *Caution:* Steep descent and stop sign ahead. Check brakes and control your speed.

39.8 Turn left onto US 220. More traffic but adequate shoulder. Road becomes Richard Street in town.

40.5 Turn right at the stoplight onto Penn Street.

40.6 Turn left onto Lafayette and into parking lot.

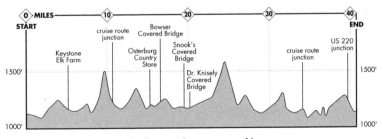

Challenge elevation profile

The cruise and challenge routes both start in downtown Bedford. They share the same roads for the first 10 miles as the route heads northeast at the base of Evitts Mountain. At Mile 5.1 the Keystone Elk Farm is a must-stop. Though high fencing diminishes your chance of a good photo opportunity, these majestic animals are still a joy to watch. In several miles, less-fit cyclists might want to walk their bikes up Yount Road. However you reach the top, stop and enjoy the views of Bedford County's undulating countryside at the top.

At Mile 10.7 the cruise turns left for the return to Bedford. The challenge turns right and heads northwest to Osterburg, where it then follows the ramble route past the covered bridges. After leaving the ramble route, the challenge route becomes hillier as it winds its way to Reynoldsdale and a possible break at Judy's Market. Another 5 rolling miles brings you back to State Route 1001 to remerge with the cruise route. The cruise and challenge then follow the same route back to Bedford.

After the ride, head west out of Bedford on US 30 for 4 miles to the historic Jean Bonnet Tavern. This native-stone and chestnut-beamed structure has been serving travelers since the 1760s. Open daily, the tavern also features a meeting room and a bed-and-breakfast. On the National Register of Historic Places, the Jean Bonnet Tavern is midway between Bedford and Shawnee State Park, mak-

One of Bedford County's well preserved covered bridges.

ing it the perfect base for cycling these routes as well as the Shawnee Lake Cruise (see Chapter 33).

LOCAL INFORMATION

♦ Bedford County Visitors Bureau, 131 South Juliana Street, Bedford, PA 15522; (814) 623–1771 or (800) 765–3331.

LOCAL EVENTS/ATTRACTIONS

♦ Annual Fall Foliage Festival. Held in downtown Bedford the first two weekends in October; (814) 623–1771. More than 400 craftspeople, lots of entertainment, food, apple cider making, antique car parade, and more. Free.
♦ Old Bedford Village, 220 Sawblade Road, Bedford, PA 15522; (814) 623–1156 or (800) 238–4347. Collection of more than forty authentic and reproduced buildings along with craftspeople and interpreters depicting the rigors of early American life. $8.00 adults; $4.00 students.

RESTAURANTS

♦ Jean Bonnet Tavern, 6048 Lincoln Highway, Bedford, PA 15522; (814) 623–2250. Stone walls, chestnut beams, large fireplaces, and hickory chairs provide a memorable dining experience.
♦ The Eatery, Corner of Pitt and Juliana Streets, Bedford, PA 15522; (814) 623–9120. Gourmet stacked sandwiches and salads. Housed in Artisan and Antique Merchant Center.

ACCOMMODATIONS

♦ Jean Bonnet Tavern, 6048 Lincoln Highway, Bedford, PA 15522; (814) 623–2250. Historic, antiques-filled stone B&B serving travelers for more than two centuries. Moderate.
♦ Oralee's Golden Eagle Country Inn and B&B, 131 East Pitt Street, Bedford, PA 15522; (814) 624–0800. Beautifully restored 1794 inn in center of town. Moderate.

BIKE SHOP

♦ Hink's Bicycle Service, 1361 Miller Road, Imler, PA 16655; (814) 276–3300.

RESTROOMS

On the ramble route:
♦ Mile 0.0: Osterburg Country Store
♦ Mile 4.2: fish hatchery, if you take the detour

Beautifully restored Old Bedford Village depicts early American life.

On the cruise route:
♦ Mile 0.0: various locations in Bedford
On the challenge route:
♦ Mile 0.0: various locations in Bedford
♦ Mile 15.0: Sunoco Station and market
♦ Mile 15.3: Osterburg Country Store
♦ Mile 19.5: fish hatchery, if you take the detour
♦ Mile 26.5: Fishertown Country Store
♦ Mile 32.6: Fisher's Country Store

MAP

♦ *DeLorme Pennsylvania Atlas & Gazetteer,* map 74

Shawnee Lake Cruise

The Shawnee Lake Cruise is a short but challenging ride through the forest and farmlands of historic Bedford County. Cycle through Milligan Cove, a heavenly valley nestled between steep Allegheny Mountain ridges. Marvel at the old White Sulphur Springs Hotel, and imagine bathing in its rejuvenating waters in another era. Cycle through Colvin Bridge, one of Bedford County's oldest covered bridges. Plan a picnic along the Shawnee Lake shoreline, and relax on one of its beaches. After your road ride, sample a few miles of the state park's mountain bike or hiking trails.

Shawnee State Park is named for the Native Americans who briefly lived in the region during their migration westward in the 1700s. The state park features 451-acre Shawnee Lake, a scenic recreational lake popular for its fishing and fine beaches. Fine hiking trails traverse the park, and several accommodate mountain bikes. Seek out a park map that details the trails.

At 23 miles, the cruise is not very long, but the ride does make up for it with toughness. This ride is not really suitable for the beginner; intermediate cyclists will be challenged by several of its climbs. Right at the start, a short 0.5-mile hill greets you as you leave the low-lying lakebed. At the top of the hill, look for the park office on the left. You can pick up maps and other information here.

In several miles you'll roll into tiny Mann's Choice. In 1848 Congressman Job Mann pressured for a post office at this then-unnamed village. Mann was to name the village after he received official approval. Before he was able to do so, postal maps were made that included a temporary designation of "Mann's

Start: From the Diehl Fishing Pier parking lot just off Pennsylvania Highway 96 in Shawnee State Park.

Length: 23 miles.

Terrain: Moderate. Includes several climbs that are too difficult for beginners.

Traffic and hazards: All roads on this route are paved, low traffic, and rural. Use caution on PA 96 and Pennsylvania Highway 31, as traffic is fast but light. Be careful on the steep descent beginning at Mile 13.5.

Getting there: From Bedford take U.S. Highway 30 West for 9 miles to the center of Schellsburg. Turn left at the stoplight onto PA 96 South. Go 1.5 miles to the Diehl Fishing Pier parking lot on the left. Plenty of free parking is available.

Choice." The name was never changed. If you need supplies, pick up something at Mann's Choice Grocery in town—your only choice, man.

Another climb welcomes you after you leave Mann's Choice. Your reward is one of the most beautiful spots in Pennsylvania. This very rural 6-mile stretch runs through Milligan Cove, a gorgeous valley nestled between Buffalo and Wills Mountains. While wildlife abounds in this deep, forested valley, people and cars are scarce. Take your time through here and enjoy Bedford County at its finest.

At Mile 7.5 the rustic White Sulphur Springs Hotel pops right up in front of you. This impressive resort was built in 1894 and became a popular health spa in the early 1900s. The resort is now private and, unfortunately, not open to the general public. The hotel's wooded property is absolutely stunning, and you'll find yourself jockeying for an ideal spot for a photo.

Later in the ride, on Mill Road, you'll cycle through one of Bedford County's legendary covered bridges. The Colvin Bridge spanning Shawnee Creek was built around 1880 and is often called the Shiller Bridge, for the doctor who once owned it. After another photo, look for Bedford's Covered Bridge Inn just past the bridge on the left. Consider spending the night at this quiet B&B bordering Shawnee State Park and overlooking the covered bridge and trout stream. After your bike outing, do some fly-fishing or take a short hike from the inn through the park for a picnic along peaceful Shawnee Lake.

LOCAL INFORMATION

♦ Bedford County Visitors Bureau, 141 South Juliana Street, Bedford, PA 15522; (800) 765–3331.

♦ Shawnee State Park, 132 State Park Road, Schellsburg, PA 15559; (814) 733–4218.

Have the entire beach to yourself at Shawnee Lake in Bedford County.

LOCAL EVENTS/ATTRACTIONS

♦ Annual Street Fair and Ox Roast, Shawnee Valley Fire Hall, Schellsburg, PA; (814) 733–2575. Late August/early September. Parade, entertainment, crafts, games, and food.

RESTAURANTS

♦ Shawnee Inn Restaurant and Bar, RR 1, Box 139a, Schellsburg, PA 15559; (814) 733–4733. Located just 0.5 mile off the route in Schellsburg.
♦ Lakeview Lounge and Restaurant, 1461 Shawnee Road, Schellsburg, PA 15559; (814) 733–2091. Local hangout, popular for beer.

ACCOMMODATIONS

♦ Bedford's Covered Bridge Inn, 749 Mill Road, Schellsburg, PA 15559; (814) 733–4093. Attractive B&B overlooking trout stream and historic covered bridge. Moderate.

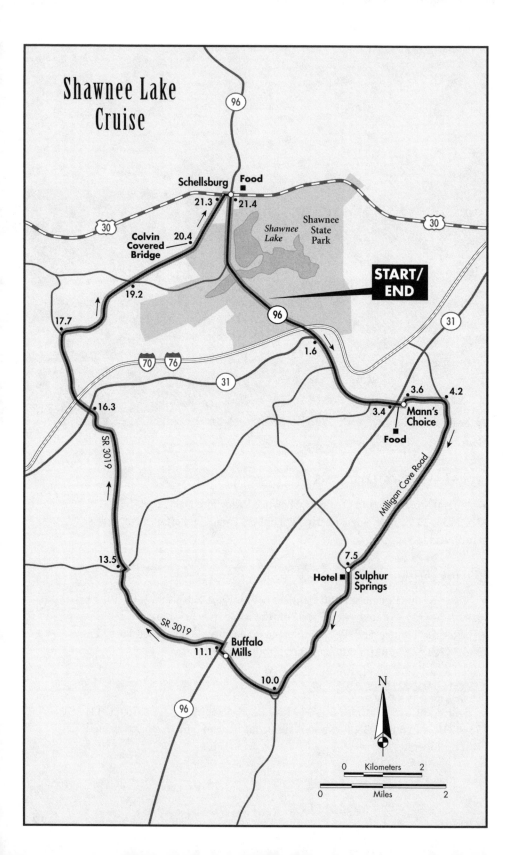

Shawnee Lake Cruise

96

Food
Schellsburg
21.3 • • 21.4

Shawnee Lake

Shawnee State Park

30

30

START/END

Colvin Covered Bridge
20.4

19.2

17.7

96

1.6

70 76

31

31

16.3

3.6 • • 4.2
3.4 •
Mann's Choice
Food ■

SR 3019

Milligan Cove Road

13.5

7.5
Hotel ■ **Sulphur Springs**

SR 3019

Buffalo Mills
11.1 •

10.0

96

N

0   Kilometers   2

0   Miles   2

- Shawnee State Park Campground, 132 State Park Road, Schellsburg, PA 15559. For camping reservations call (888) 727–2757. Located on the route.

BIKE SHOP

- Hink's Bicycle Service, 1361 Miller Road, Imler, PA 16655; (814) 276–3300.

RESTROOMS

- Mile 0.0: Diehl Fishing Pier parking lot
- Mile 3.4: Mann's Choice Grocery
- Mile 21.4: various locations in Schellsburg

MAPS

- *DeLorme Pennsylvania Atlas & Gazetteer,* maps 74 and 88

CRUISE MILES AND DIRECTIONS

0.0 Turn left out of the parking lot onto PA 96 South. At the top of the hill there is a park office on the left where you can pick up information. Across from the park office is the Shawnee State Park Campground.

1.6 Turn left at the stop sign onto PA 96 South/PA 31 East.

3.4 Go straight at the stop sign and flashing light onto Pitt Street in Mann's Choice. Go 1 block and turn left at the stop sign onto Main Street. Mann's Choice Grocery is on the left at this intersection.

3.6 Turn right onto State Route 3017/Rest Home Road.

4.2 Continue straight on SR 3017/Milligan Cove Road.

7.5 Turn left at the stop sign to stay on SR 3017/Milligan Cove Road. Just after the turn, the White Sulphur Springs Hotel is on the right.

10.0 Continue straight on SR 3017, where Milligan Road goes off to the left.

11.1 Turn right at the stop sign onto PA 96 North. In 0.1 mile turn left onto State Route 3019.

(continued)

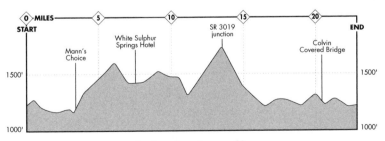

Cruise elevation profile

13.5 Turn right at the stop sign onto Glade Pike, then make the immediate left to stay on SR 3019. *Caution:* Steep descent ahead.

16.3 Continue straight at the stop sign to stay on SR 3019. You'll cross PA 31.

17.7 Bear right onto Skip Back Road.

19.2 Continue straight on Skip Back Road where Hillegass Road crosses at an angle. Becomes Mill Road.

20.4 Cycle through the Colvin Covered Bridge. Just after the bridge on the left is Bedford's Covered Bridge Inn.

21.3 Turn right at the stop sign onto US 30 East and bike through Schellsburg.

21.4 Turn right at the stoplight onto PA 96 South. (*Note:* If you continue straight on US 30, the Shawnee Country Market will be 0.3 mile ahead on the left. In another 0.2 mile the Shawnee Inn will be on the right.)

21.7 Lakeview Lounge and Restaurant is on the left.

22.8 After cycling over Shawnee Lake, finish the ride at the lot on the left.

McConnellsburg Challenge

T he McConnellsburg Challenge is a challenging tour of Fulton County, lying deep in the heart of the Southern Alleghenies. Starting in the historic town of McConnellsburg, the challenge skirts towering Tuscarora Mountain before dropping down to the agriculturally rich Great Cove Valley. After a tough climb over Scrub Ridge, the route turns north with a succession of demanding roller-coaster hills. The ride finishes with a bang as a thrilling 2-mile descent drops the cyclist off in the center of McConnellsburg and offers a chance to experience the town's history, charm, and hospitality.

Although McConnellsburg is quite a haul for most folks, a trip to the Southern Alleghenies is a rewarding experience. Recreational opportunities abound, and the region's small towns offer warmth and hospitality. McConnellsburg, county seat for Fulton County, contains an interesting mix of architectural styles, and portions of the town have been placed on the National Register of Historic Places.

Pick up what supplies you need in town or at the convenience store just 0.2 mile into the ride, as the challenge consists of considerable climbing. Just outside town you'll pass through the JLG Industries complex, the world's largest manufacturer of aerial platform lifts. The JLG plant is the county's largest employer, but once you pass it the ride remains very rural the rest of the way. In fact, turkeys and chickens top the county's population charts. People run a distant second, with cows a close third. Fortunately for Fulton County, only people get to vote.

Start: From the Fulton County Chamber of Commerce parking lot at 536 East Poplar Street in McConnellsburg.

Length: 40 miles; 33 miles by taking a short-cut.

Terrain: Hilly. Challenging route with several major climbs and numerous moderate ones. For the fit, experienced cyclist.

Traffic and hazards: Use caution when cycling the 10-mile stretch of U.S. Highway 522. The moderate traffic is offset by an adequate shoulder. Be careful on the descents; several are steep. Maintain control.

Getting there: From Breezewood take U.S. Highway 30 East for approximately 18 miles. Take the exit for US 522 South and go 0.8 mile to Lincoln Way East in the center of town. Turn left onto Lincoln Way; go 0.3 mile and turn left onto Sixth Street. Go 1 block and turn left onto East Poplar Street. The Fulton County Chamber of Commerce and Tourist Promotion Agency is on the right. Parking is free.

The first few miles contain some gentle climbing and offer a chance to warm up. You'll be cycling in the shadow of Tuscarora Mountain, which majestically looms to the east. Only climbing into the foothills, you're still rewarded with an enjoyable descent of several miles to the valley floor. The only caution here—the cattle crossing areas.

The Southern Allegheny Mountain region is characterized by ridges running southwest to northeast. Though you will have some great valley riding, crossing some of these ridges is inevitable. You'll get your first taste at Mile 9.0, when a difficult 2-mile climb is necessary to traverse the southern end of Scrub Ridge. If the climb takes too much out of you, consider the shortcut offered at Mile 13.3. Timber Ridge Road not only offers relatively easy cycling and incredible valley views to the west but also removes 7.6 miles from the challenge. I recommend taking the longer route. After all, the drive here was a challenge—be challenged.

When you enter tiny Needmore, stop at GeneO's if you "need more" food and drink. You're now at the lowest elevation of the ride. As you make your way back to the north, you'll face a succession of roller-coaster hills while slowly gaining elevation. Use caution; many of the descents are steep. Be careful on the 0.1-mile segment on busy US 30. The portion of the challenge to the north of US 30 remains very rural, with moderate hills. One last 1.5-mile climb sets you up for a fantastic finish down Peach Orchard Road and back into McConnellsburg.

Back in town, consider a walking tour of the historic district—if your legs will let you. Better yet, pamper yourself with a night's stay at the McConnellsburg Inn. This stately 1903 B&B was built for a retired Civil War captain and is a perfect place for your recovery.

Ideal cycling roads abound in rural western Pennsylvania.

LOCAL INFORMATION

♦ Fulton County Chamber of Commerce and Tourist Promotion Agency, 536 East Poplar Street, McConnellsburg, PA 17229; (717) 485–4064.

LOCAL EVENTS/ATTRACTIONS

♦ Fulton Fall Folk Festival. Held the third weekend in October. Large county-wide fair featuring historic house tours, food, entertainment, farm folk heritage skills exhibits and demonstrations, gristmill tours, quilt show, and more. Coincides with an antique tractor and machinery show. For information call the chamber of commerce at (717) 485–4064.

RESTAURANTS

♦ Johnnie's Diner, 709 Lincoln Way, McConnellsburg, PA 17233; (717) 485–3116. Local favorite located near the ride's start.

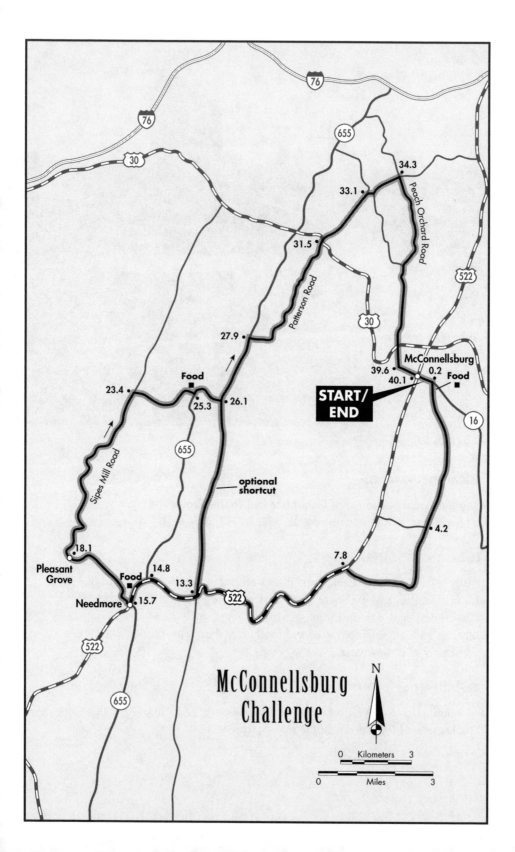

76

76

655

30

34.3

33.1

31.5

Peach Orchard Road

522

Patterson Road

30

27.9

McConnellsburg

39.6   0.2

Food

40.1

23.4

Food

START/
END

26.1

25.3

16

655

Sipes Mill Road

optional
shortcut

4.2

18.1

7.8

Pleasant
Grove

Food   14.8

Needmore   15.7   13.3

522

522

655

McConnellsburg
Challenge

N

0   Kilometers   3

0   Miles   3

0.0 Leave the visitor center by turning left onto Poplar Street. Turn right onto Sixth Street and go up to Lincoln Way East. At the stop sign turn left onto Lincoln Way East.

0.2 Turn right onto South Seventh Street. (*Note:* If you need food, continue straight for a McDonald's and Johnnie's Diner. Out of town, South Seventh Street becomes Cito Road.)

4.2 Continue straight at stop sign onto State Route 1001/Cito Road.

7.8 Turn left at stop sign onto US 522 South/Great Cove Road.

8.5 Harr's Grocery Store is on the left.

13.3 Continue straight on US 522/Great Cove Road. (*Note:* For a shortcut, which cuts off 7.6 miles, turn right here onto State Route 2005/Timber Ridge Road. Follow Timber Ridge Road for 5.2 miles. When you reach the stop sign at Pleasant Ridge Road, bear right. You are now back on the route at Mile 26.1 Continue for 1.8 miles and pick up the ride at Mile 27.9.)

14.8 Continue straight. Pennsylvania Highway 655 joins US 522.

15.2 GeneO's Grocery is on the right in the village of Needmore.

15.7 Turn right onto State Route 3007.

18.1 Turn right at the stop sign onto State Route 3013/Sipes Mill Road. Follow for 5.3 miles.

23.4 Turn right onto State Route 4002/Ebenezer Church Road.

25.3 Turn left at the stop sign onto PA 655 North/Pleasant Ridge Road. Just after the turn, Deshong's Korner Store is on the left.

26.1 Bear left to stay on PA 655. (*Note:* The shortcut reenters the route from the right at this intersection.) After 1.5 miles, use caution on the upcoming descent.

27.9 Turn right onto State Route 1007/Patterson Road.

31.5 Turn left onto US 30 West. There is a nice shoulder, but use caution. Go 0.1 mile and turn right onto SR 1007/Breezy Point Road.

33.1 Bear right to stay on SR 1007.

(continued)

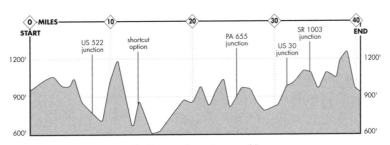

Challenge elevation profile

34.3 Turn right onto State Route 1003/Peach Orchard Road.

39.6 Turn left at stop sign onto State Route 1004.

40.1 Continue straight on Lincoln Way East at the stoplight in the center of town.

40.4 Turn left onto Sixth Street, then make a quick left onto Poplar Street to end the ride back at the visitor center.

ACCOMMODATIONS

♦ The McConnellsburg Inn, A Bed-and-Breakfast, 131 West Market Street, McConnellsburg, PA 17233; (866) 485–5495. 1903 Victorian inn. Moderate.

♦ Cowans Gap State Park Campground, 6235 Aughwick Road, Ft. Loudon, PA 17224. Beautiful campground about 10 miles from McConnellsburg. Call (888) 727–2757 for reservations.

BIKE SHOP

♦ Fat Jimmy's Outfitters, 16487 Lincoln Highway, Breezewood, PA 15533; (814) 735–2453.

RESTROOMS

♦ Mile 0.0: visitor center
♦ Mile 0.2: McDonald's and Johnnie's Diner
♦ Mile 15.2: GeneO's
♦ Mile 25.3: Deshongs Korner Store

MAPS

♦ *DeLorme Pennsylvania Atlas & Gazetteer*, maps 75, 89, and 90

Appendix A

SELECTED BICYCLING ORGANIZATIONS

NATIONAL

Adventure Cycling Association
P.O. Box 8308
Missoula, MT 59807
(800) 755–2453
info@adv-cycling.org
www.adv-cycling.org
A nonprofit recreational cycling organization. Produces bicycle route maps
and offers a variety of trips.

League of American Bicyclists
1612 K Street NW, Suite 401
Washington, DC 20006
(202) 822–1333
bikeleague@bikeleague.org
www.bikeleague.org
Works through advocacy and education for a bicycle-friendly America.

Rails to Trails Conservancy
1100 Seventeenth Street NW
Tenth Floor
Washington, DC 20036
(202) 331–9696
rtcmail@transact.org
www.railtrails.org
Connecting people and communities by creating a nationwide network of
public trails, many from former rail lines.

STATE

Bicycle Federation of Pennsylvania
P.O. Box 11625
Harrisburg, PA 17108
Tom Helm
pabikefed@paonline.com
Statewide advocacy group.

PennDOT—Harrisburg
555 Walnut Street, Ninth Floor
Harrisburg, PA 17101
(717) 705–1493
www.dot.state.pa.us
Publishes the *Pennsylvania Bicycling Directory,* the *Bicycle Driver's Manual,*
and *Bicycle Pennsylvania Bike Routes.*

Bicycle Access Council
P.O. Box 92, 465 Dairyland Drive
Dallastown, PA 17313
(717) 417–1299
www.bicycleaccess-pa.org
info@bicycleaccess-pa.org
Nonprofit advocacy organization also serves as forum for Pennsylvania
cyclists.

Pedal PA
P.O. Box 385
Harleysville, PA 19438
(215) 513–9577
www.pedal-pa.com
info@pedalpa.com
Offers a yearly cross-state tour as well as other offerings in Pennsylvania
and the Northeast.

Appendix B

WESTERN PENNSYLVANIA RIDES
BY CATEGORY AND LENGTH

RAMBLES (16)

Ligonier—11 miles
Mingo Creek—14 miles
Bedford County—16 miles
Presque Isle and Erie—16 miles
Beaver County—17 miles
Cook Forest—18 miles
Ryerson Station—19 miles
Oil Creek—20 miles
State College—20 miles
Prince Gallitzen—20 miles
Cambridge Springs—21 miles
North East Wine Country—22 miles
Hickory Valley—23 miles
Pymatuning—23 miles
Canoe Creek—28 miles
Ohiopyle—30 miles

CRUISES (20)

Bedford County—18 miles
Pittsburgh City—19 miles
Lake Arthur—21 miles
Shawnee Lake—23 miles
Ridgway—24 miles
Twin Lakes—24 miles
Saxonburg—28 miles
Ryerson Station—29 miles
Hickory—30 miles
Kinzua—30 miles
Ligonier—30 miles
Slippery Rock—30 miles
Somerset Miracle—30 miles
Mingo Creek—30 miles
Cambridge Springs—34 miles

North East Wine Country—34 miles
Cycle the Southern Alleghenies—35 miles
Beaver County—37 miles
Greene County Country—38 miles
Pymatuning—41 miles

CHALLENGES (13)

Oil Creek—31 miles
Punxsutawney—39 miles
McConnellsburg—40 miles
Bedford County—41 miles
Ligonier—41 miles
Altoona—42 miles
Ohiopyle—42 miles
State College—45 miles
Ridgway—45 miles
Lake Arthur—46 miles
Elk View—48 miles
Slippery Rock—51 miles
Prosperity—54 miles

CLASSICS (5)

Volant—60 miles
Indiana County Metric Century—65 miles
Ligonier—65 miles
Ohiopyle—65 miles
Indiana County English Century—101 miles

ABOUT THE AUTHOR

Jim Homerosky is a veteran cyclist who bicycle tours throughout the United States and Europe. The former engineer and ride coordinator for the Williamsburg Area Bicyclists is also the author of *Road Biking Virginia.* He and his wife, Wendy, reside in McMurray, Pennsylvania, and Williamsburg, Virginia.

Jim Homerosky and his wife, Wendy

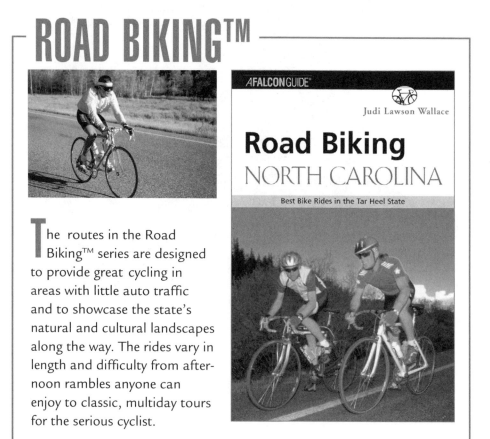